Praise for

Happily Ever After

"Now that divorce has become a major rite of passage for North Americans, along comes Sarah Hampson with an important new book that combines respect for marriage, love and child raising with the changing expectations of how we want to live our lives. Hampson's thoughtful and moving take on life after divorce will inspire all women in mid-life who have come of age after their marriages ended. And—hallelujah—it gives divorced men and women a much-needed context for their experience."

Susan Swan

"She finds a good balance between the personal and the professional, humour and nostalgia, and even men and women."

The Globe and Mail

"With great compassion and insight, Sarah Hampson takes the reader on a journey through the dilemma of divorce: its confusion and pain as well as the clarity and contentedness it can bring." Jeannette Walls, author of *The Glass Castle*

"Compassionate, bracing and rich in life-tested wisdom, this is a book that mid-life women have been waiting for. Sarah Hampson points the way from the bruising disappointments of love gone wrong to new possibilities for growth and connection."

Rona Maynard

"Sarah Hampson's book on the upside of divorce is like having a glass of wine (or two) with your girlfriends: it offers good medicine, laughter and hope." Marni Jackson

Happily Ever After Marriage

A Reinvention in Mid-life

SARAH HAMPSON

Vintage Canada

VINTAGE CANADA EDITION, 2011

Copyright © 2010 Sarah Hampson

Published in Canada by Vintage Canada, a division of Random House of Canada Limited, Toronto, in 2011. Originally published in hardcover in Canada by Alfred A. Knopf Canada, a division of Random House of Canada Limited, in 2010. Distributed by Random House of Canada Limited.

Vintage Canada with colophon is a registered trademark.

www.randomhouse.ca

LIBRARY AND ARCHIVES CANADA CATALOGUING IN PUBLICATION

Hampson, Sarah
Happily ever after marriage : a reinvention in mid-life / Sarah Hampson.

Includes bibliographical references.

ISBN 978-0-307-39769-0

1. Hampson, Sarah. 2. Divorced people—Canada—Biography.
3. Middle-aged persons—Canada—Biography. 4. Self-reliance.
5. Interpersonal relations. 6. Love. I. Title.

HQ811.5.H34A3 2011   306.89'3092   C2010-904092-9

Text design by CS Richardson

Printed and bound in the United States of America

2 4 6 8 9 7 5 3 1

For my parents, Joan and Chris,
and for my sons, Nick, Tait and Luke

Out of the manifold events of his life, his deeds, his feelings, his thoughts, he might make a design, regular, elaborate, complicated or beautiful; and though it might be no more than an illusion that he had the power of selection, though it might be no more than a fantastic legerdemain in which appearances were interwoven with moonbeams, that did not matter: it seemed, and so to him it was.

—*W. Somerset Maugham,* Of Human Bondage

CONTENTS

Author's Note   XI

Prologue   I

PART ONE: YOU WILL BE A BLUSHING BRIDE
DRESSED IN WHITE

1. My Mother Wore Lipstick in the Chevy   11
2. What the Feminists Forgot to Teach Us   34
3. Love Conquers All, Doesn't It?   45
4. Losing and Gaining Selves   57

PART TWO: YOUR LIFE WILL TAKE SOME
SURPRISING TURNS

5. The Hamlet Years: To Divorce or Not to Divorce?   75
6. The Colossus Generation   88
7. Destination: Splitsville   95
8. Un-marriage Ceremonies   111
9. Ghost Dad   119

PART THREE: A PLEASANT SURPRISE IS IN
STORE FOR YOU

10. When the Veil Finally Lifts   131
11. Emotional Flu   144
12. Tulips in the Spring Are More Reliable   157
13. The Dating Pool Is Very Shallow   170
14. Living Happily with My Bitch Wrinkle   185

PART FOUR: YOUR DISAPPOINTMENTS WILL
BECOME YOUR STEPPING STONES

15. Vows of an Ex-Wife   207
16. Neighbouring Solitudes   220
17. Lessons in Love   233
18. In the Ring of My Own Light   243
19. Playing My Cards   259
20. Life Is a Carnival   272

Epilogue   281

Notes   289
Acknowledgments   304

AUTHOR'S NOTE

Six years ago, my husband and I were divorced after eighteen years of marriage and three children, and since then, I sometimes find myself looking at people and wondering how they live. Who loves us, and how well, can determine how we make our way through the world. And so I watch. Does she have a spouse? If so, is it a happy marriage? Are they widowed? Divorced? Do they have children? Who and where is their family? Wondering how people make their marriages work when yours failed is like wanting to know why the young guy from the marketing department got promoted and you didn't. You thought you had what it takes. You worked hard at it. You consider yourself smart. But somehow, it didn't work out. And here you are, in a place you had never imagined you would be. Are others kinder? More generous? Patient? Better at picking a mate? Luckier?

This is what happens when you are outside the marriage bubble. Suddenly, you are in a parallel universe, across some mythic river in a place where you are the un-wife—and you and your un-husband are on the un-married side. And once there, as some kind of compensation for the hardship of the journey, you develop relationship X-ray vision. You know more than if you had never inhabited the bubble. Illusions (and delusions) drop away. Everything is clearer. You see yourself, your ex—refugees from the land of happily-ever-after—and others, even those still in the bubble, in a new light.

I have always been interested in people. For close to ten years, I have written an interview column in the *Globe and Mail*, and never once have I felt bored. People are always different than what I had assumed, even celebrities. I come away from an interview with a different impression—sometimes better; sometimes worse—of the person than I had going in.

And now I am surprised at myself too. Through marriage and divorce, I had become a subject, newly mysterious. What makes her tick? What does she want? Why couldn't she have what she thought was hers? What were her mistakes? Her triumphs? What made her who she is? And I could no longer make assumptions about the way my life would work out, or anyone else's, for that matter. Many of my beliefs had collapsed; my assumptions proven wrong.

One day in 2007, I was sitting at the table in my kitchen and an idea presented itself, whole. *I should write a relationship column*, I thought. I would call it Generation Ex. We are living in a culture that promotes marriage and sanctions divorce: a revolving door of the heart. In the course of the boomer generation's maturity, there had been a rise in the divorce rate to plateau at almost one in two marriages. And there was the oft-repeated and fascinating statistic: the majority of divorces that happen to people over the age of forty were initiated by the wife. I wanted to dig through the emotional archaeology of marriage and divorce—what brings us together as well as what pulls us apart. I wanted to try to understand how we are redefining the way we couple. The column debuted in April of that year, running in the new Life section.

The response from readers has been overwhelming. My inbox consistently fills with notes from people of all ages: some married, some divorced, others never-married or widowed. They offer comments, their own stories—and gratitude. Their experiences of love, hope, disappointment and of being alone—the courage it takes and the fear it can awaken—are validated by what I write about not only my own marriage and divorce but those of others. The dialogue with strangers helps me too. It is always easier to write when you know that people will find it helpful. I don't feel quite so silly for feeling the things I sometimes do. And so although in this book I explore broader themes of mid-life post-divorce, the column and the generous responses from readers were its inspiration.

Sarah Hampson
January 2010

Prologue

It was a turning point in my post-divorce life. Every year since my ex-husband and I had divorced five years earlier, I had been with family or a boyfriend on New Year's Eve, and we had always passed the evening happily. But now, as we were about to usher in 2008, I was truly on my own for the first time. I was not planning to visit my parents, as I often do, in London, England. None of my siblings lives in Toronto. And my children were all old enough to have their own plans. Luke, my youngest at seventeen, was in his last year of high school and out at a friend's house. My middle son, Tait, twenty, was also out with friends, and the eldest, Nick, at twenty-two, was on a four-month sojourn to India after having graduated from university. Instead of planning something, I had figured I would just try to be Zen about it and see what unfolded.

Sure enough, the week before New Year's, friends who live nearby invited me to come for dinner. I was pleased to receive the invitation. On the evening of, I dress up and walk up the hill in my midtown neighbourhood to their house. We are a typical boomer crowd, all over forty-five, engaged in work of some sort and in various relationship permutations. The hosts had married a few years earlier. His first marriage ended in divorce; her first husband died suddenly. Together, they have a blended family of six children. Another couple, a vibrant pair, have a long, happy marriage, somewhere in the twenty-five-year range, with two careers, five children under the age of seventeen, and a connection as crackling as electricity. The other pairs are made up of divorced people in new partnerships. I am the only one on my own—a situation in which I have become perfectly comfortable.

As midnight approaches, we are still seated around the long oak dining table, talking and drinking wine. About twenty minutes before the clock strikes twelve, our host gently taps the edge of his wineglass to silence the room. He has an idea: Why don't we go around the table so that each person can say what he or she hopes for in the coming year?

The first guest to his right, the woman with the five children, wishes for the health of her brood. Her husband raises his glass to her from across the table, and winks.

"Another year of wonderful travel," the woman next to her says. In her late forties or early fifties, she has a smooth, pretty face and a slim, toned body that suggests yoga and latte afternoons. No high-stress cortisol-induced belly fat for her.

Her partner also exudes a Freedom 55 calm. Both divorced, they have been together for over a year. From across the table, he mentions some of the exotic places they have been in the past year. He seems as jovial of spirit as he is deep of pocket.

Next up: a divorced man in his fifties. He looks across the table to his fortysomething girlfriend, whose divorce papers just came through earlier that week. "I hope that Jill will be my wife," he says.

A collective gasp rises from the guests. He holds the gaze of his lover.

"Oh," she splutters, reaching for her napkin to dry her eyes. They have been dating for under a year. Marriage has been discussed, but she wasn't expecting such a public declaration.

Seated next to her, I am weeping now too.

"Sometimes, I just look at him sleeping, and think how lucky I am to have met such a sweet man," she whispers to me when she sees my reaction.

Everyone congratulates the couple. The ritual around the table continues, but no one else's hope for the new year can compare.

"Serenity," I say when it's my turn. "And safety for my children," I add.

Soon after the last guest makes his wish for the next year, the countdown to midnight begins. We stand to raise our glasses to the future. The couples kiss and hug, and then each of us turns to wish the others the best for the next year.

Shortly after midnight, people begin to take their leave. I kiss my hosts on the cheek, thank them for including me.

"Are you okay to get home?" the host asks.

"I'm fine," I say as I walk out into the night, waving my hand over my head as I concentrate on the steps in front of me.

Snowflakes float down in the darkness, covering the ground in a light dusting of white. Everything looks fresh, waiting, untouched, for whatever will happen next. Gingerly, I negotiate the hill in my high-heel boots. People traipse along the sidewalks, laughing. The snow closes the city in. We inhabit a snow globe, the lights from downtown making a silhouette of buildings—figurines of people, arm in arm, in a suspension of white.

My cell phone rings.

"Happy New Year, Mom!" Luke exclaims.

I can hear his friends in the background, loud music.

"Happy New Year to you!" I say back.

"How are you?" he asks.

"Fine. I had fun. Heading home now."

"Okay, see you later," he says. "Have a good night."

Tonight, I have allowed him more flexibility on his curfew.

"Okay, love you."

"Love you, Mom," he says before hanging up.

A few minutes later, Tait calls. We wish each other Happy New Year and sign off with our usual "love you." He, too, is living at home, but only temporarily.

I turn into my street. It is deserted, the street lamps dropping pools of light into the darkness. I had left the outside light on for myself. I unlock my door and enter, and for a moment, stand in the silence of the house.

Happy New Year, I say silently to myself. I look at my reflection in the mirror in the front entranceway. The person staring back looks lost.

"What are you doing?" I ask.

It is close to one-thirty in the morning. I phone my friend Joy.

"Everyone left a little while ago. I'm just cleaning up. Where are you?"

"Home," I say glumly. I am sitting on the sofa. The night presses up against the window, lonely and insistent.

"You don't sound so good."

"I'm not."

Girlfriends are sometimes like those firemen you see outside burning buildings. They hold the edges of a large round landing pad, reassuring you that you will be safe if you jump. In divorce, especially if they have jumped before you and know that you can land safely, they rescue you.

I had met Joy fifteen years earlier. She was the photographer paired with me on assignment for a house and garden magazine. I had begun freelancing for magazines, after opting out of a lucrative job in advertising to stay at home with my three boys. Working from home, and in between children's naps, runs to the boys' schools, occasional daycare, soccer matches and, of course, the grocery store, I wrote. This was my first location assignment, whereas Joy had been in the business for years. "I lose three pounds a day when I am shooting," she told me on the second day we spent together. "It's all the energy I expend through my eyeball," she explained. I looked at her. She was completely serious about her passion for her work. From that day forward, we have spoken almost every day, through her divorce, which came the next year, and then through mine, almost ten years later.

I tell her about the evening, the wedding proposal.

"That's beautiful," she offers.

"It was."

"And?" She knows there is more.

"I cried."

"Ooöh," she says in the way she does when she knows I am upset.

"I'm alone. The kids are out," I explain.

In the early part of life, New Year's is a marker of the anticipated progress ahead. I will graduate from high school. I will go to college. This is the year I will get my first job. I will marry. We will buy a house. We will have a baby. We will have another baby. And another. I will quit my job and stay home . . . But now?

"Come on, it's not so bad. What are you doing?"

"Having a cognac." I sound like a sullen child, and I know it, but I don't care. "It's the perfect storm," I say.

"What is?"

"My life." I will turn fifty in the year ahead, I remind her. There is no more denial about being middle-aged. The children, whose well-being has been my primary focus, are leaving home. I'm glad to be divorced. But at the same time, I'm afraid of being alone forever. And it doesn't help when I read U.S. census data, stating that the least marriageable individuals are MLWs—my shorthand for mid-life women—who are highly educated and make a good salary. It feels like a cruel irony, an emotional price we have to pay for independence: that which enabled us to divorce—economic autonomy through work outside the home—is what decreases our chances of ever finding love again. Lovely.

"Am I always going to be alone?"

"Of course not," Joy says.

Joy is always unequivocal, a shot of clarity. When I cannot be my own husband, addressing my needs, talking myself out of a panic, she steps in and takes on the role to cheer me up, motivate me, console me. And I do the same for her, when she needs me to. An exemplary MLW, she has the look of someone who has edited out all but the essential, the good and the positive from her life. She is fit, beautiful. Men adore her. But she is happy on her own. She has seen herself through various crises with admirable calm.

"Don't you ever feel lonely?" I asked her once.

"Sure," she replied. "But only for a few minutes. And then I snap out of it. I like my own company."

When I was new to living alone and struggling with the adaptation, she told me something that stayed with me. "It is your chance to be good to yourself, Sarah, to honour yourself. When you are good to yourself, it changes the way you feel about your life." She buys fresh flowers for her house every week. She gets up early enough to enjoy an hour-and-a-half-long breakfast ritual that includes classical music, the newspaper and a full-cooked meal.

Now, she is talking to me about her New Year's evening. Earlier in the week, she had suggested I join her at her house, but by then I had accepted my invitation up the hill. She tells me about the friends she had over and how happy she was to have them around.

"Look, it's only one night," she tells me. "Don't be sad. It will be better in the morning."

I feel like Scarlett O'Hara with no grand staircase to sit at the bottom of as I wish for better things in the uncertainty of tomorrow. "I know," I mumble into the phone. We talk for another few minutes, say good-night.

I rise to look out the window over the street. The snow has stopped. The footprints of people who have passed along the sidewalk are visible now. Evidence of where they've come from and where they're headed is no longer hidden under the silent, forgiving grace of a white blanket. A journey is never forgotten, I tell myself, not completely; and perhaps it is only through knowing it that one can see a way forward.

PART ONE

You will be a blushing bride
dressed in white.

I.

My Mother Wore Lipstick in the Chevy

My mother thinks I should take up bridge. "You never know who you might meet," she says brightly. We were having one of our regular Sunday afternoon telephone conversations, a ritual we have maintained for years. This one took place a few years after my divorce, when I was adapting to being single again.

My mother believes in marriage and thinks men are as important to a woman's life as a good pair of shoes. That is how her generation was brought up—and what I was encouraged to believe. "It is just what we all did," she explained to me once about her early marriage at twenty-one, a decision that put an end to her nursing education. Her belief in the goodness of marriage has been reinforced by her experience. My parents have been married for fifty-five years, and they have endured spats of bad weather, confident the squall would soon end and that calmer seas lay ahead. Certainly, as one of five young passengers in the ship of their union, I always felt snug and safe.

"But I know how to play bridge," I say.

"How well?"

"I get by."

"Well, you can always get better, and it's fun!"

For her, bridge with her friends is an important part of life. My parents have a flat in London and a house in Sussex, an hour southeast of the city. In both places, she has her circle of bridge friends, and when she returns from her afternoon games with them, she is buoyed by stories of their bidding, who played what how, and the news about grandchildren, health and recent travel that floated up in gaps of concentration.

"I don't know, Mom. Maybe." Somehow bridge makes me feel that knitting will follow. Or that my hips will start to creak.

"What about ballroom dancing?" she suggests. "Wouldn't that be fun?"

"A possibility," I reply patiently.

When I was young and had moved to a new city for a job, I told her that I didn't know very many people, and she suggested that I join a church group. In my family, the solution to almost all complaints and anxieties is to *do* something. There was, and still is, little tolerance for self-pity or emotional stagnation.

When I think back on my childhood, I remember it as richly peopled—I was sandwiched between two older siblings and two younger ones—and full of adventure. I was inculcated in the importance of family. We were always *doing* something as a team. I was never alone. My father, who was born in

Montreal as my mother was, wanted us to know our native Canada, from sea to sea. We went on canoe trips as a family in the wilderness. "It's glooorious!" my father would say, as he floated in a lake, no matter how cold or weedy-looking. He has a way of floating on his back, in a semi-reclined position, as if seated in an invisible lawn chair. "Come in," he would call to us, oblivious to how his determined enthusiasm would backfire, entrenching us further in various forms of teenaged sullenness.

Once, my elder sister, Daphne, who never liked camping much, sat on the beach in a funk, talking with the exaggerated, faux patience of an annoyed school teacher to the flies that landed on her arm. "All right, little Buzzie, you've had enough fun now. Time to leave," she would mutter through clenched teeth from beneath her floppy sunhat. She would slap away at the fly, but if she had been able to march it off her arm by the edge of its wing, I swear she would have.

Long ago, I remember my father saying that he liked his work in the corporate world because he could "manage potential and possibility," and I often think that was how he saw his role as a father. And there were enough of us to be a little company—one of pimples, hormones and scuffed knees, that is. We three senior ones anyway, Geoffrey, Daphne and me, even had our own collective name, GeSaraDa, and used it to christen the forts we made in the woods.

My father took all of us on as if we were a motivational project. Even on rainy mornings during those camping trips, while my mother and all of us stayed snug in our tents, he would stand outside and rouse us with "Rise and shine! Pancakes are ready!" Out we would crawl, crumpled and grumpy, to sit under a tarpaulin around a wet picnic table, eating his thick, lumpy, disgusting pancakes. "Come on now. They're delicious," he would say, as we rolled our eyes.

Shortly after my lonely New Year's Eve, I tell my mother that I am thinking about taking up flying.

"In a plane?"

"Well, yes, Mom. Not in a video game."

"A big one?"

"No, a little one. Sort of a tin can with a lawn-mower engine." I have already taken an introductory lesson in a Cessna 150 at a small airport north of Toronto. I love the feeling of being beyond birds, piercing the sky.

"Oh, don't do that!" she says, clearly horrified. "I don't want you to die!"

"Don't worry. I'm just trying it out," I reassure her.

It's a bit of a cliché as a pursuit, I realize, especially for women, many of whom pursue it in mid-life. I mean, what are we doing? Wanting to prove our ultimate liberation, sexual and otherwise, by showing ourselves and others that we don't have a fear of flying? (If true, that would be your fault, Erica Jong.) It's more about being cool, to be honest. Staying adventuresome in mid-life is a strong incentive. Besides, it's a hell of a way to make an entrance. At an afternoon party in the country years ago, the host's mother, who was in her sixties, arrived in a small plane by herself—a red one, to boot. As she taxied up the grassy strip, she upstaged everyone. An alternative activity is golf, I suppose. Many MLWs have embraced golf like a new religion, but on that subject I find myself paraphrasing Hermann Goering: whenever I hear the phrase *tee-off*, I reach for my pistol.

I know my mother wants to help. Her agitation reminds me of my own plight as a mother of grown children: you never stop worrying, no matter how old they are. In a conversation she had with a friend, which she later told me about, they were talking about their lives and their accomplishments. My mother never worked for pay. She was a corporate wife, following my father faithfully, with five children and pets in tow, every time his job for a multinational company necessitated a move. "You have your children," her friend said. "They were your career."

Once, when I was headed out to Los Angeles to do an interview for the paper, she phoned me to wish me a good trip. I told her where I would be staying and how long I would be there.

"Now don't talk to any strangers," she said at the end of our conversation.

"Okay, Mom." I allowed a pause. "But that's my job."

We both laughed.

She is not quite sure what to do with me—a divorced mid-life woman. My elder brother is divorced too, but in a new, happy relationship. My other siblings are in long, stable marriages. We all married young and contributed to a brood of fifteen grandchildren. On some level, we wanted to continue what we had been the beneficiaries of.

⌒

"We were just lucky," my father says of the successful union with my mother. Perhaps it was his way of reassuring me that the failure wasn't so much the fault of the individuals involved. But my parents' success was more than luck.

In part, my parents benefited from being part of the same tribe—a motley band of WASPs whose history in Canada dates back to the late 1880s. Ancestors arrived in Montreal, then the commercial centre of the country, in the decades following Confederation, when opportunities were abundant. A society flourished as wealth was created. Anglo superiority kicked in, in some ways aping British society with a New World class system. They took themselves very seriously. Gentlemen of industry pictured in a souvenir book for the Montreal Board of Trade to commemorate its fiftieth anniversary in 1893— including both my mother's paternal grandfather and my father's paternal grandfather—described their work in noble terms. The small biographies make a dry goods merchant sound like a force of unity in the great Dominion.

My parents and their friends went to the same parties, skated the same rivers, tobogganed the same hills, ate the same food (much shrimp cocktail), sang the same hymn ("Praise, My Soul, the King of Heaven") at all important life passages and bought shoes in the same store on Green Avenue in lower Westmount. It was almost as though my parents' marriage was arranged. Their parents knew of each other before they met as potential in-laws. That world was a little too small for my liking. The tendency to marry a member of another "good family" seemed old-fashioned to me—a throwback to the days when marriages were made to secure the participants' wealth and land titles.

My mother and father had similar expectations—an important one being betrothal at a young age followed quickly by marriage. They met at a "not out" party thrown by a mutual friend in 1952. My mother was seventeen; my father, nineteen.

A "not out" party was a formal affair in a private house. "Not out" meant that the women had yet to be presented as debutantes at the St. Andrew's Ball, held at the grand Windsor Hotel. That event involved members of the Black Watch, dressed in their uniforms of kilts and red jackets, piping the women into the ballroom, where they were presented, with a curtsy, to some lesser Royal or visiting Lord.

When it was my mother's turn to be a debutante the following year, at eighteen, she invited my father as her escort. Two years later, they were engaged.

⁓

But if their marriage adhered to the social expectations of their era and class, it was also clearly about love. As a child, their affection for one another gave me comfort. They called each other "Hon" more often than they used their first names. Sometimes, my mother would suddenly get up and plop herself down on my father's lap. "Oaf," he would say, surprised, pretending shock, as if the weight of her was too much. "Hug," she playfully instructed him. "Kiss," she said, bringing her face close to his, and tapping the side of her face, indicating where he should plant one. Even now, their behaviour is the same.

Recently, my mother showed me a scrapbook she kept of her youth. From magazines, she had cut out pictures of popular movie stars—Jimmy Stewart and Elizabeth Taylor and Cary Grant, among others—and pasted them on the pages. She had also kept memories of her courtship with my father, including a letter from him, thanking her for a weekend spent with her parents, and a note he wrote wishing her well on her night shift as a training nurse. He had given her a chocolate bar, the wrapper of which she had fixed to the page with tape. There is a large black-and-white picture of them on their first formal date, at a restaurant in Montreal, in 1953. She told me then that it took ages for my father to get up the nerve to kiss her. The week before her wedding day, my mother turned twenty-one. My father was twenty-three. By the time she was thirty-two, they had five children.

I never had to wonder where my mother was—a memory that made it difficult for me to leave my children when I returned to full-time work after the birth of my first two sons. She sent us off in the morning, and when we came home for lunch, she was there, making us a sandwich to eat at the table. She always dressed in skirts and blouses. If I went out with my mother in our Chevrolet station wagon—nicknamed Nelly— to do errands after school, when we were stopped at a red light, she would often look at herself in the rear-view mirror. She would push at her bouffant hair and check her lipstick, smiling broadly at her image, looking for red smears on her teeth.

At night, she would transform into the Wife. If they were going out to a dinner party, before they left she would come to say good-night and give final instructions to the babysitter when we were young enough to need one. Perfumed and pretty in a dress and pearls, she was foreign somehow, lean- ing over to kiss us. Our mother was now his, not ours. And just as we saw the edges of their intimacy, we witnessed the fringes of their disagreements. The summer that I was four- teen was particularly difficult. My mother was thirty-eight, with three hormonal teenagers, two younger children and two golden retrievers. My father was away a lot on business. When we were staying in a rented cottage in Cape Cod during a two-week holiday, I remember my mother saying, "Well, maybe we should just get a divorce." But no argument ever erupted in front of us. My father looked at her, silently, as he put down whatever it was he was reading. "Don't be ridiculous," he said. And when he returned to reading, she made a face at him and blew a raspberry in his direction.

More often than not, my mother deferred to my father in family matters. He set out a monthly household allowance for her to follow. The Depression had been a factor in their youth, despite the comfort of their childhoods. As a result, they had respect for money and the discipline of frugality. We adhered to a strict, no-frills budget. Our diet consisted of fish sticks, frozen peas, meat loaf, Kraft Dinner, shepherd's pie. My mother made a dish called Frickatelli, with hot dogs in rice and tomato sauce. Only on our birthdays were we allowed a glass of orange juice at breakfast. For years, we drank milk that was a combination of real milk and the powdered variety, mixed with water, to make it last longer. Toward the end of the month, if she had run out of money and needed to ask my father for more, an argument often ensued—behind closed doors. My two sisters and I say that our determination to make money of our own, even if only part-time when we were busy with young children, was partly fuelled by not wanting to be in the same position as our mother, who had little economic autonomy.

But for all the inequality in their relationship, at least in those years, there was also a deep commitment to each other and their family. We moved around frequently in the first twenty years of their marriage. It was our family that was the consistent element, not our school, not the neighbourhood or city or province in which we lived, not our friends. We were our own little country. Despite the peripatetic quality of our life, our parents provided constancy. My father worked for the same company his whole career, enjoying a sure and steady rise up the corporate ladder. My mother was always there when we came home, wherever home was. Rituals remained the same. In the late afternoon, after homework time and supper preparation, she liked to rest on her bed. When I came in to talk to her, she often asked me to lightly run the tips of my fingers over her back, under her shirt. "Like that. Perfect," she would say. "Keep it up for ten minutes, and I'll pay you ten cents."

My parents did not live at a time when the Pill allowed them to easily opt out of parenthood or to engineer our arrival. They had children because they had them—not always perfectly planned; welcomed and loved, but not idolized. My elder brother and I are eleven months apart—for just over a week every year, we are the same age.

My parents' relationship to one another, which always seemed like something special and different from what they were to us as parents, had an immutable, self-contained quality. And I think that partly accounted for its success. They treasured what they had together, just the two of them, as much, if not more, than they enjoyed their interaction with the family as parents. And they rarely let one sphere intersect with the other.

When we were young, we would be sent off to bed after our baths so they could have their adult time. On some weekends, we would go to visit my maternal grandmother at her farm-house outside of Montreal in St. Andrew's East. There were plentiful apple orchards and weather-worn sugar shacks deep in the woods. She had been widowed in her early fifties, so my parents brought us often to visit her there, to fill up the ram-bling house and her life.

At night, branches from the big trees scratched the win-dows, and the walls groaned in the wind, like the hull of an ark on high seas. Geoffrey and I would often slip out of bed and into the hall, flatten ourselves like inchworms on our tummies and wiggle closer to a wide, black grate in the floor-boards. The one we liked best was right over the living room. It was a perfect window into the adult world below, a place of crackling fire, music and conversation, where we could see my mother, legs neatly crossed, laughing, and the top of my father's head, hair brushed neatly, wearing a blazer, both of them drinking from heavy tumblers and leaning in to tap the tops of their cigarettes into a ceramic ashtray the size of a pond. It fascinated us that our parents lived a separate exis-tence beyond our understanding in a parallel universe.

⁓

"It's not easy being single in your forties," my mother said to me when I was on the brink of divorce. As an older woman, my eligibility was diminished, she thought, and she was express-ing her worry—perhaps as an incentive for me to remain married—that I would not find a new husband. She is aware of the loss in "social capital"—the term psychotherapists use—that comes in the wake of divorce, when a former spouse

tact with the ex's family and those friends who side
: other. She would like to be able to make my life more
tionally happy. Recently, as a joke, she sent me a gim-
micky item that read *Grow a Boyfriend!* A tiny plastic he-man in
a white undershirt came with a promise: *Mr. Right grows 600%
his size in water!*

Social currency for a single woman is also not the same as
when she is part of a couple. A few years ago, when I was in a
relationship, I was invited to a neighbourhood dinner party
with a group of other couples who had met my boyfriend.
It was the first time I had been included in their social circle.
"That's because you're with a man," my mother observed
when I recounted my week to her in our regular phone call.
"Otherwise, a single woman is seen as a threat."

When I talk to her, I tell her I am happy on my own—
even if that's not always completely true. "I have great friends.
I love my work. The kids are doing well. I'm fine, Mom.
I'm happy."

"I'm proud of you," she says. "You've made your life work."

Sometimes I feel that she projects her own fears of being
alone one day onto me, so I didn't tell her what a single, never-
married woman I know said to me when I asked her how she
coped with occasional loneliness. "You learn from the widows,"
the fiftysomething explained. "You keep busy."

A few times, I have spoken to my mother about widowhood.
So many of her friends have lost their husbands. "The men just
drop like flies," she often says. When my father, never one to
admit frailty of any kind, changes a flat tire, shovels a path of
snow or carries heavy suitcases up flights of stairs, she expresses
her anxiety by joking, "Don't have a heart attack today."

Stupidly, about two years ago I gave her a copy of Joan Didion's the *Year of Magical Thinking,* a meditation on the sudden loss of her husband. It is beautifully written, elegiac, I reasoned. My parents are both avid readers. But later, when I asked if she had read it, she said she hadn't. She had thrown it out. "I didn't want it in the house," she explained.

"I think people react differently to grief," I told her once, when we went out, just the two of us, for lunch when I was in London.

"How would you know that?"

"I don't know. It's just what I imagine—that you can't know or plan for how you will feel."

"You're right, I think."

"It's one of those things you only know when you're in it."

"Like divorce?"

I nod at her acknowledgment that our marital experiences are so different. "Or, like a good marriage," I say.

We laugh.

"Some of my friends are just fine," she says, returning to the discussion about widows. "They get on with it. They find things to do." She pauses to eat, finishes her bite. "And some women are quite relieved when the old duffer passes on."

We laugh again.

My mother has never been on her own. She moved from her father's house into one shared with her husband. In their forties, I remember my father telling her, "I've known you longer than I haven't known you." Now in their seventies, they discuss health in the same absorbing way they used to discuss children. "It's just the stage we are in," she says, explaining that when their friends get together, they all have a conversational rule. "We are allowed to talk about health issues for only ten minutes. We could go on for hours, if we wanted to."

It is hard to imagine how one would cope without the other. My siblings and I naturally express worry about the eventuality. Their marriage has largely defined both of them. "We do things together," my father once said when we were on holiday as a family, to explain why he was waiting patiently for her to get ready to go to the beach, which was mere steps from the front door. In the morning, my father usually sets the table, placing all the little homeopathic pills they take, and a baby aspirin, next to her place and his. Over the morning papers, they do the anagrams and other quizzes together. "Brain fitness," my mother says, tapping her temple. At Christmas and on their birthdays, they shower each other with presents, each delighting in the other's reaction.

My mother never lets anything change the way she conducts herself, not a crisis, not advancing age. She rarely appears at the breakfast table without having "put my face on," as she says, which means lipstick and a bit of eye makeup and rouge. Once a week, she goes to her local hairdresser and comes home with a high helmet of smooth, hairsprayed hair. When she swims, she holds her head above water, wearing a bathing cap like a fancy Easter bonnet. One year, when we were together for Christmas, she filled my stocking with little presents, one of which was a single napkin ring. I took it as a reminder about keeping up one's standards when living alone. I was not to start slouching toward the Frigidaire in my pjs.

She and I tiptoe around our generational gulf. We respect each other's geography, which mostly involves me charting mine for her. I know hers well through observation and the often-unkind judgment of a daughter. For the longest time, I thought hers was an unfulfilling life. But I see now how short-sighted that was. My generation's brand of woman-hood confounds her. When my two sisters and I started having babies and trying to figure out what our balance of work and family should be, our mother expressed admira-tion over our individual permutations of the Juggle. "I don't know how you girls do it," she said.

She is the product of a forgotten time, when many women and certainly most of her friends didn't pursue work. A career was a sort of distasteful sideline, suggesting that their hus-bands were unable to support them, and divorce was some-thing people did not do.

When I told her that I had pitched the *Globe and Mail* on the idea of writing about marriage and divorce, she reacted with some astonishment.

"And you're going to write about your own?"

"Well, yes. Why not be truthful?"

"Interesting," she replied in a small voice. My parents come from the sort of background that frowns upon personal display. A woman who laughs too boisterously was consid-ered unbuttoned somehow, lacking discretion. A person—and certainly a woman—should be in the newspaper only three times: for birth, marriage and death announcements.

"It's what everybody does now—they write about their own experiences. Because of blogs, I guess."

"What?"

"Blogs—first-person accounts on the Inter—"

She cuts me off. "I know what blogs are."

"Well, like that, then."

My parents are not ones to be left behind the times. They e-mail like teenagers.

"And besides, how could I not write some of my story when I'm asking people to tell theirs? It would be cowardly."

"Oh," she says.

"And you and Dad are going to be in it."

"No."

"Well, just a bit. It's a good thing you live in England," I joke.

As much as she tries to understand the state of mid-life post-divorce, and the fearless exposure of the truth about marriage that it often invites—a violation of its sanctity, some might say—she is still on the other side of that mystical river, in a different bubble of experience, like women who have never had children trying to fully grasp the sea change ushered in by motherhood.

But if I once questioned the nature of her marriage, I now envy her for the life she and my father built together. They share a lifetime of memories. Even if I marry again—tomorrow—I will never know that.

⌒

We choose partners whose personalities are the same, the opposite or a combination of both or one of our parents. That's what the Oprah-endorsed Imago Relationship Therapy maintains anyway. (They encourage participants to recognize which parts of their partners are their mothers or fathers, and then address, in a positive way, the unmet needs from childhood—because parents apparently leave all of us with some.)

Like many people, I have thought about the influence of my parents, and the example of my father as a man and a husband. As I was growing up, he could be authoritarian, strict and formal. When I was sixteen, he allowed me to have a drink before dinner—only a thimbleful of sherry in a small glass, despite the fact that my friends and I were drinking beer on a regular basis and had, on several occasions, snuck into a tavern downtown behind the old Montreal Forum.

He preferred my sisters and me in feminine clothes. "Is that what you're wearing?" he would say, slightly disapprovingly, as he folded down a flap of his newspaper, when we were going out as a family and one of us appeared in pants rather than a skirt or dress. Invariably, we would retreat back upstairs to change into something more appropriate. It wasn't that we were being encouraged to be dependent as future wives. We were all inculcated with a strong work ethic, and expected to work at a summer job after the age of sixteen. And the expectation that we would all go to university was very clear. But I was raised with a version of femininity that was not so much about being a woman as being a lady—demure, never pushy.

My father was the patriarch, and we obeyed him. He insisted that we learn proper table manners. Most Sunday lunches or evenings, we would eat in the formal dining room. When the meal was finished, we had to ask him, "May I be excused from the table?" We learned to respect our elders. We didn't dare talk back to him or to our mother. He never once called his mother-in-law by her first name, Margaret, or the name we called her, Gagi, even though she insisted. He addressed her, always, as Mrs. Evans. Well into my thirties, I used Mr. or Mrs. for my parents' friends too.

When Geoffrey and I were about seven and six, respectively, we shared a room in our family home in Toronto, where we lived for a year. One night in the summer, we lifted the heavy curtains that covered the long window between our beds to look at our parents in the garden during one of their parties. My father happened to glance up at our window, and saw us there, the tops of our heads. We dropped like stones into our beds, under the covers, feigning sleep. We heard the slam of the back door, the sound of his feet coming up the stairs. He asked us what did we think we were doing, out of our beds, when we had been told to go to sleep. Maybe we murmured some attempt at explanation or apology. It didn't matter. He spanked us, each separately, on our bare bottoms.

He was often remote—a scary authoritarian figure in many ways. I may have wanted a husband who was more emotionally available, but that didn't mean I avoided men who took control. I revered my father's calm guidance. He always knew what to do, especially in a crisis. I will never forget an evening when we went out to the theatre in the West End of London, when I was home from university. Before the performance began, we were standing on the ground floor, in the foyer, having a drink, as is the custom. In a far corner, a man suddenly drew a knife and began to slit his throat in a suicide attempt. There were screams. People recoiled in horror. My father walked over to the man and grabbed his hand, forcing him to drop the knife. "Don't do that," he told him sternly. Shortly after, the police arrived and led the man away, while the patrons filed into the darkened theatre, glancing with expressions of admiration and curiosity at my father from the corner of their eyes. We were in awe too, of course, following him like minions after their monarch.

⁓

Several years ago, I had the opportunity to
Gurley Brown, the iconic former editor of *Cosmopolit..*
zine, and author of *Sex and the Single Girl*, the book that promoted sexual liberation and made her name in the 1960s. She
was eighty years old when we met, and she had come to Toronto
to accompany her husband, David Brown, a noted film producer. We started talking about love, marriage and sex (what
else?), and without any hesitation, she was soon telling me
about her octogenarian libido. She explained, smiling wickedly
through her bright red lipstick, that it was good, very good—
which was a bit more than I needed to know. I recall that she
even told me about some techniques for the bedroom.

I asked what the secret was to her long marriage. She and
her husband had wed in 1959 and survived all her success and
his. Never marry the charmers, she said. Forget the men who
whisk you off your feet, who wine and dine you, who are out
to impress you with their fast cars and nice clothes and fat
wallets. She held up one boney forefinger to make her point.
"Go for kindness," she advised. That's what she had done.
"You want someone who will be your best friend, who will
support you and want the best for you."

I never focused on kindness as a trait in the men I wanted
to date when I was younger. It seemed too bland an attribute,
something expected of a little brother, not a lover. I wanted
something more exciting. But I see how vastly underrated
kindness is. I see that it is what nurtured my parents' marriage. My father was and is not an uncomplicated man. His
moods are many, but kindness is the most constant.

He encouraged my mother to go to university, which she did, part-time, when she was forty. And when she and one of her friends wanted to work outside the home, he helped the two women to set up an art gallery in downtown Montreal, a venture that made minimal profits. Upon their move to London, England, in 1978, he supported her when she studied decorative arts. He treasured his relationship with her. On Valentine's Day, he would send her a goofy card in the mail, with *Guess who?* written in a script that was meant to be that of a mysterious suitor.

A typically retro Dad, seated behind a newspaper most of the time rather than on the floor with us building forts, his love was rarely expressed in words, but it was never questioned. When my younger brother was brought home from the hospital after his birth, I remember feeling that I had lost my place. I had been the baby of the family for almost seven years. In the nursery, my father motioned for me to sit on the wobbly platform of his knees. A few minutes later, he took me into the living room to sit beside him on the piano bench, just the two of us. He played something. I can't remember what. His long, thin hands floated over the keys, rising and descending gracefully, like birds.

The message in all quarters of our upbringing was that marriage was the life glue, which I'm sure helped propel me into marriage at twenty-five. It doesn't surprise me that I was one of those young girls who dreamed of being a bride. I was raised in a culture that revered it. When I was eight or nine, I liked to fasten a white ballerina skirt to my head like a bridal veil, my hair scraped back off my face. I walked slowly toward a mirror in my nightie and would gaze at my reflection, as if I were the husband admiring the beauty of his wife. And then I would practise a kiss by pressing my lips against its cool surface. I rehearsed life as a mother too. My brother and I loved to play family with our stuffed toys. His room in our house in Montreal had a blue rug, which we pretended was a sea. His bed was the ship, and we would go to far-off places with our brood of monkeys, bears and a kangaroo. Rescues were often necessary, as some insisted on diving into the sea. Our game was called The Hansons—our own rendition of Hampson.

In our extended family, there was the curiosity of Great-aunt Mabel, a spinster, as they called unmarried women then. Mabel suffered from macular degeneration, which forced her to wear thick glasses. As she aged, she developed a widow's hump on her back from poor posture. Her lack of physical beauty served as explanation of her ineligibility, underscoring a pernicious paternalistic message that women are happiest when pretty enough to be held in a man's gaze. She was painfully shy when she was a girl, we were told. The youngest in a family of three and the only daughter, she had cared for her father after her mother died (which was expected of daughters in those days). By the time he died, she was in her early forties, well past the traditional marrying age.

Throughout my childhood and into my adulthood, we went for tea at her house, where she lived on her own for nearly fifty years. She would feel her way along the walls. She never used a white cane. She acted as though she could see. As children, we knew not to laugh when she almost missed while pouring the tea from her china pot into the cups. Her best story was one she repeated often. She was walking down the street in her neighbourhood one day and fell down an open manhole. The men in the bottom of the sewer were very kind. They helped her up the ladder and gave her back her purse. We loved her, but she was a strange creature, who didn't quite fit. I thought of her as someone who had been left behind somehow, abandoned, as the traditional opportunities of life—marriage, children, work—passed her by. Not that this was ever expressed by her or any of us, of course. She was included in our family rituals like a treasured relic.

Even in the story of Granny, my paternal grandmother, who was not an easy woman and never seemed to enjoy domestic life, the lesson was that marriage meant more than we sometimes think. A spoiled and somewhat vain woman, she had grown up the last of sixteen children. Her father had a boot and shoe business, although, when pressed, she would only allow that the family was "in fine leathers." (One of their biggest contracts had been supplying the army during the Boer War.)

In the dining room of my grandparents' house, where we would often go for Christmas dinner and other occasions, a portrait of her hung on the wall behind her chair at one end of the table. In it, she wore a dress of black silk satin, designed by Oleg Cassini. "Buster," she would often say to my grandfather as we settled down to dinner. "The portrait light is not on." A tall, round man with a face as gentle as Sunday (his nickname came at birth because he was ten pounds), he would get up from his seat at the opposite end of the table and dutifully flip the switch.

But if my grandparents' marriage survived on repressed, patrician manners, its sudden end, when my grandfather died, turned my formidable grandmother into a vulnerable widow. She developed a nervous habit of biting her lip. She adjusted to the change eventually, travelling with friends and inviting the family on holidays together. But she was never again as fierce. All those years of being impatient with him, of reminding him to do this and that, of being annoyed about the qualities he didn't have, were suddenly replaced with fondness for the lovely traits he did have. It wasn't just that she was alone but that she was without him, the very man who had once made her seem so discontent.

It is often said of children of divorce that they emerge from childhood damaged by the conflict they endured, soured to commitment in their own relationships by having witnessed their parents' broken promise of everlasting love. But we all carry some kind of weight from childhood, even a wonderful childhood—a burden of expectation, if nothing else, that you will have what your parents had, that you will fulfill your dreams, that the world will be as fair as it seemed back then. I sometimes think that the happiness of my childhood was a liability as I became an adult. I had a burden of trust. I thought husbands were like taxi drivers. If you chose to take one, to become a passenger, they would get you to your destination safely. That was their job, wasn't it? They had a licence. They would know the way.

2.

What the Feminists Forgot to Teach Us

In 1994, I returned for my fifteenth reunion to my alma mater, Smith College, a famously feminist, all-women's university in Northampton, Massachusetts. I happened to visit the school's museum, where I saw a painting by Gustave Courbet entitled *The Preparation of the Bride*. The 1850s-era work depicts a young bride surrounded by women who are helping her prepare for her wedding. But for many years, scholars had questions about it. Why is the bride's head slightly tilted? Her arms limp by her sides? Why is she slumped in her chair?

An X-ray in the 1970s, when the painting was sent to a Courbet retrospective in Paris, provided the answer. Courbet had painted a scene of women preparing a dead girl for a funeral. But after his death, when the painting was about to enter the art market after the First World War, the central figure was changed to that of a bride, to make the work more saleable. Another artist painted over the original scene, and Courbet's title, *The Preparation of a Dead Girl*, was changed to *The Preparation of the Bride*. Some scholars, notably Linda Nochlin, the feminist art historian, think that Courbet painted the wedding scene as it appears; that the bride was meant to look as she does. Nochlin explained the work in terms of wedding customs in the Franche Comte, a territory of France at the time. *A wife is a dead girl*, I thought. How fitting that the controversy had come to light in the 1970s, at the peak of feminism's second wave. The anti-marriage interpretation was inescapable. If I had seen the painting when I was a student, I would have dismissed the idea of bride as victim. I did not identify as a feminist, not completely. The school was a hothouse of feminist rhetoric at the time, which many of us took in as we might a Thoreauvian treatise. Some adopted it wholeheartedly; some questioned it; others rejected it. It was all up for debate. I found it interesting but I never saw myself as a hard-core feminist. But ten years into my marriage, the painting made me laugh. And it made me uncomfortable.

I had originally come to Smith in the fall of 1977 as a transfer student from the University of New Brunswick to study English literature. Like many students, I revelled in the school's message of limitless possibility and lapped up the feminist messages if that meant I was spared the bourgeois expectations of pot roasts on Sunday and nice tweed skirts. My clothes at the time consisted of long Laura Ashley skirts and Victorian-style blouses and vests, worn with workboots from Canadian Tire. "I don't want to be like you," I had said to my mother in an outburst when I was in high school.

"I will never be a wife!" She had her outlets beyond the domestic realm, but like many girls, arrogant in youth, I had decided what kind of person I thought her to be. Like most other housewives I witnessed, she seemed stuck in her domestic life, like a coin in a piggy bank.

The 1960s and 1970s didn't make much of a dent in the WASPy world we inhabited, although some of the influences seeped under its heavy wooden doors. I remember my parents' friends arriving at our house for cocktails before a ball, many of the women dressed in paper mini-dresses, their hair teased into high beehives. In 1969, when the birth control pill was legalized in Canada, we were living in Vancouver, a city of maxi skirts, VW Bugs and hippies on English Bay, whom we gawked at like tourists from the back seat of our big blue station wagon. My mother volunteered at a clinic to help dispense contraceptives—her nursing instinct, I think—and I remember her expressing astonishment at the freedom they represented.

When we returned to Montreal in 1971, I was sent to a private girls' school called The Study, where in 1952 my mother had been head girl. There I experimented with marijuana and alcohol, and began smoking du Maurier cigarettes at fifteen, blowing the smoke discreetly out the window of my room at the top of our stone house overlooking Montreal's downtown and the St. Lawrence River. Mine was a standard rebellion. Mostly, I was continuing my ladylike education. We learned to waltz in gym class in our running shoes, tunics and bloomers, girl with girl. I often joke that I first learned about the great mystery and glory of sex from reading Leonard Cohen's *Beautiful Losers* in grade ten. Our English teacher, Mrs. Willmott, dressed in a knit dress, with her strawberry-blond hair in a pert cap, saved me somehow when I fell into consciousness that year, suddenly aware of myself, all alone, in a big wide world. From behind her large glasses and with her slightly bucktoothed grin, she gave us entry into another world. I adored her.

When I graduated from high school, I wanted to get away. In Quebec, students finish high school at the end of grade eleven, and the educational system encourages them to attend one of the province's two-year Collèges d'enseignement général et professionnel (CEGEP) before going to university. I skipped the process and entered the University of New Brunswick just after turning seventeen, a year or two younger than many of my peers. But I hated the casual atmosphere, and when I complained to my father he suggested I apply to colleges in the United States.

I applied sight unseen to various schools. In the end, I narrowed it down to a choice between Smith and Mount Holyoke, both women's colleges in the same valley in western Massachusetts. In the summer, my parents drove me down to have a look at the campuses. I loved Northampton, a small town founded in 1654, where Smith is located. There were many factors in my decision, and one was the saying that a student guide told me was often used to distinguish the type of women who attended the two sister schools: Smith to Bed, Mount Holyoke to Wed.

I decided on Smith.

The school was a curious blend of traditional and progressive ideas. Some parts of campus life made me feel like I was in a finishing school for young ladies. I had a room in Talbot House, a brick dormitory built in 1909 with a gambrel roof, a wide, white porch with a swing, and ivy growing up the sides. Students wore what seemed like a uniform of Fair Isle sweaters, khaki pants and Top-Siders. Many of them knitted or did needlepoint in their spare time. At night, most wore Lanz nighties, long flannel floral-patterned gowns with puff sleeves and stitched lace around the yoke. They floated about the house, settling down like instant tents, their gowns draped over their knees, to eat popcorn and talk late at night in the carpeted hallways.

But if many women seemed to have stepped from the pages of *Town & Country* magazine, their academic ambition turned them into intellectual Amazons. We enthused or complained about our courses the way women I used to know discussed their boyfriends. Once, soon after my arrival, my friend Molly Hamill, a fellow English literature student who had been assigned to be my "big sister"—a tradition at Smith—invited a small group of us to go to a pizza place in town for supper. On our way home, Molly stripped off her T-shirt to run bare-breasted through the darkened, quiet streets. "We are Smithies!" she cried. We all followed suit, laughing at the townies who turned to stare. Friday nights were often spent in the library. For exams, Smith went by the honour system. You could take your final exam when you wanted to, which meant that some classmates would know what was on the final before others. But there was never any chance that someone would divulge its content. It was every woman for herself.

The campus ideology was in transition, straddling different eras of expectations for a woman's life. Four years earlier, to mark the school's centenary, Smith had hired its first female president, Jill Kerr Conway, a writer and historian whose highly praised memoir, *The Road from Coorain*, was a moving story of an Australian girl who emerged from her isolated childhood on a sheep farm to take on the male-dominated world of academia. T-shirts from the hundredth anniversary were sold in the school store: *One Hundred Years of Women on Top* read one. Even the classic: *A Woman Needs a Man Like a Fish Needs a Bicycle*. Among the alumnae, there were fascinating exemplars of how we might live our lives: among others, Gloria Steinem, the social activist and founder of *Ms.* magazine; Betty Friedan, who had used a questionnaire during her fifteenth reunion as research for the *Feminine Mystique*; Julia Child, who introduced Americans to French cuisine through her bestselling cookbooks and television shows; and Sylvia Plath, the celebrated poet who had taught at the school. "We have one in the White House and one in the slammer," students would say a few years later, in reference to Nancy Reagan and Jean Harris, the Smithie who was convicted in 1981, the year Ronald Reagan was elected president, of murdering her lover, Dr. Herman Tarnower, the famous cardiologist and Scarsdale Diet doctor.

Varieties of women blossomed at Smith as freely as wildflowers. It was all an exploration of our gender. There were Sylvia Plath wannabes, deeply immersed in their poetic sensibilities, wafting about campus. The women who flirted outrageously with the men bussed in from Yale and Harvard for the weekend parties were called Debs. Not unlike Reese Witherspoon's character Elle Woods, in *Legally Blonde*, they wore pearls and colourful ribbons in their ponytails. Prince Albert of Monaco, then a student at nearby Amherst College, once came to a party at Talbot House, protected from the husband-seekers by wingmen. Members of the school's Lesbian Women's Alliance would visit the dormitories during scheduled meetings to promote understanding of their sexual orientation. Some women decided to be LUGs, or Lesbians Until Graduation. Their preferred hangouts were in town, where a vibrant lesbian community made an afternoon at a café feel like an anthropological field trip into an alternative lifestyle.

I steered away from the preppie parties. Instead, I became involved with a professor in his fifties. I was annoyingly serious at that juncture in my life. "Do you always have to be so deep?" a handsome boyfriend once asked me after we had gone to a movie (Woody Allen's *Interiors*) and I was busy analyzing it. He dumped me, that particular guy, and I really don't blame him. Imagine a smoky café, preferably windowless: I was the girl in the corner, debating Emily Dickinson poetry with sophomoric pretension. "Experience is sharper when you begin innocent," I wrote of the affair with the professor a few years later in my journal. I didn't like men my own age very much. I found them silly, boring. I wanted to push myself into something unknown and a bit dangerous, a situation that I believed would hasten my maturity. The affair made me feel clever, even though I kept it mostly to myself. I felt superior to my peers who contented themselves with clean-shaven frat boys. See what I mean? Insufferable. Even Smith was a continuation of my protected life, in a way. I wanted to know what lay beyond its perimeter. In town one afternoon, I saw a book by Joyce

Carol Oates that had a bright pink cover, the title in bold letters: *Do With Me What You Will*. I took it to that professor's class. I usually sat a few students away from him around a large round table. I put the book on top of my pile of notebooks and turned it slightly to face him. I have no idea whether he noticed it. And I never asked. Not a girl gone wild. Just a girl gone very, very naive.

"He made a mistake with you," Molly said to me during our final year. "He usually picks a senior. That way, the affair is brief. They graduate. But you were in your junior year. He blew it." The affair had lasted one semester. Although I saw him in my final year, we were merely friends. I was hurt—I didn't understand why he had cooled things off—but I never felt that I was a victim. Who, me? I felt exquisitely beautiful at twenty, experimenting with my sexual power like a forbidden substance.

Messages at the school about how to navigate our romantic lives were mixed and incomplete. There was no attempt to discuss how the wife identity had not changed with the times. In her book *The Meaning of Wife*, Anne Kingston astutely charts the "wife landscape" with contemporary, historic and literary examples, including the husband-leveraging Hillary Rodham Clinton, the train-wrecked Anna Karenina, the misadventurous Lucy Ricardo, the rebellious Nora in Henrik Ibsen's *A Doll's House* and the attic-dwelling Bertha Rochester in *Jane Eyre*. Even now, the wife has not been liberated from her freighted past, Kingston argues.

When Anne Morrow Lindbergh visited Smith in the spring of 1978 at the age of seventy-two, she spoke about her life as a wife, mother, homemaker, aviatrix, writer and, at that time, a widow of four years. Fifty years earlier, she had graduated from Smith. In her senior year, she had met Charles Lindbergh, the dashing American aviator, through her father, who was a diplomat. She accompanied him on his flights and became the first American woman to earn a first-class glider pilot's licence. But she had what she called "a lot of unlived woman's life in me." She went on to have six children, the first of whom, Charles Augustus Lindbergh, Jr., was tragically kidnapped and murdered in 1932 at the age of twenty months, a story that became the news event of the decade.

"No woman has to go through all these stages," Morrow Lindbergh made a point of saying to us. "You are free today—due to many of the feminist victories—to stay unmarried and to have no children. Some women cannot have children or do not want them. You can decide to have fewer children or to have your children late. It is possible for you to get on the escalator of a career and ride up to the top floor, and many of you can and will. . . . Don't let anyone pressure you into thinking that you can't have marriage or children or a career or all three or any combination you choose."

The school had only recently embraced a feminist approach. The male presidents before Kerr Conway had helped instill a patriarchal view that women's education was part of their grooming as future wives of powerful men. There was never any discussion then about assessing who would be the right kind of husband, not like today, when dating experts try to make the choice and pursuit of spouses as clinical as a business deal. It's as if they view their advice as the last weapon of female empowerment. Marriage governs happiness. It doesn't matter how well educated you

are, how well employed, how physically attractive, how kind—
who you marry is the one decision that will determine much
of how life unfolds.

When I was at Smith, no one helped us understand how
to approach marriage, children, a work–home balance, or even
how to handle personal finances, for that matter. (The school
has since made financial literacy an important part of a
woman's education.) Friedan's book *The Second Stage*, in which
she argues for a revolution in the management of the household, was not published until 1981, when she returned to the
school to speak. We were just meant to go out and succeed, to
have it all. The only time that the idea of conflict in marriage
and motherhood came up was in a movie about divorce in
1979, the year we graduated. In *Kramer vs. Kramer*, Meryl Streep
plays a Smithie who leaves her husband (Dustin Hoffman)
and her son and moves to California to "find herself," only to
realize that she wants custody of her child after all.

At the graduation ceremonies for our class, the feminist
poet Adrienne Rich, who had come out as a lesbian in 1976
after a failed marriage, gave the commencement address.
"What does a woman need to know, to become a self-conscious, self-defining human being?" she asked rhetorically.
"Doesn't she need to know that seemingly natural states of
being, like heterosexuality, like motherhood, have been
enforced and institutionalized to deprive her of power?"

My friends and I thought her speech was ridiculous—the
parts we managed to absorb, that is. Many of us harboured
romantic fantasies while paying lip service to feminism. We
were juggling ideas of how to be women, toying with them,
really, and the one that never ceased to have power was a

traditional one. Valentine's Day was a major event on the campus. Students would gather around the front door of the dormitory, when the postman was due to make his delivery. Each would snatch the card addressed to her, if she was lucky enough to get one, squealing with delight. Bouquets of flowers arrived during the day, and the recipients paraded off to their rooms, carrying their gift for all to admire. Those who didn't get any were left feeling like utter losers. Some of my friends—Molly among them—were preparing to marry their boyfriends. All the steely Smithness of the determined, smart women we were encouraged to be, and which we gladly adopted, could easily slip beneath our desire to be loved—to be chosen.

3.

Love Conquers All, Doesn't It?

"I can't believe it. You too? Bullied into marriage?"

"Well, sort of," I say.

I am talking to a new divorced friend, who lives nearby in Divorce Alley, my name for my midtown neighbourhood of skinny townhouses, the perfect landing places for people who are downsizing. Several neighbours are divorced. Others are empty-nesters. Some are newly married, but once they have a few children, many move to more loosely packed neighbourhoods, where detached houses and wider, greener gardens give families space to grow.

Ellen and I have just done the marriage-tale exchange, her potato gratin for my beef stew. She told me that she got married largely because her mother pressured her, telling her she was too picky about her suitors and that "it was time."

She was in her early thirties. "And my biological clock was setting off alarm bells," she says. Her husband was twelve years her senior. Established in his business, he had an air of authority. "Oh, he was probably a father figure," she allows breezily. Her own father was ill. He was hanging on until his youngest daughter married, she felt. That the families knew each other gave the match a feeling of inevitability. The marriage lasted ten years and produced two children.

And I have given her the top-line facts of how I met my husband-to-be. For all my feminist leanings, my story was traditional and the details that now seem so telling for how the marriage would turn out were invisible at the time.

I had been living in London, England, for a year and a half, after graduating from Smith. But with visa issues that prevented me from continuing to work in my chosen field of advertising, I moved to Toronto. The problem was that in the midst of the 1981 recession, no one was hiring. A creative head of a large agency suggested I go to a small affiliated advertising company in Halifax, where I could get some experience with the view to returning to Toronto when the economy improved. *Why not?* I thought. I had relocated my entire life. I was twenty-two.

The agency had offices near the waterfront and a busy client list, and I was the only copywriter. Within three months of moving there, I was romantically involved with one of the partners. A father of three children, Eric said he was unhappy in his marriage. He had almost left a few years before, but he thought he should try to make it work. He was thirteen years older than me.

When I think back on our courtship, a collage of memories twirls through my mind. I remember the first time he leaned over to kiss me. We were in his car, parked outside my apartment. I remember going to Point Pleasant Park with him at lunchtime. We walked to a bench in a clearing and talked the whole time, barely eating our sandwiches. I remember watching the Halifax harbour from the large window in his office. We sat back to back, supporting each other, like bookends with an imaginary future between us. There were dinners at waterfront restaurants. There were late-night talks seated on the floor, eating pizza. On weekends after he left his wife, and when he didn't have his children, we liked to drive along the highway to Lunenburg or Chester, along the south shore, to see history tucked into the coves, treasures of time and place.

He had married young, soon after his mother had remarried following his father's death from cancer. He knew on his honeymoon that he had made a mistake, he said. But he wanted a family. I knew nothing about unhappy marriages. I knew they existed, of course. But to hear about the workings of one, its interior climate, was like peering into someone else's heart. He often spoke about his wife in a disparaging tone—a huge red flag I now know to pay attention to. "But you must love her as the mother of your children," I said to him once. "Yes, I suppose I do," he replied, looking forlorn. I was drawn to his melancholy at being trapped, of wanting more. For all his competency, there was a vulnerability. Every part of my being clung to him like scattered metal filings to a magnet.

I was in that experimental period of youth, rejecting my parents' model in an attempt to find my own. I never liked men from the same background as mine. It was like looking in a mirror. Eric came from a working-class family in Battersea, England. He had moved with his parents and younger sister to Germany and then to New Brunswick. His father had been in the military. That you could go out in the world, often just on a whim, as I had come to Halifax, and encounter someone who you think sees the world in the same way, feels like magic. A connection across class, gender and time feels like you have travelled to Mars and found a spoon buried in the red sand. It has something to do with feeling that you have come home, that you have been found. "She pushed all the right buttons," Liam Neeson once said of his late wife, actress Natasha Richardson. "Certain people push one or two. But she pushed buttons I didn't even know I had."

Eric was the first man I knew to whom I could really talk, who cried sometimes, who openly discussed his feelings, who had deeply conflicting ones, who was curious about mine, who dug down into them, interested to find out what else was there. It was a kind of knowing that parents, who love their children deeply and feel they understand them, can never compete with. Once, in my final year at university, I had written an emotional letter home expressing some of my concerns about school, my anxieties and how much I loved my parents. "We were worried there was something wrong," my mother said to me, concerned that I was fretting too much. I hated to worry them. Besides, in adolescence, divulging thoughts to our parents as we cross from innocence into adulthood feels uncomfortable. The maturing mind sprouts characteristics, just as the body does, that you don't want your parents to see.

With Eric, I could completely unspool myself. And as he explored my questions about the world, he quelled them.

He took my hand often, when we were driving along the highway or flying off to some meeting elsewhere in the Maritimes in propeller planes. A shelter, his hands were—solid and square and dry. He would tuck my hand under his, and with his thumb, stroke the back of it, gently.

In the fall of that year—six months after joining his firm—I was offered a job with Ogilvy & Mather in Toronto. I had been writing to agencies, sending samples of my work, in an effort to get hired. It had never been my plan to stay in Halifax. I left and returned to the apartment I had shared with a friend in Toronto. I loved Eric, or thought I did, but wasn't sure what would happen. I was cavalier about it all, which also helps explain my lack of hesitation over getting involved with a married man. I was in that self-referential stage—a romantic adventurer high on my ability to seduce others. I didn't step back to think about consequences.

But by the time I had moved back to Toronto, he had left his marriage. Every night, he would phone me. And I missed him, more than I had thought I would. I would tell him about my day. My job was challenging and exciting. But the conversation would always end with him telling me that I had made a mistake by moving back to Toronto, that he loved me, that he needed me. He came to visit me, and all my girlfriends were impressed with him. I'm not sure if we ever analyzed love relationships the way young women do now. I just figured it must be true love, if he needed me that much, if he couldn't bear to be without me and if I missed him so. Was it infatuation? Real love? His need for control? My desire for a father figure? I was too young to know that what looks and sounds and feels like love isn't always love.

Part of me felt he had left his marriage for me, even though I knew he had been unhappy for a long time before we met. I felt bad that he was so bereft because of something our involvement had precipitated.

Three weeks later, I quit my job. I went back to Halifax. My parents were not happy. "I can't tell you what to do," my father said on the phone from London, but he made it clear that he didn't understand my decision. Eric was still married, even though he had moved out of the marital home. My parents would have preferred that he sorted out his family life before I lived with him. And maybe they thought the relationship would fade once I moved away to pursue my career in Toronto. I remained defiant. Eric and I found a large apartment to share. It was the first time I had ever lived with a boyfriend. We travelled to London so he could meet my parents. He was charming, and they liked him. That Christmas, my parents paid for me to come home to question me on my own. I told them more about Eric, my life with him, and how much I loved him. I felt rebellious, as young people do. At that point, parents are somewhat powerless, and mine likely knew that if they expressed bigger disapproval, they would push me deeper into his arms. I wanted something bigger than my protected childhood and adolescence, a more creative life. My parents had often dismissed my thoughts not because they considered them odd but because they wished to spare me the anguish of thinking them. At least, that's what I decided. I loved the great, beautiful drama of life. I was obsessed with meaningfulness. And I felt that my parents and others in that circle were only interested in the surface of things. I wanted to make my own way.

For a year I stayed in Halifax, while we waited for his divorce papers to come through. But I was restless. Although I never acknowledged it to myself at the time, I felt that I had moved back to Halifax without thinking carefully enough about the decision. I didn't fully acknowledge it at the time, but I resented Eric for persuading me to leave a good career opportunity and take a step backwards. Once again, I began to write to agencies in Toronto to look for a job. Soon, I got a copywriting position at Ted Bates Advertising.

"I will only move to Toronto if you marry me," Eric said. He was standing by the fireplace in our apartment. I can see his face—not soft or pleading, but defiant. He was giving me an ultimatum. It's not just women who give them.

I said yes.

⟋⟍

I am not sure how to pinpoint what makes us love another, although I know why we wish we could. It has a deeply trans-formative power. Part of me agrees with Theodore Roethke, who wrote, "Love begets love." We often fall in love with people who are in love with us. And there are always some subconsciously calculated transactions at play in our roman-tic decisions. One partner adds to or subtracts from the other's image or needs.

"Bruce came along and he offered me what I was missing in myself—bravado, aggression, decisiveness," Barbara Clerihue Carter, a commander in the Canadian Navy, says about her ex-husband. She wasn't yet sure of herself as a female leader. Her husband functioned in a typically male way, which she liked and, for a time, thought she would have to emulate if she wanted to be successful. "I thought he could get me out of my abstract mind," my friend Joy says of hers. "I think I offered him a sort of wild side and he offered me a solid, more traditional grounding," explains another woman about her former marriage.

Established and successful, Eric offered security. I had moved around a lot, and maybe I needed to establish a place for myself in the world. Being a wife was one way to do that. It was a clear path at a time when I wasn't completely sure what I really wanted.

Eric added to my confidence too. He owned a snazzy sports car; whisked me off on surprise trips; bought me presents, flowers; wrote love notes. He was a master of the grand gesture—I bought the breathless Harlequin romance ideal. Tall and handsome with a beard and bright blue eyes, he looked like a character from a Merchant Ivory film, a sea captain or something. Every woman in the office—there were four, including me—was secretly in love with him. He signed his name, I remember, with a grand flourish, a bold statement.

I met his wife and thought I understood why he had chosen me over her. I believed his criticisms of her. He repeated the classic line of many divorced men: my wife doesn't understand me, but you do. One time when we picked up his children at their house, I watched her in the side mirror as we drove away. She was standing in the doorway of her house, her arms by her sides, watching us disappear into the distance. I never once wondered about her side of the story. The Other Woman rarely asks anything of the one woman who knows the truth. It is the nature of female friendships that we often share everything, and when it matters most, nothing.

In return, I gave him youth, I suppose. I was a fresh start, a safe landing. I liked the departure from where I had been as a single girl to this new place, where I could begin to carve out a new way of being. My particular Montreal WASP ethnicity was part of my identity, although which part and how strong it was, I was never sure. I was as much in rebellion against it as I was in solidarity with it.

The first time Granny met Eric, the summer before our marriage in September 1983, we all had dinner—my parents, the two of us, some of my siblings. When it was time to leave, we filed out the door, one by one, to say good-night to Granny, who stood in the foyer. She was the matriarch of the Hampson family, and we all revered, if not feared, her. When it was Eric's turn, he put his hand out to shake hers, but she placed her arms firmly at her sides, like a soldier. She said good-night in a small, clipped voice, but she would not shake his hand. I was the first grandchild with plans to marry. She did not approve of my choice. He was divorced, for one. Already a father. Older. I was shocked at her rejection of him, but tried to laugh it off. What did she know about what women of my generation wanted? What did she know about what I wanted?

I stepped into the role of stepmother with the same breezy confidence that many women do. Eric's three girls, then twelve, nine and six, treated me like a glamorous big sister. It was fun. They were adorable. Eric and I took them to movies. We went swimming at the Y. They could visit us in Toronto, he assured them. We would go back east for some summers. Eric was willing to sacrifice a lot. He would have to wind down his portion of the business or manage it from afar until he figured out the best solution. His children would remain with their mother. The move and child support would stretch his financial resources. He moved to Toronto with little money, but he was confident in his ability to start over, which he did successfully. Smart and talented, he always had money-making ideas.

I was flattered, I think, by the high stakes of it all, by the drama, by the feeling that love would prevail. I felt swept up in a big romantic story: a man is so taken with a woman that he is overcome with wanting her and will make sacrifices to have her. They make movies like that. But I didn't fully understand the impact my decision to marry a father of three would have on his children. Or on me.

When I think back on that period, I am stunned at my own naïveté and the pain I helped inflict on his children through my ignorance and desire to have my own family. If I had taken more time to think through the decision to marry him, would I have gone through with it? I see now that I had a tendency to err on the side of confidence. I thought I could do anything. I was naively certain, like Wile E. Coyote, the *Looney Tunes* cartoon character who speeds off the edge of a cliff until he realizes that he's running on thin air.

But there were other factors. I was not good at confronting and sorting out the conflict of my own emotions. If I'd wanted to break up with him, could I have? I don't know. The decision to marry had something to do with not knowing how to say no to something that seemed so big, even if I harboured doubts about his tendency to persuade me to do as he pleased. And I couldn't begin to figure out how to get out of something the strength of which I could not deny. I equated love with marriage, I suppose. I believed that one inevitably led to the other. But the decision also had something to do with what Jane Fonda described as "the disease to please." She had grown up in a strong patriarchal family and subconsciously had come to see her value as measured by what men thought of her.

My Smith indoctrination fell away. On the night before our wedding, I wrote Eric a letter in a present I gave him of an antique tea caddy, where I hoped we would keep all our special notes. I found it after our divorce with several letters still inside. He must have forgotten about it.

In part, my wedding-day note read, "I want to really be something and I want you there all the way beside me. . . . Forgive me sometimes for my thoughtless ways. I want to be a good, honest, loving wife for you." He was able to make me feel bad about my own ambitions that went beyond being a loving partner. I didn't know how to reconcile the two. On our first anniversary, I wrote another. It begins: "I think sometimes when I talk to you that I am the luckiest—and happiest—person in the world." The next sentence? "I have many faults, I know that through being and living and loving with you. I want so much to be a good, honest wife. . . . I shall continue to work hard at being a better Sarah—the one you know and love so deeply."

⌒

"I always felt glad that Eric would look after you," my mother tells me sometimes.

I nod. Maybe I did need to be looked after. Maybe that's why I got married.

"You were happy, Sarah," she said to me soon after the divorce. "It wasn't all bad."

"Of course not, Mom," I reassured her. "A lot of it was wonderful."

4.

Losing and Gaining Selves

When I remember how I donned the mantle of wife, I like to think my wedding dress glows in the dark. It's down in the garage now, on top of a tall cupboard in a professionally sealed white box wrapped in heavy plastic that hasn't been opened in over twenty-five years. If I had known how it would transform me, I would not have enjoyed shopping for it, standing on a small pedestal in front of a three-panelled mirror, surrounded by cooing salesladies who congratulated my mother on what a lovely bride her daughter would make. That dress was radioactive, capable of reorganizing the molecules of the young woman arriving at Smith, so boldly sure of herself and rebellious, into those of a dutiful wife, who five years later felt the need to reassure her husband that she would try to be "a better Sarah."

I had no idea that night before my wedding how profoundly my life would change and how little I would be allowed to grow with the man I'd chosen. Women always feel the internal pressure to be perfect, which partly explains what happened. I remember that feeling when I sprouted breasts and first got my period. "Oh, you're a woman now," my mother gushed, hugging me. And I, too, felt differently about myself. When I see a young teenage girl gazing at her reflection in a mirror, mesmerized, I recognize the preoccupation. *Who am I now?* they wonder. Their beauty and youth have power they are not sure how to inhabit. When I became a bride, I stepped into a different persona yet again.

Cultural and familial influences played a part in my interpretation of the role. Upon news of my engagement, Gagi gave me her sterling silver vanity-table set: a small jar for pins, a brush, hand mirror, comb, shoehorn and button fastener, which had been engraved with her initials and given to her upon her engagement. It suggested a preoccupation with appearance, if nothing else; a need to be someone's complementary reflection. Part of a wedding present from my parents was bed and bathroom linen, monogrammed with my new initials.

At first, everything seemed perfect. The year after our wedding, my paternal grandmother died suddenly, and my parents decided that Eric and I would get her heavy mahogany dining room table, chairs and impressive sideboard. We were the first to be married in my family, the most settled, with a new house and, by that time, a child on the way. A million memories came with that furniture: Granny at one end of the table, under her portrait; Grandpappy at the sideboard in his velvet smoking jacket at Christmas, carving the turkey; my siblings and me arranged around the table's perimeter, in our good clothes, on our best behaviour. Suddenly, there I was at one end of the table, Eric at the other, living the traditions of my past. I was proud to uphold them. I felt that I was fulfilling an expectation, like graduating from college. I morphed into a slightly hipper version of my mother, giving dinner parties with my new china and silverware in the way I remembered her giving them. I was enjoying the creation of a home. It was as though I had been carrying an unborn idea of how to be a wife all my young life, without knowing I was pregnant with it, and once I put on my dress and said my vows, it emerged, fully formed, big and loud.

The wife behaviour is a riptide in the feminine psyche, invisible on the surface. Many women feel enough of its pull, even without marriage, to know that if they ever waded into one, they soon would be far out to sea, unable to get back to shore by themselves. "I feel if I had the role of wife, I would become someone else. I would then start behaving like a wife," Oprah Winfrey said on *The Tonight Show with Jay Leno* to explain her decision not to marry Stedman Graham, her longtime companion. And some are conscious of it, of course. A divorced friend explained to me recently—without irony— that she felt positive about her romantic future because "I am good wife material," by which she meant that she is slim, athletic, social and knows how to keep a nice house.

After the initial honeymoon phase, I began to struggle, not only under the wife's retrograde script, but also out of my own notions of what it means to love. Hard as it may be for me and the feminists to accept, the desire to give oneself over to someone—or something—is common. Do we malign men for subjugating themselves to their work identity? Do we think it weak or misinformed or somehow retro for people to devote themselves to their God? Isn't a selfless devotion to something outside of ourselves—to art, say, to music, to sport—seen as a passion? And there is something about such passion that makes us forget about ourselves, even want to lose ourselves. When I spoke to J.M. Kearns, author of *Better Love Next Time*, he spoke of marriage as similar to religion. "When you get together with someone and decide to make them the centre of your life, and you will be the centre of theirs, and you're building everything around them, including children, that is a huge belief system." Yet the desire to channel one's energies into someone else—a spouse, a child— is considered diminishing, while the focus of self in other pursuits is admired.

Like the man subsumed in his work, the wife devoted to her husband is a sacrifice that can be taken to unhealthy (and unflattering) extremes, of course. And I soon felt that I was sacrificing more than was healthy. In her memoir *Resilience*, Elizabeth Edwards, the now-estranged wife of John Edwards, then a Democratic presidential hopeful, describes her disappointment in her husband's affair with Rielle Hunter. "I am imperfect in many ways, but I always thought I was the kind of woman, the kind of wife to whom a husband would be faithful," she writes. Some inadequacy of her own was partly to blame, she suggests. The "good" wife wasn't good enough.

But for many women, wanting to be a "good" wife is nothing more than a simple desire to live up to her responsibilities, just as a "good" husband tries to live up to his. Becoming a husband involves sacrifices too. In my own sons, I have seen a modulation of self that takes place as they share their lives with girlfriends. Still, the culture is preoccupied with women's adoption (or not) of roles, suggesting criticism of them, the very thing feminists purport to want to eliminate.

I didn't know what the balance was—or could be—between what I needed for myself and what I was willing to sacrifice for others. Just as I was becoming an adult, stretching myself into my maturity, like a hand into a new glove, I had to think about how others expected me to be. I had to try to fit someone else's glove. I was confused. My head filled with youthful romantic notions about losing oneself in love, losing firm boundaries. I thought real love involved complete surrender. I longed for it in a way—to be swept away, to be remade. But it didn't happen. Some little voice inside—a Me who could be snarky and ambitious and judgmental—would not be silenced. She was difficult. Not sweet. And I felt guilty that I couldn't be otherwise. In a journal I labelled "After-marriage," I wrote an entry in the first year: "I think about my role, my so-called preconceived ideas about what it means to love somebody, and I fail, because I'm so concerned with maintaining my selfhood."

Upon marriage, Eric insisted that I change my surname to his. I balked at first—so much of who I was felt like a Hampson. And it rubbed against the grain of what I felt at Smith. But I relented. I wanted to please him. I know many women whose husbands felt the same way. "Failure to take his name indicated to him that I would be unable to psychologically be his partner, unable to compromise," a friend of mine said of her mate. I understand when a woman gives up her maiden name (or "blends" it with her husband's) as a show of love and devotion. "It was a sign of complete commitment," one young woman explained of her choice to drop her maiden name. Measha Brueggergosman, a celebrated Canadian soprano who was born Measha Gosman, and her Swiss husband, Markus Bruegger, decided on a combo surname because, as she explains, "My name is my identity. But I also wanted to make sure that there was something in my identity to signify my spiritual connection to my partner." Hyphenation wasn't an option. "It has the semblance of a trial period, a temporary quality that could be dismantled," she says. Some women feel so clear about who they are and what they want that they don't see the loss of their maiden name as significant. "I can't rail against oppression I've never experienced," wrote Kelly Grant, née Kelly Patrick, in the *National Post* about her decision to assume her husband's surname.

But when one person gives up a surname for another, it is almost always the woman. There is the rare man who drops his, but the decision is often made as compensation for the superior power he knows he has in society. "I never suspected that as a man I had been given an extra portion of power in the global allotment," wrote Josiah Neufeld (né Thiessen) on the *Globe and Mail*'s Facts & Arguments page. His fiancée, Mona, had explained her fight to be taken seriously as a woman, which made the loss of her surname difficult to bear. As compensation—to balance their power—he decided to take hers. "I did it because any form of power comes with duties. I'm obliged to take responsibility for my power, to learn its effects—even unintentional ones—to see what it does to others when I'm not watching, to use it in the best way possible. Sometimes, to relinquish it."

My surrender was not complete—perhaps a sign of my own confusion about the decision. Of course, my parents automatically began addressing their letters to me as Mrs. with my husband's surname. They used it socially, as Eric did. For important pieces of identification, such as my passport, my health card and driver's licence, I adopted his surname. For some other things, I used a hyphenated version. But for work, I stayed with Hampson. I had a career under that name, a reputation, I argued. But even when I gave up my job in advertising and reinvented myself as a magazine writer ten years later—a perfect opportunity to adopt a new name—I stayed with Hampson. I didn't know then that in years ahead my maiden name would become a lifeboat from my sinking marriage.

There were other transitions to sharing my life with someone else that made me uncomfortable. Eric wanted control of the finances. Again, I resisted. I was happy to contribute to our expenses. I simply wanted control over my own money. To avoid arguments, I eventually agreed, although I kept some money aside for my personal use, an amount that he and I determined together.

I was doing what my mother had done—hand over the financial reins to her husband. I knew there were other, more equitable, ways of managing a household. But Eric was more knowledgeable about money than I was. We had a large mortgage on our first house. And I was soon busy with babies. It was part of our division of labour that he handled it. Still, I began the habit of hiding things I had bought for myself. They would go in the closet, and when I wore something new, if he asked about it I would say I had bought it ages ago: "This thing? It was on sale, too cheap to pass up." If I bought something for the house, which I loved to do, I would lie about the cost. It was a fraught, circuitous pattern of self-denial followed by self-assertion. I put myself last, denying myself things I wanted, but then resentment would build and I would splurge on something. It was like an eating disorder. Starve myself. Then binge. And never tell.

Recently, I came across a short passage of fictitious dialogue I had written in a creative writing class when I was a young wife. It reveals some of the feelings I was trying to process.

He sat forward and took a long pull on his cigarette. The children were down for the night, finally. Fed. Bathed. Storybooks read. Kissed. Tucked in.

"I don't know, Em. We've been through this all before."

I stood in the kitchen, preparing a simple meal. "You talk about it as if it were a book," I said.

"Well, it sometimes sounds like one," he replied, looking over at me. "A bad one."

"Thanks a lot."

"Well, come on, think about it." His glance returned to the ceiling.

"You want it just to go away. To put it back on the shelf."

He remained silent for a moment. "I want to help you if I can."

"Maybe you're not the one who can," I said, petulant.

He sighed deeply. "Talked to your mother recently?"

"Yeah."

"Well, what did she say?"

"She said it was me."

He chortled softly and winked at me from across the room when he caught my glance. "Your mother always did have a soft spot for me," he said.

"Great, isn't it?" I laughed too. "The ultimate weapon."

"You're too hard on your mother," he said after a moment's pause.

"I think she's a little hard on me."

"Okay, maybe," he conceded. "But you're bringing this all on yourself. Everything's okay."

"Thinking everything's okay is half the problem," I shot back. I wasn't even sure what we were talking about now. My lost work identity. Being a stay-at-home mom with three children, a dog, a Chrysler van. Living in yuppie perfection in Toronto.

"Mediocrity afflicts half the nation," he said. He rolled his eyes.

"Well, I want to be in the other half, thank you very much."

"Just who do you think you are." He spit out the sentence, thrusting his chin forward the way he did when overcome with anger. "Madonna hates mediocrity. Is that where you read it? In *Vanity Fair*?" His laugh was short and just below his breath. "So now you think you should champion the battle against mediocrity?"

"You're unfair." I was quiet. Stirring something. "I just want to make sure I have really lived by the time I'm finished with this."

"With what?" Calm, cool.

"With this! My life!" I was shaking, my hands in the air, exasperated. He had pushed my buttons, and he knew it.

"And that means ruining a marriage?" He said it softly, in a friendly voice, as if he were asking for tea.

"How can you ruin something that was never built?"

"Ooh. Don't start," he said, shaking his head.

My back was to him. "I have started."

I couldn't go on, though. He was lying back on the soft pillows, his eyes closed, tuned out. I did love him, or so I thought, so I wanted to believe. It sometimes felt like just good behaviour, though, like remembering to excuse myself politely from the table when I was small. Good behaviour wasn't enough to keep a marriage together.

I was unable to acknowledge these feelings in any productive way. My subconscious may have been whispering to me, but I wouldn't listen. I couldn't.

Our married years were packed full of activity, a great distraction. We were constantly renovating our house, and then buying and fixing up a new one, living through the dusty chaos, always, it seemed, while I was about to deliver another baby. I couldn't pinpoint the source of my unhappiness, and something else always seemed more important than dwelling on it. My parents lived in Australia at the time. My siblings were scattered over two continents. I was among the first of my friends to marry and have children. There was no one to whom I could talk openly. And if I was confused, I thought that was part of the process of marriage. We were in that period of family transmogrification that happens in every union, when you take what you knew as a child and erase some parts and meld others with what your mate knew and wants to keep or drop. You forge something different, something new, for yourselves.

In the years following our marriage, I continued to work in advertising. My career had gone well, despite the interruptions of my pregnancies. Maternity leave was not as generous then as it is now. With the first baby, in 1985 when I was twenty-seven, I took four months off, and eighteen months later, with the second, I took only three months. Lack of mat-leave provisions aside, it wasn't wise to leave the advertising industry for long. Alliances would shift. Accounts would change hands. An art director would find a new copywriter to partner with. Every time I came back to work, I felt that I had to re-establish myself.

But I was quickly tiring of the business, especially by the time I was twenty-nine with two young children at home. I was not a fun, happy-go-lucky ad chick anymore. In the late fall of 1988, we flew to Sydney, Australia, to shoot a commercial for Dentyne gum, one of the first ads to be allowed in movie theatres under the guidance of Garth Drabinsky at Cineplex Odeon. We were there for almost two weeks—to cast, to shoot, to re-shoot, to record dialogue, to party. One of the married account directors phoned my hotel room one night, asking if he could come up. He was invoking what he called the "out-of-hemisphere rule," meaning that infidelity was allowed at a certain distance away from home. I declined. As a group, we went to beaches, to musicals, to restaurants. "I feel like I'm on holiday with people I don't want to be on holiday with," I complained to the art director.

I was not fully engaged in my work and found it hard to compartmentalize my home and work lives. I was not able to reconcile their dissonant spheres. At work, I was constantly thinking about my boys.

My colleagues were almost all single and in their twenties. After hours, they headed out to the bars, where much of the relationship-building among the agency, clients and creative teams continued. I, meanwhile, just wanted to rush out the door right on the dot of five to get home to my babies and relieve the nanny. We had hired a young woman from England to live with us as the children's caregiver, but I was often making mental note of their nap times, snack times, playtimes. I would even phone home to ask what they had eaten for lunch and how long they had slept. I could not completely let go.

Two years later, I was pregnant again, and I asked to work part-time until the birth of my third child. When Luke was born, I quit.

Having babies at home made it easy to exit from a career I had soured on. Eric and I decided we would make sacrifices so I could be at home and try my hand at freelance copywriting in an attempt to find a better balance. He had folded his agency in Halifax and found a job in design and marketing in Toronto. Within a few years, he had set up his own design firm with two partners. Financially, we were doing well. I descended into diapers, play-dates and generally sleepless nights with three boys—a four-year-old, a three-year-old and a newborn.

I found a solution, for a while anyway, to my confusion about who I was in being a mother. People talk about the timing of the decision to have children—before or after a women's career has been established—but I do not recall making any such calculation. For me, the desire to be a mother was so simple, so straightforward, it was a relief. Perhaps a part of me thought that being a wife meant having children. It was a way to cement our relationship as a married couple, a fulfillment of the script, expected not just by my family but by society. The popular saying *First comes love, then comes marriage, then comes a baby in the baby carriage* must have worked its way into my subconscious. Eric wanted children too. Despite the fact that he already had three children, he never expressed doubt about having more. He encouraged the idea. We wanted them: we had them. I marvelled at the perfection and intelligence of the pregnant body. While I was writing stupid ad copy or cooking a turkey, it was knitting together a human brain, arteries, organs. Brilliant! It was like having a fantastic sports car you now had a licence to drive.

It is amusing to me when women debate whether their children should take the surname of the father. I know of some who ensure their children have both surnames. One family I know gave one child the father's surname and their second child the mother's. But what mother doubts that her children belong to her? I didn't need a surname to tell me. I knew from having studied the whorls of damp baby hair on their newborn scalps, the crinkled horns of their earlobes, the moons in their fingernails, the fat folds of their knees.

A woman I know once explained that she took her husband's name because she didn't want her children confused or upset by the fact that she had a different one. They would be one team, she said. Children don't care about names, though. They don't care about what you do for a living or whether you have discovered the career you are meant to have. They care about who loves them, a fact any adopted child or stepchild, who has lost a parent, knows.

"I found it tremendously satisfying to give completely of oneself to another creature: body, mind, flesh and blood, food and drink," said Anne Morrow Lindbergh that day at Smith when she was discussing her phase of busy motherhood. The devotion my boys gave me was pure, simple, as mine was to them. It was unquestioned, unlike so much else in my life at that time. Sure, the daily grind of motherhood was tedious and annoying, but the intimacy was unlike anything I had known, so much of it physical, created by contact with their bodies. I had felt their elbows and knees scrape the inside of my uterus; the weight of them on my chest seconds after birth. I scrutinized the colour of their shit, noted the hours of their sleep, the contents of every meal, what they liked and didn't. I knew if they were getting sick by a slight change in cry. They enthralled me. The love I felt for them was big, effortless, new—better than the fraught relationship with my husband, and far more gratifying.

Each son provoked love in a way that was specific to him, for the things he liked me to do or say. Without thinking, I developed a repertoire of mom behaviour for each—having "frog sessions" with Nick (talking in a deep voice while I manipulated his big green frog puppet); instigating the "Kissing System" good-night routine with Luke (a pattern of kissing each cheek, earlobe, eyebrow and eyelid, followed by forehead, nose and finally lips); and giving Tait a nightly heart pat (a gentle tapping of my fingertips over his sternum). I loved creeping into their rooms at night to watch them sleep, and their scent!—as clean and comforting as bread baking in the oven.

When I would go to the park with my toddlers, to watch them on the swings or the jungle gym, I liked it when every woman would turn her head when a child shouted, "Mom!" We were all one, stripped of our real names, selfless nobodies whose children needed us.

Of course, I knew that I could escape their enormous demands when it suited me or time allowed. I could work on a writing project, go to a meeting, book off an afternoon with a sitter to do research. But I enjoyed the self-effacement. Being a mother was a welcome distraction from the difficult business of searching for myself, and an opportunity to discover a part of myself I hadn't known existed.

PART TWO

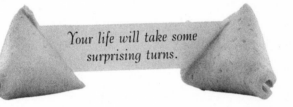

Your life will take some surprising turns.

5.

The Hamlet Years:
To Divorce or Not to Divorce?

I need to give myself a divorce for a present this year.

It was the voice of treason talking to me again as I approached my fortieth birthday, about fifteen years into our marriage. I had heard it many times in my head. Unprompted, it would speak up, sometimes even with humour. It was truth insisting on itself, but even so, it can be hard to take seriously. It is asking you to drop a nuclear bomb on your life.

I didn't know what to do about my unhappiness. I had been going to a psychiatrist. I was trying to sort it all out. I had suggested therapy to Eric, but he didn't want to go. After we finished the kitchen renovation on our last house, I remember opening the new fridge and thinking, *Everything looks so perfect, but my life is a mess.*

People often wonder when you know. They ask about the

moment it was clear that the marriage wasn't going to work. And for some, of course, it is very clear. "The day in 2004, June fourteenth, I came home unexpectedly at lunch," says a fifty-year-old divorced mother of two. "I thought, 'I should phone the house and let him know I am popping back so he can clear out the girlfriend,' but then decided that I had to see for myself. It was the first time I ever even thought he had a mistress, and I don't know why I thought of it. Something triggered my intuition, I guess. So a half-hour later, I walked in on him with his girlfriend—a married friend of mine with whom he'd been having an affair for about a year. In my home. I had a form of post-traumatic stress disorder after. For about a year, I'd feel like retching every time I pulled into the driveway."

Or you get a call as did Evelyn Keyes, the beautiful actress who played Scarlett O'Hara's younger sister, Suellen, in *Gone with the Wind*. For three years she lived with Mike Todd, a producer, until he sent her to the premiere of *Around the World in Eighty Days*, a film they had both worked on, and then called her to say, "Listen, I have to tell you. I've fallen in love with Elizabeth [Taylor]." Tom Hayden, Jane Fonda's third husband, told her he was leaving her for a younger woman on the night of her fifty-first birthday.

There is a tipping point for many, that one final, even small, act that changes everything. "We were making love, and we were in the missionary position, and I looked up at him and I thought, 'I can't grow old with this man doing this,'" recalls a woman, now in her seventies, who divorced in her forties. A divorced father of three told me he knew his marriage was over when he called down to his wife, on the dock at their cottage, to tell her that their house guest, a business colleague of his, had arrived for the weekend, and she refused to come up. He could suddenly see that she was not the partner he wanted.

For many, though, the denouement of a marriage is protracted, and to pinpoint when it all started to go wrong is like trying to determine when the aging process, which progresses with each new sag or impertinent wrinkle you hadn't previously noticed, actually began. And, to make matters more confusing, there are many "postcard moments" at birthdays and holidays, which interrupt the regular flow of life and calm you down, make you think things will work out. Besides, marriage is comprised of many layers of compassion. Forbearance is part of its fabric. Forgiveness darns holes as they appear. New developments stretch it thin in places and leave it thick in others.

Marriage counsellors explain that the decision to divorce often takes five years. And they point out that the energy that goes into deliberation would be better spent on addressing the problems in the marriage. Still, even when engaged in therapy, people often conclude that they should divorce. Couples counselling sometimes serves to clarify why a split, not a reconciliation, is in order. And while it's true that therapy can save a marriage, it can also delay the inevitable. "In the three 'lost years' before I left, we went to marriage counselling," a friend admits. Some insights were helpful—"he said that I never supported him in his career . . . he said he wanted to be the centre of the family and be surrounded by supportive, caring people"—but her attempts to address them were unsuccessful. "I tried an experiment. For weeks on end, I spent each evening engaged in active listening about his day, his hopes, his concerns. He said that he was really feeling closer after a while. Sad thing was, he never reciprocated." In the end, therapy provided relief, but not the kind she was expecting. "It felt like a huge weight had been lifted off my shoulders." She never would understand what he had wanted from her as a wife. "I finally felt that I wasn't a nutcase for not being able to know."

For me, things began to shift as the boys became increasingly independent and I found a meaningful outlet in the world beyond the family. After I opted out of my advertising career, I still wanted to make money, not just to contribute to the household, but to have some agency outside the home. But if I was going to leave the boys, even for an afternoon, I wanted the work to have as much importance to me as they did. For a while, I did some freelance work in advertising, just small print campaigns through people I knew, but then I discovered journalism. The first piece I published was an essay about summer for the *Globe*'s Facts & Arguments page in 1991. From there, I pitched stories to various magazines, and soon I had a regular stream of work.

It was the perfect career. When the children needed me, I could be completely present, taking them to doctor's appointments, cooking meals, picking them up from school—and then I could step across a threshold, into the small office in our home where I wrote. That I published under my maiden name, that I was paid to think, to engage in the world as an observer, felt like wonderful self-affirmation. I remember one fall afternoon when I stood in the garden of our house, raking the leaves while the children tumbled around like puppies. How perfect that I could be calm and still in the centre of my life, I thought, as its various parts—children, husband, career, friends—swirled around me. I was no longer fragmented.

Eric was supportive at first. He bought me books on writing. He fixed up the office so I had a place to go. Before that, when we were in a smaller house, he had let me use a space in the basement of his office downtown, so I could escape the household. For a few years, we had outside help with housekeeping chores and babysitting, and when that proved too expensive and unreliable, we put Luke in daycare after his half-day of junior kindergarten, so that all three boys would be in school for most of the day.

As time went on, the pride Eric took in my work began to fade and was replaced by unease that I was growing away from him. Perhaps that's because I was doing something that was different from what he knew, meeting people beyond those we socialized with as a couple. "I don't want to be Mr. Hampson," he said once when I wanted him to come with me to a function. "You're not the person you were when I married you," he would often complain. What he meant, I think, is the girl who looked up to him as her mentor, her guide to maturity. "But I don't want to be that person," I would respond. It wasn't as though he felt emasculated by my superior income—a problem other wives have described. Freelancers earn a pittance. I was finding my own way, and somehow that threatened him. At least that's how I read his lack of support, which in turn fuelled my resentment. I may not have been making very much money, but I had a psychic income. My sense of self was getting richer. And as that happened, my unhappiness grew. I didn't understand his lack of support. And soon I felt stifled by it.

Marriages are kaleidoscopic, made up of good and bad, difficult and beautiful, dark and light. Jane Fonda told me in an interview that she thought the story of her struggle with abusive, controlling husbands was instructive for readers because "we can be very strong and very weak and vulnerable at the same time." Certainly, both Eric and I loved our family, those summer afternoons at a cottage or in a park, when the children played at our feet, slipping in and out of our arms like dolphins. And managing three boys so close together was not always easy. I needed the support of a husband, as he needed me as their mother. I remember one summer day, when Eric was away on business, that began with a Lego war between Nick and Tait (one had a piece the other needed for his ship), Nick trashing his bedroom in frustration and me being wished dead. In the afternoon, Luke fell and split open his knee while the boys and some of their friends were playing in the backyard, and we took him to the hospital emergency room, where he got stitches. That day ended with a glass of wine—several, in fact. I couldn't wait for Eric to return.

Unhappy as I was in my marriage, my ability to take action was also hindered by a concern about Eric's health. Two days after being released from hospital following gall bladder surgery in the early 1990s, he had suffered a pulmonary embolism. "You're extremely lucky," the attending doctor told him. "Most people would have died of a heart attack."

When I think back on that illness, I reme/
I remember gratitude. Fear, because he wa/
and I needed him. And gratitude because, aga.
seemed, he recovered. It felt like a miracle, the lesson
which was to treasure the time we had together. I also know,
as I became increasingly distraught in the marriage, that the
worry over his health became a sort of warped expression of
my unhappiness. I feared his health might deteriorate again.
It had happened before, and he was often sick with lung
infections, coughing for months on end. I wasn't wishing
him dead—a common line of thinking among unhappy
spouses, I'm sorry to say—I was just worried that he was
not well and that I should look after him as best I could,
and love him.

Wishing a husband dead is the coward's way out, of
course. Widows have it easier than divorcees, we think. "I have
divorced friends who often say they envy me because my husband died and I got out of the marriage without having to
share the assets," a widowed friend of mine explained. Widows
also avoid the turmoil and stigma of a divorce. It's all very
tidy. Several people have confessed to me that they have
wished their spouses dead. "Only in really bad moments,"
one young father told me. A woman whose husband left her
for someone else was more explicit: "You don't think I wanted
him to drop dead after what he did? You bet I did." One
therapist explained it to me as "an expression of rage." It's
passive aggression, really. You don't want to be the one to put
an end to the marriage. If fate brought you together, you
want it to end your marriage too. But I also think it's an
expression of helplessness.

So we carried on, despite the problems. That's the part some people don't understand. "You liked the package," a friend of mine mused soon after we split. She meant the image of it, I think: the handsome husband, the house, the beautiful children. And maybe that was some of it. It all looked good from the outside. (Eric was also extremely charming to my friends, especially the female ones. "If you leave him, he'll be snapped up in a second," several said.) All marriages are opaque. But ours, both the interior and exterior views, was also my reality. It was what I knew; it was my identity and my pride. And like many women, I took emotional responsibility for the marriage, feeling that if I didn't try to make it work or smooth over the difficulties, I wasn't living up to my promise as a wife and mother.

My friend Joy and I would talk every morning. "It is your life," she would tell me in those years, when I blurted out my problems. "You deserve to be happy," she repeated like a mantra. But I couldn't separate that from wanting to do the right thing for my children, mostly, but also as a wife. "If he doesn't physically beat you, you don't leave," I remember hearing a woman my mother's age say about unhappy marriages. Eric never did, of course, and he was often just as capable of affection as he was of great anger. I once had a dream that he admitted to being unfaithful, and in it I felt relief. Now, I could tell him it was over. There was a clear-cut reason.

⁓

Divorce lawyers report an increase in consultations about divorce around Christmas, which is not surprising. The holiday is a crucial opportunity, like a birthday, for a couple to reconnect. They need a love tune-up in the crazy race of modern life.

For many years in my marriage, we had storybook Christmases. In the beginning, I would hang mistletoe on the frame of our bed and in thresholds around the house. We would teach the children our favourite traditions, of opening stockings all together and then, one by one, going around the room as each of us opened bigger presents, in descending order of age. We put a big red bow on our dog Ketchup, a golden retriever also known as The Love Carpet, and let him have an enormous bone that Santa Claus had brought. Eric and I also created an elaborate game of clues for each other's major present. One clue on the tree would lead to a nook or a cupboard, where another clue would lead to another and so on, until finally you found your treasure—a pair of silver earrings, say, wrapped up and hidden under an overturned flowerpot in the garden.

When a marriage is coming apart, however, the holidays can be painful, partly because you feel the phantom limb of the old, effortless love. And if you're trying to re-create the former tableau for the sake of your family, and especially the children, you feel like a hypocrite.

For the Christmas of 1999 and New Year, my father had arranged, as he had in previous years, for all of my siblings and their families to get together for a holiday reunion. We were a large group, including spouses and grandchildren. For this particular year, he had found a place near a private beach in Maui.

Eric and I had been through a rough few years by that point. In 1998, I was invited by the *Globe and Mail* to write a social column on a freelance basis at the start of the newspaper war with the *National Post*. Eric dismissed the importance of it and encouraged me to turn it down. But soon after, a neighbour of ours, Howard Schneider, then the *Washington Post* correspondent for Canada, told me I was crazy not to take it. "When a newspaper offers you a column, I don't care what it's about. You do it," he said. The change in my work life caused more of a rift between Eric and me. I had to go out frequently to events. He rarely wanted to accompany me.

Then, a year later, along came the opportunity to write the interview feature soon branded The Hampson Interview, which required more of my time and effort. My career was gaining momentum. I felt great.

During that Christmas in Maui, Eric and I pulled it together. He put on a good show, helping to cook a huge New Year's feast. But out of the range of everyone else, he made cutting remarks. One evening, in front of my mother, he invited me to sit with him on the beach at sunset. He would make us gin-and-tonics, he said. It would be romantic. But when we were sitting there on our own, he looked out at the ocean and asked me if I ever thought about marrying again— marrying someone else—and said how nice it would be to have a wedding on a beach. I looked at him, stunned.

After the others left, we had a few days in Maui by ourselves with the children. One night, he began to vent about my turning down his sexual advances—I couldn't be intimate with him when there was so much tension in our relationship—and he accused me of having affairs. "You get on your back for others," he spit at me. I went to the bathroom to draw a bath, crying. A few minutes later, he came in, apologized and handed me a glass of champagne to drink while I soaked. This was his pattern: a blast of hurtfulness followed by a show of remorse. Initially, I did what I had always done. I excused his verbal assault, convincing myself that he was under stress and frustrated with me. I was doing what so many wives do—blaming myself for his poor treatment of me. The next morning, I sat with him on the beach again, and told him that we should work on our relationship, that we needed to be strong for our family. I told him how much I loved him. He was unresponsive, unwilling to look at me, as he gazed out at the water.

I got up and went for a long walk along the path that led around the bay and past some hotels. Three thoughts followed in quick succession. The first was *Everything will be okay*. Then I thought about some improvement I could make in the house. Curtains. I actually thought about stupid curtains. And then an unfamiliar one screeched into my consciousness. *This is what you always do. This is your dysfunctional pattern*. I stopped. I had always responded to Eric's aggression by trying to prove that I really did love him, and followed this with some plan to add a feather to our nest. Or he would. He had once phoned me after a verbal rant to suggest we buy a piece of furniture he knew I wanted. My desire to cocoon was an effort to mummify myself in denial.

The next day, we flew home. I wept almost the whole way. Mid-flight, a flight attendant leaned over to ask me if I was all right. She thought I was afraid of flying. I waved her off, shaking my head. "I'm fine," I said. Eric was sitting across the aisle from me, with two of the children on either side. One of them was seated beside me.

"Why is Mom crying?" Luke asked.

"Oh, she's just sad that the holiday is over," he lied.

But the holiday *was* over. I would finally have to face the problems in my marriage. I was going home where I had little support, which scared me. My parents knew I was unhappy. Sometimes, on my regular Sunday calls with my mother, I would cry and say, "I hate being married." But they didn't know what to do, and I wasn't telling them about everything that was going on.

When we got home, I started seeing a therapist again every week after having stopped going years before. I insisted Eric come with me for marriage counselling. He did—for one session. He didn't like the scrutiny. After several sessions, the therapist asked me, "Why do you protect the children, but not yourself?" I couldn't answer her question.

One afternoon, I was soaking in my bath on the second floor of our house. (The beauty of the freelance life is that bath breaks are allowed during the day.) The late-afternoon sun shone through the window. I thought, *Well, you are either the person Eric says you are—selfish, not organized, not a good housewife. Or you are the person your friends outside the marriage describe—kind, funny, thoughtful.* And it occurred to me how simple the choice was: Why would I want to be the person Eric thought I was, anyway? He criticized me as a way of keeping me in my wifey place. I closed my eyes, and I imagined a peace, a serenity, on the other side of my marriage. I wanted to live without conflict. I was sure it was possible. I could almost feel it. *I want to go there, to that calmer place.* It was a flimsy, thin vision, but it had a certain weight too, and it quickly gathered force. For the first time, I was envisioning a possible life without a husband.

I was also beginning to see that what had made me stay in the marriage—the welfare of my children—was, in the end, why I should go. I didn't want them, as potential future husbands, to think this was what marriage should be, and I didn't want them to know only a mother who was often sad. And I could see that they were growing up, that they were strong and healthy and that they would be fine, whatever I decided.

"You are responsible for your own happiness," my father said to me, when he came for a visit and saw my distress at one point in my long deliberation. He wasn't going to tell me what to do. He never had. He simply wanted me to trust in myself. He wanted me to do whatever I thought best when it made sense.

That spring following Christmas in Hawaii, I sat working at my desk one afternoon, thinking about everything that had transpired. *I don't feel married anymore*, I thought. I felt a mixture of relief, sadness, fear. On the beach holiday, I had read Alistair MacLeod's novel, *No Great Mischief*, and the last line—"All of us are better when we're loved"—sent me crying into the ocean. Salt tears, salt water. So true, those words are, and I knew that what I was living with was not love, not the kind I wanted, anyway. In the quiet of my home office, I looked down at my hand with the wedding rings and started to pull them off. For years, I had never been able to remove them, even if I wanted to.

But this time, they slid off as if greased with soap. I had no idea what lay ahead, but I was willing to find out. I could not go on as I had.

6.

The Colossus Generation

"You're not always easy," my mother once said to me when I complained about my husband. My mother was demonstrating what every successful wife or husband knows how to do: to flip a switch in the brain so you can see yourself as your spouse does. It's different from simply imagining how the other person feels. Compassion and empathy are essential too, of course, but to see yourself as he might is more like an out-of-body experience. Suddenly, you understand, for example, that for a self-contained and private man, your desire to talk a lot, laugh loudly and be extravagantly enthusiastic about people and places and ideas would be difficult for him, uncomfortable—a burden, even.

It was hard to tell my parents about the end of my marriage. I felt that I was failing in my ability to give my children what my parents had given me. I had become a traitor to the values that defined my family. And I knew that it would worry them. Some parents fear that their divorced children will ask them for support or need to return home. I know couples who didn't tell their parents until they had resolved where the children would live and how they would manage. "I didn't want to burden them, and I didn't want to have their confusion add to mine," my friend Carolyn says. And then there is the question of self-ishness, an accusation that many of my friends encountered in their discussions with their mothers about divorce. "It's the me me me syndrome," offered a seventy-five-year-old woman when I asked about her view on contemporary marriage. "If it's not perfect, then you leave."

I now tell my mother that I see something enviable in the lives of couples who came from the Make It Work school of marriage. Their traditional model of marriage may be easily mocked—we like to tar all such women as Stepford Wives—but it had a certainty to it, a set course, a clear definition of roles. In some cases, it was intolerable, involving abuse and infidelity. I have listened to some women my mother's age who stayed in toxic marriages, who remark how lucky we are to have the option to leave. But it's hard not to believe that because they felt divorce was socially unacceptable, they toughed it out through the bad patches. "Don't think I was always happy," my mother has told me. They gritted their teeth and sucked it up. More than one person who has been in a long marriage has told me that the second score of years—after the children are grown, after you have seen each other through some ups and downs—are easier and better than the first twenty.

Some in this earlier generation see the high rate of divorce as an unfortunate outcome of contemporary consumerist culture. We are addicted to quick fixes, to instant gratification. "Marriage is a journey, and things turn around," offers Maggie Scarf, a mother of three and a grandmother of eight who has been married for fifty-five years. Instead of recognizing that emotional pain signals a problem that needs to be worked on, couples often feel it's easier to throw the marriage away and get a new relationship, one that seems a better fit. The immediate sense of relief wins over the possible rewards of long-term relationships, which are more substantive, but require patience, a long-term view, say the anti-divorce voices. (Progressive pro-marriage experts at least acknowledge that while people have been shown to be happier, wealthier and healthier in marriage, the benefits accrue more to men than to women.)

What marriage was for our parents is clearer than what it is, or has become, for us. Women and men of my generation had to figure out the modern terms of marriage while we were in one. It's like taking a horse that's been trained to trot around a ring and suddenly expecting it to leap over the rails and gallop across the field.

For me, the situation became intolerable. I could not have continued in my marriage for another twenty years. Like many women just entering their forties, I could look ahead another fifteen, twenty years, and see Dotageville on the horizon. If I had stayed, I'm not sure what would have become of me. At the very least, my husband and I would have been one of those older, long-married couples who sit glumly across from each other in a restaurant with little desire to engage.

I have met women who supported their husbands, Silda Spitzer—style, after the discovery of sexual infidelity. It's not that my generation is unwilling to make an effort. The parents and siblings of a male friend of mine told him for years that his marriage was dysfunctional. "What you need is a divorce," they advised him, long before he split from his wife of twenty-two years. He stayed for so long because he was a father of three and he loved his family.

And if it makes anyone feel any better, there is confusion over both male and female roles in modern marriage—at least that part is equitable. Many men are puzzled about what their wives want. They're flying without GPS.

Husbands are often in a quandary. The culture tends to give men little instruction about women beyond how to win their affection and get them in bed—a catch and capture expedition, basically. Once he gets her in the boat, he's not sure how to keep her happy—and alive. It helps if he has grown up with alpha sisters, of course. One man I know explained that his two sisters (one older, one younger) were the force that made him into a menschy husband, finely attuned to his wife's being. Generally, however, men grow up unschooled in the art of understanding women. As husbands, they often feel they cannot win no matter how they try to modulate their behaviour. They complain that their wives want them to be more involved, but when they are, they are criticized for being too controlling. And when they try to listen to what women want, they are told they are too soft or too wimpy. Their wives want a man who takes control, and who knows what he wants, who he is.

"Women have been struggling to redefine their role in society and in marriage, and men have been asked to stand aside and not interfere," says a man who has been married and divorced three times. "We watch women take on huge amounts of responsibility and workload in their quest to 'have it all,' and we do our best to make ourselves useful," he says. Another man explained a similar confusion. "It sure surprised me," he said of his divorce after twelve years of marriage. "I thought everything was okay. We have four great children. I like to cook. But suddenly, she comes home with a belly-button ring and a tattoo and says she is not happy."

Some say a feminist overcorrection is at fault. Acting out of a collective belief that their gender has been taken advantage of for hundreds of years, many women swing to the opposite extreme, compensating for the legacy of self-subjugation with uncooperative aggression. On the Smith campus in the late seventies that feeling gave rise to man-hating diatribes. It was women—or "womyn," as many feminists of the time preferred to write it—against the all-mighty patriarchy. But that attitude, which lingers today, strips many men of the roles (provider being a key one) that traditionally helped them feel they were earning the badge of manhood. For many, becoming a man is a status that requires proof of competency. They have to show they are men through actions, before they can claim the title. Feminism has denied them that opportunity without providing an alternative.

Interestingly, the shift has created problems for women too. Many take the reins in all aspects of home life, the housework and child-rearing as well as the job of making money and running the household finances. She becomes a superior wife, the archetype du jour, played out in numerous commercials featuring the bossy Mrs. and the hapless hubby. The have-it-all exhortation has led to the do-it-all wife who cannot adjust her domestic standards to accommodate how her husband may diaper a baby or scrub a pot. So, she huffs. She instructs. She treats him like a child. But then she grows resentful that her husband lets her have control, even though she took it. (Yes, what women want can often be confusing.) Do I have to be the one who does everything around here? she complains. The dynamic of superior wife/inferior husband leads many to divorce. The women give up. They feel like they're living like single women anyway. What's the point in staying together? they ask themselves.

Certainly, working women's economic independence has sharpened their critical assessment of marriage. If they no longer need marriage financially, they can be more analytical about why they remain married. A 2008 poll showed that women overwhelmingly (48 percent) said that they made the decision to divorce because of abuse issues—verbal, emotional and physical. I heard of one successful mid-life woman, who chose to end her marriage because of a tension she felt when her husband was present. There was no abuse, but she always felt that she was walking on eggshells. I understood what she meant—it was how I often felt too, toward the end of my marriage, bracing for the shift in mood in the household when Eric walked in the door at the end of the workday. Years ago, I remember listening to a woman, who was about seven years older than me, describe how she knew her marriage was over when she could no longer bear the difference between the respect she enjoyed at her workplace and the frequent disrespect she suffered at the hands of her husband at home.

I am part of the Colossus Generation, straddling the old ideas of marriage and the changing expectations of how we want to live, to love and to be loved.

*

7.

Destination: Splitsville

The final chapter of a marriage doesn't always end with a spectacular fight, a brilliant put-down, a drunken rant. It can end in prolonged silences, resignation, depression. It can end because no one has the energy to unravel all its knots. And when you have children, the calendar is always full with someone's birthday, a school project, a family event, an important holiday. It is easy to put off a monumental decision like divorce. You barely have time for a yoga class let alone the end of your life as you know it.

And so after that afternoon at my desk, when I slipped off my wedding rings, another year passed. Yes, another year. I feel embarrassed to say that, but thinking back, I only remember fear and anxiety. The big, breezy confidence I once had was gone. I put my rings back on a few times, only to remove them again when I felt stronger. Eric didn't notice their absence until one day about two or three months later.

"Fine," he snapped. "If that's how you feel. Let's separate."

He was unhappy too. All marriages have two sides, two stories, which is why they're tricky to write about. But I don't know everything he felt. All I know clearly are my thoughts. When he called for separation, I was surprised. I wanted him to ask me why I had taken off my rings; what I was feeling. (The whole thing sounds very passive-aggressive, but hey, a marital implosion is never healthy.) I tried to tell him, but we got nowhere.

We had both descended into paralysis: he wouldn't work through the issues, and I wasn't willing to bury them under another room makeover. In the end, his approach—as I later came to see it—was to provoke me, pushing me to decide the fate of our marriage.

"I need to know by the end of the week what you're going to do," he would say to me. I think he figured he could call my bluff, make me see that I couldn't, wouldn't, leave, and that I should just be nicer or something. Finally, with the help of my therapist, I realized that my response should be simple and straightforward.

"You're right," I said to him one night in the spring of 2001. "We need to separate."

The decision took the wind out of his sails. I don't think he ever thought I would do it.

After consultations with my family and lawyers, we decided to have a one-year separation, as a trial, but also, should we decide to divorce, as a buffer period of adjustment for our children.

I would remain in our family home, and he would move to a house on a farm within commuting distance of Toronto. My parents owned the house, but we had used it as our own for the duration of our marriage. Eric loved it there, and planned to purchase it from my father if and when we divorced.

We worried about when to tell the children. Should we tell them in the summer at the end of school? But then they would be going to camp. Wouldn't they worry about what was happening at home while they were away? "It's better just to tell them," advised my brother, who had gone through the same thing. "They likely already know something is wrong. The uncertainty is worse. Once you tell them, you can get on with making the adjustment." Still, we deliberated. Finally, we decided to tell them at the end of the summer, just before the start of school. Their daily routine would be a comfort, we reasoned, and their schoolwork a distraction.

In September 2001, when the terrorist attacks in New York City unbuttoned the world, I momentarily lost my nerve. But a month and a half later, we decided to move ahead with our plans.

Eric went out to the country on a Saturday, and I visited with the children the next day. Everything would remain the same, we said when we sat down at our family meeting. They would go to the same schools. We would live in the same house in the city. They could come to the country on the weekends. Before we left that evening, I stood in the main room of the cottage and watched Eric through the picture window. He was tending to his garden. I felt sad, but I was glad that we had made the announcement calmly, without hysterics. The boys absorbed the news through large eyes. There were no tears.

On the drive home, we were all quiet, and I didn't attempt to fill the silence.

"I knew. Didn't you?" Tait, then sixteen, asked his older brother, who was almost eighteen.

"Yeah," he replied.

When we got home, they all watched TV. An hour later, one of them came into the kitchen to ask what was for supper.

And that was all, for the moment. Many of my friends have reported a similar non-reaction. Children can take in only so much information at a time. I would come to realize that the announcement of divorce simply opens a conversation that will go on for years.

Irony takes no prisoners, of course. The generation who began to use the noun *parent* as a verb—a reflection of how seriously boomers take the role as a crucial society-shaping agent—has also taken to divorce the way they embraced free love in the 1960s. Divorce has the potential to undo all their diligent efforts to raise happy, productive children. They programmed their children's extracurricular lives with violin lessons, karate, math tutoring, soccer practices, and now here they are, introducing them to the concept of love's limitations.

The process of divorce is not helped by the fact that modern parents tend to make children their equals, whereas many of our own parents were authority figures. In a story about family, I once briefly described my parents' approach to us as one of "benign neglect."

"Benign neglect?" my father said when he'd read it, as if someone had just given him a boiled egg for a Christmas present.

"I mean it in a good way," I replied.

In the child-centric world of modern parenting, tots are treated as though they are remarkable geniuses. (And frankly, let me just say as a tiny digression, that they often are. I treasured the miracle of my boys' sudden sentence construction and their individual and haphazard invention of perfect words. People do have "eyebrowns," if you ask me.) But children are also naturally self-absorbed, so it's not a bad thing to balance that with a dose of reality.

We were listened to, of course, and my parents endured endless skits that my siblings and I put on for their amusement (and their entry fee of a penny), many of which involved my elder sister and I wearing our nighties as ball gowns and toothbrushes with strings attached to make dangly earrings. My brother was roped into playing Prince Charming, bending down in his pillowcase cape to fit our mother's shoe onto the foot of that particular performance's Cinderella. But we were never encouraged to think of ourselves as the centre of the universe—at least, not for long. And if my father's career necessitated a move to a new city—like when we all went off to Geneva the year I was six—there was always this certainty, this equanimity. My parents believed we could and would adapt.

The crisis of divorce demands that the needs of the children be put first and that their worries be acknowledged and contained, but I also think that some of that unquestioned authority of a 1950s-style parent, who will calmly lead his children into a new reality, is necessary. At the moment when everything is falling apart, you have to pull yourself together—that's what therapists advise, anyway. This is never easy. I have heard of a mother who told the children of an impending divorce while her husband was out—a ploy to get the upper hand in the affection battle. And I know of a girl who found out about an affair her father was having—one that would lead him to ask his wife for a divorce—by happening to read the lewd messages he was texting his girlfriend on his cell phone.

Children don't need to be protected from your profound disappointment or your tears. Real emotion gives the children permission to be sad. But they don't benefit from witnessing uncontrollable grief, anger or excessive worry. They are not your friends. Boundaries are necessary. They need you to be a parent, strong and capable, and to simply tell them the basics—where they will live, who will pick them up from school and who will take them to soccer practice—not that Daddy had an affair, say, or that Mommy is now gay. A platitude such as "Daddy and I just don't love each other anymore, but we love you" is a safe one. They should be told that divorce is an adult matter, and that the family will continue, just differently.

"Don't whitewash and don't denigrate," a child therapist told me when I sought help on how to deal with my ex in the aftermath of divorce. If left to their own critical thinking, free of persuasion (and the horror of alienating parents who deliberately malign the ex-spouse), children do, over time, see their parents for who they are—and aren't. It can be hurtful, no question. Disappointment in love, and in others who sometimes do the wrong thing and act irresponsibly, should come to them only when they are adults, which it invariably will. It should not come to them through the people who are supposed to care the most for them.

We all eventually recognize our parents as imperfect. Who among us hasn't wished that one or both of his parents hadn't been slightly different, more encouraging of his talents, say, or more focused on giving direction, more involved or less interfering, less judgmental? Even the most diligent parent, when the children are grown and independent, often acknowledges her own spotty record by saying to them and to herself that she did the best she could under the circumstances. Still, it's one of the great liberations of maturity, I often think, when you realize that you became who you are because of (and in spite of) your parents' influence. Your shortcomings aren't all their fault, just as your accomplishments aren't all their successes. You have the choice to make of your childhood what you will, to compensate for some of its deficiencies and to draw on some of its strengths—or not. One of the things I often tell people, including my own children, is that few, if any, of the extraordinary individuals I have talked to for my interview column come from a conventional background.

Divorce speeds up that realization of a parent's fallible humanity—forces it, in fact. And is that always a bad thing? A U.S. study of grown children of divorce found that an amiable divorce is better than a bitter one, but there is no such thing as a "good divorce." Pro-marriage advocates argue that while children can rise to the occasion of their parents' divorce, they lose their childhoods.

I know this. All divorced parents know this. Please. Give us some credit. It's why few enter divorce lightly. I would argue that the focus on the grown children of divorce, and studies that document their poor outcomes, is a form of social censure, an echo of a fearful society that is ambivalent about the mutant state of modern families that divide and then sometimes attempt to blend with lumpy results. It's more productive if we all simply acknowledge that the milk has been spilt in the announcement of divorce, and while everyone will cry over it, we should think of ways to make something with it (pancakes, anyone?) rather than scold parents for having spilled it in the first place. Consider: stepfamilies will soon outnumber any other kind of family.

The use of the term *broken family* is also a form of passive disapproval. The fact of the matter is, we all know there are plenty of "intact families" that are horrifically dysfunctional, causing more harm than a divorce might. Experts now say that many divorce-statistic children with poor outcomes were more affected by the parental conflict during the marriage than the split. The marriage was toxic to them; the divorce a relief.

Society worships the sanctity of the traditional family, and blinds itself to its potential evil. People forget that murder-suicides in families usually happen in a suburb with nice schools, parks and a crossing guard at the intersection. They wring their hands, saying, how could this possibly happen? Neighbours tell reporters that the family seemed really nice and normal—they walked their dog, they mowed their lawn—as though it's a great surprise that anything cruel could happen behind white picket fences. They view *Desperate Housewives* as entertainment, not an amusing statement on the fake veneer of civility.

"Divorce was one of the best things that happened to me," says Max Sindell, creator of the website survivingyourparents divorce.com and author of *The Bright Side: Surviving Your Parents' Divorce*, written while he was at university. Sindell was six years old when his parents divorced. A series of upheavals followed. Upon divorcing his mother, his father, who had three children from a first marriage, moved to another state and remarried, only to divorce again. He has since remarried a fourth time. Sindell's mother remarried and moved several times.

Sindell is not saying divorce is great. And, arguably, he wouldn't have felt compelled to write about his parents' separation if he didn't have some significant processing to do in his own inner life. But his goal is to empower children of divorce and help them see it as a potentially positive experience. "There's no question that having parents fight, split up and move on can be stressful and damaging," he allowed. "But if you keep talking about that, it can become a self-fulfilling prophecy. I really want to change the narrative. Whether or not you think that divorce is good or bad, people are going to get divorced, and kids are going to be dealing with it. I try to be helpful."

Children don't need to be told that divorce sucks. And overselling the doom and gloom of it can reinforce the feeling that they are damaged goods. "I don't want to be a child of divorce," a mother of two recalls her ten-year-old son saying when she and her husband announced their split. "He did not want to take on that identity." No one wants to be labelled or reduced to a statistic.

Sindell devised the Divorced Kids' Bill of Rights, which includes, among other things, an entitlement to awareness (to know what's going on), to be heard and to be neutral. "It's about no secrets, no surprises," he explained. "If parents are thinking about moving somewhere or having [their children] change schools, or having a new partner move into the house, those are big life-altering decisions that have to be discussed with children." He has a close relationship with both parents, he says, which he attributes partly to the divorce process. Even at six, he could see they were unhappy together. When they announced their split, "my initial reaction was one of relief." He stepped up to the opportunity it gave him to mature. "You can prove to your parents that you can have the responsibility, that they can trust you, and that, in turn, gives you more freedom," he said.

Divorce is a symptom of the revolution in the reorganization of the household. I suppose we could all climb into some time machine and travel back to when we were an agrarian society or cave dwellers, when men had one set of duties, women another, because we needed each other in order to survive, our roles economically interdependent. That would be a way to eradicate divorce. Better, though, is to look at the fissures in the modern family as part of our evolution as a society—one that needs the support of others, not their negative judgment. Divorce has many devastating psychological effects in the short term, but a longitudinal study has shown that six years after divorce, the vast majority of children are adjusting well. Why leap automatically to frightening conclusions? Children are resilient, and parents would function better, when separated, if they were relieved of the guilt that they have ruined their children's lives.

⌒

Eric and I began our separation as exemplary partners. We spent Christmas together in the country almost two months after we had told the children about the decision. In the spring of 2002, Eric suggested that perhaps we should get back together. But I didn't feel that he was willing to work on fixing our problems. I felt that he simply wanted to avoid the financial hit of divorce.

"Our marriage is over," I said to him.

I had found my centre. I had talked over my situation with many friends, and my family, now that it was out in the open. Eric had had a brief affair with someone else, and so had I. I had enough distance to be sure of what I wanted—and what I didn't. Even through a minor health scare for him, I held on to my conviction. In the late fall, after discussions with our respective lawyers, we began preparations to sell the house.

Soon he was involved with a new girlfriend who had two children from a previous marriage. Once she sent Luke home on a Sunday night with a lunch packed for school the next day. I was outraged, suffering from acute mother-replacement angst. But I learned to tone down my defensive reaction, and one day a few months later I phoned her to leave a message, requesting that she call me. I wanted to explain something about the boys that I thought would be helpful to her when she saw them. I was hopeful we could have a mother-to-mother chat.

"You called?" she said when she returned the call a few days later.

I told her what I was concerned about.

"Well," she said, apropos of nothing. "Eric and I are getting married."

"Oh." I was caught off guard. Eric had said nothing to me. "He likes to be married," I blurted. It wasn't the most gracious response, but it was the best I could do on short notice.

Later that day, when the children returned from school, I asked them if Eric had told them about plans with his girl-friend. They then told me that their father had announced his intention to marry two days earlier, but they hadn't informed me. They hadn't been sure how I would react.

"You're not upset?"

"No. It's okay," I lied.

They visibly relaxed. "Now we just have to find someone for you," one of my boys said sweetly.

In reality I was reeling. I had pushed him to leave but Eric's plan to remarry so soon left me feeling like a replaceable part, as though our long marriage had meant nothing. I am not sure why it is that even when you have divorced someone, news of your partner's remarriage can be a blow. When the ex of a friend of mine heard she was remarrying, he immediately broke up with his girlfriend. "I think it just made him see that the person he was with was not right for him," my friend mused. "My remarriage caused him to assess his own relationship." There is a bond, still: what you once did together shaped your life; and now, what you do apart, one compared to the other, gives it definition too.

Most divorced couples I knew told each other first of their plans to remarry, so the children would not be in the awkward position of having to worry how the other parent would react. Eric hadn't shown me that courtesy. Worse, Eric and I still did not have a separation agreement. The house had yet to go up for sale. In an echo of my past with him as the New Woman, I had seen his girlfriend in his car one time, looking up at the house, when he dropped by to retrieve something. He hadn't left me for her, but I still felt abandoned. I was the estranged wife this time, watching from the window.

My freelance interview column for the *Globe and Mail* was the one thing that was certain about my week, giving it structure and shape. I would go out to do the interview in person and transcribe the tape of the conversation in my home office. On the night before my deadline, I would ask my eldest to be in charge of getting his younger two brothers into bed on time. I had to go to sleep at 9 p.m. so I could rise at 3 a.m. to have the finished piece at the paper first thing the next morning by 7 am, before I had to help the children get ready for school. In the middle of the night, I was calmer. The street outside my window was dark and empty. The world lay still. With the children safe in their beds on the top floor, I felt like a captain in the wheelhouse of a ship, guiding it through the night while the passengers slept.

"We will get through this," I would say aloud to the children, gripping the wheel of the car as I drove them to school. I was trying to convince myself as much as reassure them.

The children would often tell me their concerns about Eric's behaviour. When we were a family, Eric was a good father and always seemingly strong. But he was not accustomed to being single and divorce creates emotional instability. Shortly before his engagement, he and his girlfriend had briefly broken up, an unexpected turn of events that had caused him to weep once in front of the boys.

"Dad was better when he was with you," said one of them, visibly shaken over seeing his father so upset.

"He's a grown-up, and he'll be fine," I replied, holding his hand. "All grown-ups go through difficult times." It sounded like the right thing to say.

When the house went up on the market, Eric was unavailable to help clear out the debris from our eighteen years of marriage. I filled the car with old clothes and unwanted household items to drop at Goodwill. I packed boxes of his books for him to collect. He came several times to the house and perused its contents, as though in a shopping mall, contemplating what to purchase.

One Friday night, the older boys had friends over. I let them have beer even though they were underage. I knew they were experimenting with alcohol and figured it was safer for them to do so at home where I had rules. Their friends' parents had to know. No hard liquor allowed. And everyone had to be out by one a.m. But that night, just before departure time, one of their friends threw up before being escorted home. After the children were in bed, I got down on my hands and knees to scrub up the barf from the carpet. The real estate agent had scheduled an open house for the following morning. "If you can't handle the boys, you don't have to have custody," Eric said the next day when I phoned him to tell him about the incident, hoping for his participation in preparing the house for sale and looking after the children. He was being confrontational. He knew it would upset me to not have custody. But he wasn't willing to help me manage.

More help was my psychiatrist who lived nearby. Every Thursday, it was my Sisyphean task to trudge up the hill, rolling my anxieties and pain into her office, where she put things in perspective and gave me insight into Eric's behaviour. I was in bad physical shape as well, having developed a herniated disc in my back after moving some of the boxes in our house. I couldn't stand for more than ten minutes without excruciating pain shooting down my right leg. Years later, I read of a health study from the University of Chicago and Baltimore's Johns Hopkins University involving nearly eight thousand divorced and widowed men and women. Researchers found that the subjects were more likely than their married counterparts to suffer from serious health conditions like heart disease, diabetes, even cancer. This didn't surprise me. I was literally coming apart, I felt, and unable to stand on my own two feet—a metaphor that didn't escape me.

"My work is a holiday from my life," I told my psychiatrist once. I never missed a column, not even during the week that we moved. If I didn't file, I wouldn't get paid. And luckily, when I sat at my desk, the nerve pain abated. Jeanne Beker, Canada's premier fashion arbiter, once told me that when her husband informed her their marriage was over, her career "was the one thing that I knew wouldn't betray me." I could submerge myself in my work, like a swimmer in a cool, refreshing lake.

The legal process of my divorce was difficult and emotionally draining. I soon realized I was in the dark about our finances. They were a puzzle I had not taken the time to solve at any point during our marriage. Full financial disclosure took months. Trust evaporated. Over the course of three years we had a series of child-support agreements pertaining to Eric's income and the support he owed. When he said he was unemployed during the initial separation agreement, I waived spousal support in order to have some of his money put aside for the children's education. It was discovered in a later negotiation that he had a lucrative job lined up, which he failed to disclose. If he had, his financial obligations would have been significantly different and I would not have had to waive spousal support. But I let the issue rest because by the time a scheduled renegotiation came around, a year later, he had lost his job and was claiming to have no money despite his comfortable lifestyle. I never considered the option of going to court, but relied on mediation, arbitration and, finally, when he stopped paying the child support, based on an imputed income for him, the Family Responsibility Office. In the last mediation meeting over how he would pay what he owed and help provide for education for the boys, I opted for a modest lump sum in exchange for an agreement that I would never again come after him for any kind of support. The legal fees alone—just to chase him—were exorbitant. I was fed up. It was puzzling that he refused to provide for the boys. He had paid child support for his girls and even spousal payments to his first wife until she remarried. Maybe he just didn't feel he could start over once more as he had when he married me. Still, however much risk it involved for me to cut him loose financially, it didn't matter. Once I did so, a weight was lifted from my shoulders. I had finally, completely untethered myself from him.

8.

Un-marriage Ceremonies

To cure myself of "veil brain," which is how sex therapist Lou Paget describes the adoption of the wife persona, I performed a few un-marriage rituals. Not that they are undertaken to cure anyone of the desire for love—that is never-ending, if you go by dating reports from old-age homes—but they help to underscore the over-promise (and overselling) of marital bliss, which I had completely bought. And it seems that I am not alone, among the legion of the divorced. I read about one divorced client of Celebrant USA Foundation & Institute, a non-profit organization that helps train professionals to tailor ceremonies for life's milestone events, who glued back together a broken glass in a reversal of the Jewish tradition of smashing a glass at the wedding.

Divorce parties are reportedly on the rise, an exit ritual from the wedding industry complex that lured them into marriage in the first place. People serve cocktails with names like So Long, and Sucker, and play "Hit the Road, Jack" and "I Will Survive." Some people bring presents, which is an excellent way to replace the fifteen-piece Wedgwood dinner set the ex walked off with. Burning things is big. Women often torch their wedding dresses. I read about one woman who celebrated as she watched her ex-husband's trophy deer head go up in flames. Some drape a banner reading JUST DIVORCED across the room to echo the seismic shift that marriage had brought. "My divorce party was cathartic," says a man named Rick on the website divorcepartyplanner.com.

Cathy Gordon, a performance artist in Toronto, mounted a show titled *On My Knees: A Public Divorce Ceremony*, to "do homage" to her eight-year failed marriage. Gordon put on her old wedding dress and crawled for eight hours (with the help of kneepads and gloves) to eight different places in the city, all of which had been significant to their courtship and marriage. Her last stop was the edge of Lake Ontario because, she explained to a local newspaper, she wanted to end at the water to be "born again."

My favourite un-marriage ceremony is that of Shanna Moakler, former Playmate and participant in the reality show *Dancing with the Stars*. In November 2006, when she split from her husband, Travis Barker, a drummer—for the first time, that is, as they have reunited and split again several times since—she threw herself a break-up bash in Las Vegas, a popular destination to play roulette of the heart, where many about-to-be-marrieds go to enjoy their last taste of freedom, quickie weddings occur, and the end of a union is celebrated like New Year's Eve. Moakler invited friends. They partied all night. The coup de grâce? She rolled out a three-tier anti-wedding cake. On the top of the cake was a miniature plastic bride, arms raised in victory, wielding a knife. The groom lay at the bottom of the confection, nearly dead and bleeding red food colouring over the girlishly pink icing.

My un-marriage rituals were tame by comparison. At the end of our union, after having bought, renovated and sold two fixer-uppers during the course of our marriage, my husband and I were living in a large house that was an expression of full-blown family life. It, too, had been a fixer-upper, having sat on the market for months in the recession of the early 1990s, when we bought it for a steal. And we had done some of the necessary renovation—at least we had updated the kitchen and thrown out the avocado-green appliances from the seventies. It had an expansive lawn and plenty of room for three strapping boys and Ketchup. Bikes littered the driveway. The playroom in the basement was a vast Lego-land landscape filled with inventive buildings and ships. Running shoes the size of boats filled shelves. The new kitchen had a restaurant-grade stove, granite countertops, a Sub-Zero fridge. Our house boasted much of the domestic porn of our generation.

When we sold the marital home, I tried to make the most of that difficult move. The boys and I moved into a house less than twenty years old, not in need of renovation. There was no lawn. I could open the front door and a window at the back, and the wind would practically blow the dust and dirt out. But if my living space was reduced, I used it as an excuse to remove unhappy karma. Gone was the husband clutter. I took only the things I loved. My three boys fit into the new house like loaves in a baker's cooling rack. Ketchup found his spot under a table. I threw out the sheets we used on our queen-sized bed, bought a new mattress and painted my bedroom a bold shade of pink. *Less house, more life* was my mantra.

I know one woman who took very little from the marital home and moved into a rented apartment with hardwood floors and white, pristine walls. She bought a sofa and bed to begin anew. I understand the impulse. Ask any feng shui consultant, and she will tell you about the power of possessions. "When you wake up in a room, surrounded by things with negative energy, you take that negative energy with you all day," explains Sharon Hay, director of the Toronto School of Feng Shui. She helps many divorced people restart their lives. "I start by asking where the arguments were in the house, and many couples are often arguing in bed, especially when they have children. They don't want them to hear," she points out. "Plus, if the sex was bad you don't want that energy around."

Less is often more. "I don't want any of it," a friend recalls her ex-husband telling her when they were discussing who should get what in the split of household contents. "It just reminds me of our failure." Another woman I know realized a truth about her eleven-year marriage when she contemplated whether to keep any reminders of it. "Nothing was sentimental," she confesses, "and it made me realize that my marriage had been devoid of real emotion and that we never really loved each other."

This new, simpler version of my life is why I often feel that more than a cubicle wall separates me from my younger colleagues at the *Globe and Mail*. A generation separates us too, of course. But it is the difference in our stages of life that feels most significant to me. Not that the reporters chat to one another very much during the day; the concentration in the newsroom is enough to give the impression that we are assembling nuclear bombs, not sentences. But we sit in close proximity and know something of one another's lives. They are in the acquisition years, much as I was at their age. They are getting married, buying their first house, taking on a mortgage, getting to know in-laws, having babies.

And I am in a different place. My reproductive narrative has been told. I have lived in a marriage. I have passed through what they are now entering. I would never warn them of its dangers. Why? Its promise is so beautiful, and for many, it is fulfilled.

In the last two years, two of my colleagues have announced engagements. They came in to show off their engagement rings. This is such an iconic high point in a woman's life that it's a cliché—the left hand fanned out for all to admire. I am happy for them. I did the same thing myself. I know the joy. "What happens at thirty?" one of the newly married reporters asked me when it was her milestone birthday. "Good things," I replied. "It all gets better from here." And it's true. When I was at the start of my marriage, building a life with my husband felt like we were creating a world. Bringing our children into that place filled it with the most intense purpose and happiness I have ever known.

My post-divorce ring ritual had been significantly different. I had sold my gold wedding band (inscribed on the inside with *love, forever*) as well as my diamond engagement ring. I took them to Russell Oliver, a.k.a. "the Cashman," a salesman who runs odious ads on television, in which he screams at people that he will give them cash for their old jewellery.

At his storefront, I walked in the outside door, only to be caught in the small entranceway so he and his employees could assess my potential shadiness before buzzing me through the next, locked door. I was wearing my best Saturday sweats and a Soccer Mom smile.

"Let's see what you have," a man behind the counter said gruffly, without making eye contact.

I put my rings on the little velvet counter pad.

I knew their strategy was to look unimpressed.

"Look, I want you to just give me the best price. I'm not interested in playing games," I said.

He eyeballed me then, this balding bulldog of a man who looked as though his job required training in martial arts.

He held the diamond ring up to his monocle again, non-committal.

"Is Russell here?" I asked. Years ago, for a magazine, I had written a small story about him.

The salesman pressed a button under the counter, and out popped Oliver from the back room.

I introduced myself. He recognized me.

"You were mean about me!" he shrieked, clearly recalling the piece I had written, and pointing a finger in my face.

I had simply described his ebullient personality. "But the story gave you publicity, no?" I retorted.

His face twitched like that of a skunk smelling a foe.

"I'm divorced," I announced plainly. "I want to sell these rings. I know the diamond is good. All I want is enough money to buy something new."

Oliver's eyes widened a bit behind his large round glasses. I was not the usual animal who wandered into their locked showroom. I was prey, I knew that, but I was not the kind who had sentimental attachment to her jewellery.

When I had entered the store, a man was on his way out, indignant over his treatment at the hands of the bulldog, who had told him that his prized gold watch and some earrings were "garbage."

Oliver took over the assessment of my pieces. "This is worthless," he said of the gold wedding band. "I can't resell it. The gold will just be melted down."

I thought about keeping it for my children as a token of their parents' marriage. But why? It would be a reminder of what they no longer had: the two of us together. I could instead pay for Godammo.com to melt it and mould it into a bullet. That's their divorce-happy anti-marriage service.

"Take it, anyway," I said.

"The diamond is good," he acknowledged, turning it under the light. He offered about what I had thought I would get.

Still, I asked for more. "Look, I want to sell. Just sweeten the deal a bit." I smiled.

He upped the prize by two hundred.

"Done."

Oliver counted out a wad of crisp bills. I left with a wave, and immediately headed for a store downtown, where I had seen a cocktail ring—my divorce bling, I later called it—for the exact amount of money he had paid me.

It was not by accident that the ring that came with "I do" in a church was now being handed over a seedy altar in an unceremonious transaction. It was a way to close the door on what had once been my domestic fantasy.

9.

Ghost Dad

As time passed, it was clear Eric was building a new life for himself too. A year into his new marriage, he took two of our boys out for dinner, a week late for one of their birthdays, and made another announcement. "I hate to steal your thunder," he said, "but we had a baby last week." He and his new wife had not told the boys that they were pregnant. They hadn't had a visit with our boys either. Eric was now sixty-one, the father of nine children in total, counting his two new stepchildren.

The boys were thrilled about their new half-sister. When they came home and gave me the news, they looked at me to gauge my reaction. I was shocked, stupefied, really, and yes, angry. But when I saw their delight—for my children, the new arrival was simply an exciting addition to their stepfamily—I realized that I had no business saying anything. The baby, Eric's new life—they had nothing to do with me.

As Eric set about creating his new family, he left a big hole in ours, despite every effort to save his place. He didn't take the opportunity to invite the boys for holidays or weekends. I had seen him do the same thing before, of course. He had disappeared from the lives of his three girls when he married me and started a second family. Then, the challenge of staying connected with the children from his previous marriage had been made more difficult by the physical distance between the two families. We spent some parts of the summers together—either in Halifax or they came to us—but it was not consistent. The girls became distant, angry over his absence. He would often travel to Halifax on business and not visit them, saying he was too pressed for time, one of them later told me. After my divorce, when they heard that their father was repeating his pattern and walking away from our boys as he had from them, they were upset and took it upon themselves to stay in touch with my sons.

"Well, at least he isn't dead," said a friend of mine whose father died when she was young. She, too, was trying to help. Eric was alive. There was always the chance that he might decide to become more involved, and if the children ever needed him, they could seek him out. With a parent who has died, anything left unresolved stays that way.

"There were plenty of children who didn't have a father, because theirs went off to war, or were killed in the war," my father said to help me put my plight in perspective. When a father leaves for war, he has good reason to be absent. And he often returns. But Ghost Dads—fathers who are alive but absent—can haunt their offspring. In his beautiful autobiography, *Dreams from My Father*, Barack Obama wrote about the persistent draw of his absent father, who disappeared from his life when he was two. He wrote a whole book about it, he noted, while his mother, "the one who was the single most constant in my life," was in the background. He understood that an absent parent can have more presence.

"You don't know what it's like," my boys would say to me when we talked about divorce and their father. "Your parents did not divorce."

In my attempts to help them manage it, I often feel like an overzealous friend, who insists on her special remedy for an ailment she has never experienced. The divorce will always be a part of their lives, the impact of which I will never fully know.

They get a card from Eric for their birthdays and Christmas. He rarely calls them. Once, a week before Christmas, he phoned to complain to one of the boys that there would be no plans for a visit (meaning a brief lunch at a restaurant) over the holiday because none of them had phoned him recently. When I overheard the conversation, I cried. As their father, it was his responsibility to stay in touch with his children. It was not up to them. I explained this to the boys to ensure that they didn't see themselves as the cause of his absence. I knew that children naturally take responsibility for many of their parents' troubles.

"It's okay, Mom," Tait said.

I wasn't mad at their father for not helping me to co-parent—I was over that—but for how he hurt them.

"Don't cry. You don't need to worry about us. We understand how Dad is."

Still, his behaviour often confounds them. "He has so much to be proud of," Nick said, meaning that he and his brothers were good students. "It's weird that he doesn't make more of an effort."

Recently, I was talking to an acquaintance, and the subject of my ex came up. She wondered if he was involved with the children, because she knows I write about my divorce. Perhaps she was curious as to how I could justify excluding his voice when I write my family's story. Then I told her: he has no voice by choice. She is a mother too, and her face suddenly changed expression. She explained that her father had disappeared after her parents split, and there was something a psychiatrist once told her that was very helpful. "He told me that my father was not *capable* of staying in touch with me. He just couldn't do it, for whatever reason. But because I was capable of staying in touch with him, and wanted to, I still had a choice. I could decide when and if I wanted to make the effort. It was within my power," she said.

Eric had been a very involved parent. He helped run the soccer club the boys played in. He built them things in the country—swing sets and wagons. But when we divorced, he dropped out.

I reassure my boys that their father loves them, because I know he does. I encourage them to write to him, to call on his birthday and at Christmas. And they do. They don't need me to remind them. But I wasn't always so gracious. They have seen my anger, which I know is wrong. They could see the stress his abandonment of them and his lack of financial responsibility caused me. I couldn't have protected them from that, even if I'd wanted to. Their disappointment was mostly unspoken. They were confused. "Don't tell me about it," one of them would say sometimes when I complained about trying to pay the bills after Eric suddenly stopped sending child-support cheques. But if they couldn't express their anger, at least someone was doing it on their behalf. That was my lame excuse, anyway. As time passed, I mustered more restraint. "He is your father," I would tell them. "He will always be your father. It's good to try to have a relationship with him. He has many good qualities." And they have inherited many of them. "But he can also be an example of how not to be."

Besides wanting to free them from my bias so they can make their own judgments about their father, I want the children to have both parents present for important moments in their lives, their graduations and weddings. They benefit from our ability to practise forbearance.

One of the remarkable things about the parent–child bond is that children love their parents despite their faults. I knew this not only from watching my own children but from the lessons of others. Sam Berns, founder of withoutafather.com, a website that offers online mentors and advice to youth, sought me out to explain his work. He told me about his difficult relationship with his father, who had abandoned him when he was a young teenager, after his parents divorced. The loss deeply affected him, but his love for his father never wavered. As a teenager, he took on extra jobs, and later, put himself through university. When he was twenty-three, he paid off his mother's five-figure mortgage. "You know when you love someone and they do something wrong, but you still love them, and you can't really understand why? They are the way they are. It's beyond their control. And you almost want to cover it up for them. I always felt that if I did this for my father, it was almost like it was okay. I could fix it, you know?"

His mother never spoke ill of his father, who moved away and remarried after they separated. His father never paid support of any kind. Father and son had brief, sporadic reconciliations, which never lasted. But Sam's respect remained. Before starting his website, he sought his father's permission. He would be using his own experience as an abandoned son. His father gave his blessing. Recently, his father died unexpectedly from a pulmonary embolism while on holiday in the Caribbean. Having separated from his third wife—there had been a second, brief marriage after the one with Sam's mother—he was on holiday with a new girlfriend. Sam was put in charge of funeral arrangements because his father's latest wife, from whom he was not yet formally divorced, lived in the United States.

When he went to clear out his father's small apartment, Sam learned of a man he had never known. By reading personal papers and looking through belongings, he came to realize that his father had suffered from depression and anxiety, and had had a learning disability. "What frustrates me is that the [term] *deadbeat dad* is dismissive," he explains. "It doesn't look at the underlying reasons or any real source of understanding. I wish he had told me about his mental health issues. I'm sure it must have scared him." And Sam believes that the loss of his relationship with his son caused the man pain. "It wasn't easy for him," Sam says. "I think he felt guilty." Among his father's possessions, he came across his laptop computer. One of the bookmarks was withoutafather.com.

⁓

For a moment, step inside the faint outline of an average Ghost Dad. He is not abusive, not a father your children have chosen to excommunicate for good reason. He was a decent father when married, but now, because the children live with the mother, he feels marginalized. Even a seemingly innocuous comment by the mother—referring to the other parent as "your father" instead of "Dad"—reinforces to the child that he is no longer central to their home life. Her frustration, even resentment, over being the one who must do the work of two parents causes her to say things, bad things, that the children hear. When he is late to pick them up, she grumbles that he never does things right, what a jerk, and that his girlfriend is more important to him. She forgets that little ears are listening.

"The custodial mother who continues to fight the divorce issues through the children as a means of revenge is contemptible and real," explained a father who concedes that his involvement as a parent decreased with time because his children expressed enormous resentment against him.

Many mothers remain stuck in the role of victim, always casting her ex as the bad guy. Some of that may be their misguided coping strategy. For people who are struggling with a traumatic separation, to manage the intolerable feelings of loss, they often do a reconstruction of reality and begin to see their ex-husband as a bad man, explained a social worker.

A mother may think that because the children passed through her body they are more fully hers. She may consider herself a paragon of virtue—but she is not.

Many fathers have felt the icy fingers of the Ghost Dad on their shoulder, pulling them into the shadow of their family's life. A recent study revealed that men who have faded from their children's lives report dismay and anger at not having sufficient time with their children following separation. They disappear because of the repeated feelings of loss that result from only occasional visits. Paradoxical as it may seem, they deal with feelings of loss by creating more loss. They also begin to question themselves as parents, say other experts. Some of these Ghost Dads grew up with the old-fashioned notion that a father's love is expressed solely through what he provides financially. Just as mothers have to make the transition to single-household head, so do fathers, and for them that often means an increased involvement as a parent on several levels—emotional, social and financial. He has to become Mr. Wallet and Mr. Mom.

"The kids would come on a Friday night, and they were little and they were all over the place. It was very difficult," says Ian Harvey, a journalist whose eleven-year marriage broke up in 1991 when his two children were five years old and eighteen months old. He was overwhelmed, and in the first few months moved back into his childhood home with his father. There were many nights when he sat on his boyhood bed and cried. Eventually, though, things got better. "I am obstinate. I wasn't going to quit." He found his way as a single father, learning not to make promises he couldn't keep, and not to give in to the guilt that produces the Santa Daddy, who overcompensates by showering the children with presents. He also refused to become the Disneyland Dad, who can only plan visits around extravagant outings. As another divorced father of two toddlers put it, "You can't have a conversation with [children] if they're staring at a tiger."

The Ghost Dad often lacks the ability to connect with his children. "The child has a deep longing for the parent to be there as a human being, not as a role, no matter how conscientiously that role is being played," writes Eckhart Tolle in *A New Earth*. But a Ghost Dad may feel that he has been reduced to a marginal role—that of babysitter. He is criticized if something happens, something as innocuous as a tumble in the park, while the child is on his watch. "How could you let this happen?" the mother screams when he delivers the child back on Sunday night. You can hear him sometimes say to his children, "Remember to tell Mom that you had your fruit." He feels that the mother nags him like the wife he thought he had divorced.

And then there is men's own handicapping socialization. "It's difficult for men to express their hurt," Calvin Sandborn, author of *Becoming the Kind Father*, explained to me. For much of his life, Sandborn, who is a professor at the University of Victoria and a member of a divorced men's group, emulated his alcoholic father's example of hiding emotions, which he believes was a factor in the breakdown of his own marriage after twenty-five years and three children. What he learned in the aftermath of divorce helped him create the bond he now enjoys with his three adult daughters. "I was an ignoramus as far as what was going on in my inner life," he said. Men see their lives in terms of doing, not feeling, he said. "We have been taught to regard ourselves as a body with a job to do, like a machine . . . to cut ourselves off from our heart." Instead of expressing to their ex-wives how terrible they feel about losing daily contact with their children, they view the vulnerability they experience—not being in control of their emotions—as an assault on their masculinity. "A man feels sadness," Sandborn observed. "But on some level, he thinks, 'I'm not supposed to feel sadness,' so the way men react is to blame the person who is making them feel [that way]. They get angry. There's an adrenalin rush. And that makes them feel powerful again."

Once, at a party, a divorced dad was listening to me wonder why some fathers choose absence.

"It's about cruelty," I said.

He had a different take. "No," he replied solemnly. "It's about shame."

I nodded. I hadn't considered the possibility that in the world of masculinity, you're either a winner or a loser. It's black or white. Because divorce is seen as a failure, you are a loser—and who wants to be reminded of that?

PART THREE

A pleasant surprise is in store for you.

10.

When the Veil Finally Lifts

The divorced mid-life woman doesn't have the protected, cosseted air of Wife, of being someone's other half, of being able to look across a room, or a dinner-party table, and find safe mooring in the eyes of her husband. The divorced woman surveys a room with a gimlet eye. She is unashamed. There is not a whiff of tragedy, unlike among divorcees of my mother's generation—the few I saw, anyway—who had a little too much cleavage and an air of instability about them. They were loose in the sense that they seemed unbolted, somehow. Today's divorced MLW has the look of a survivor, and if she is still mired in the emotional storm of a fresh divorce, the vulnerability she exudes is complemented by a determination to get through it.

In public, when it seems appropriate or if she feels like it, she will let it be known that she is divorced, usually in the same offhand way an owner might discuss a horse he has put out to pasture. There is regret. I am the first to admit that. The horse was once deeply loved. He was needed, useful, beautiful and integral to happiness. He is missed and likely will never be forgotten. But everyone knew that he had to go. Perhaps he just didn't want to play the same role anymore, and had made that clear in his actions. Or, maybe he was tired of the oats. She was not kind, perhaps. She couldn't care less if he was happy in the stable. Or, it could be that—to her—he had simply turned into a tiresome nuisance. In any case, the tone of the announcement that they are no longer joined at the saddle is one of breezy ruefulness.

In private, however, when divorced women get together, there is never any shortage of detail about what exactly went wrong. It's similar, I suppose, to the time as young wives when we would compare our lives: what the husbands did for a living, whether the wife had a career or was a stay-at-home mom, where a couple lived in the city, where the carpet was purchased, and the sofa, where they bought groceries, and travelled, what kind of car they drove, and where the children went to school. But now, when we compare, it's over how bad the marriage was.

He was a control freak! If the kitchen wasn't clean, he would make a disparaging comment, as though it were my sole responsibility. He would pick a piece of lint off the carpet, off the freaking carpet, the minute he walked in the door, for God's sake!

OR:

He wasn't even present for the births of our children. Always some excuse. A meeting. Some important message he had to relay to a business colleague—you know, in the pre-BlackBerry days.

OR:

He hated my success! He hated my colleagues. He said they were boring.

OR:

He was boring!

OR:

He was abusive. At least, I call it abusive. He was a master of the Art of the Put-Down.

OR:

Oh, and the sex was terrible. Bang, bang!

OR:

One time, late at night, I came into the rec room, and there he was, looking at porn, right on the kids' computer, and he was, you know . . .

OR:

Well, the first affair happened six years ago. We worked through that one. Went to therapy. He said it would never happen again. But then . . . some girl from the office. In her thirties. He said it was a sympathy thing. He wanted to help her. She was a Single Mom, and she looked up to him.

OR:

All of the above.

I have heard all the stories. And I am happy to tell mine— the short version: older man; I was an exit strategy from his first marriage; he was controlling and insecure.

It's understandable, what we are doing. We are venting as a form of communal therapy. Men do it too, but not with the same ease. I have heard complaints about ex-wives who refused to get a job outside the home, even when the children were full-time in school; who worked too much; who could not budget the family income; who maxed-out the credit cards and once racked up a $60,000 debt on a line of credit without telling the husband; who withheld sex; who had affairs; who "went spiritual" and needed to go her own way; who turned out to be gay; who had nothing interesting to say beyond kids' stuff.

Men will divulge their marital issues when asked or if they feel it's required, especially in a dating scenario. But it's not something they like to do, generally speaking.

"Can we stop talking about divorce now?" one man asked me after we had talked about our mutual marital disappointments for about ten minutes. He cocked his head cutely to the side, and shrugged. "It's not something that I like to talk about at length. I know it's important and all," he added, laying his hands out, palms upturned, as if to suggest he was an open emotional book. "But, only for so long."

It's not just that their minds work differently than women's; their support networks do too. Sure, they may discuss their divorce with their male friends over a beer after a game of squash. But the former marriage, even a twenty-year one, is usually a topic of conversation for four, maybe five sentences. It was once great. It broke. We couldn't fix it. I couldn't fix it. Hey, what did you think of the hockey game last night?

Not that I want to diminish men's emotional lives. Once, when I was being a nicely dressed wine-drinking fly on the wall—it was late, and I was a solitary writer-type on a bar stool at a local watering hole, in need of an evening "humanity bath"—I heard two guys talking about women over a plate of chicken wings. They were on a man-date, discussing how to gauge sexual interest.

"Ask her to come out with you and a couple of friends," one of the men said to the other.

"Really, you think?" his friend replied.

"It'll be good to see if there's anything between you."

"But we did have a moment at Brian's party last week," the nervous dater said.

"What kind of a moment?" his friend asked.

"A 'moment' moment," he said. "A look in the eyes."

"Yeah, well, those can be dangerous. You think it was something, but it could be nothing." He gave his friend the hairy eyeball—a warning to be cautious.

Not only women parse the language, spoken and not, of their relationships with the opposite sex.

Still, it is my experience—and the opinion of many male experts out there—that men sum up their romantic lives succinctly the way they might characterize a business deal, in guy shorthand. Men are usually quite straightforward, especially in their communication. Remember the wisdom of *He's Just Not That Into You*: when a man is interested, you know. When he is not, he doesn't call back. It's simple, really. And that applies to other areas of their lives. Men don't process in the same way women do. We do it verbally—with a glass of wine in hand. Men don't feel compelled to talk about the minutiae of life. They don't emotionally knit and unravel things. Look, they don't write divorce memoirs. I know this intimately, and respect this. I've raised three gargantuan test studies.

"Come, tell me how work is going," I once suggested to Tait.

He settled his lean six-foot-four frame into a chair and regaled me with some funny anecdotes about his work in information technology.

"How are you feeling about it?" I inquired.

He looked up at me. "How do I feel about it, Mom?" he said. He laughed. "How do I *feel*?" he repeated.

I shrugged.

"Hey, Luke!" he joked as his younger brother, a beanpole (also six-four), entered the room, carrying a glass of milk. "How do you feel about that glass of milk?" Luke held it up and looked at it thoughtfully, as if it were a work of art and he might start to lecture on the beauty of its whiteness.

But before a word was uttered, they both collapsed into guffaws.

"I think you need a daughter, Mom," Tait said, teasing me.

Men are as complicated as women, just not in the same way. And that's both a good and potentially an unhealthy attribute, at least as far as divorce is concerned. A recent Statistics Canada study revealed that men aged twenty to sixty-four, who had recently experienced a break-up of a marriage or common-law relationship, are six times more likely than men who remained married to report a period of depression. By comparison, women who had undergone a marital breakdown were only three-and-a-half times more likely than women who remained married to experience feelings of despair. It's true that this revelation could simply be proof that there are more depressed women in marriages than there are sad, married men. But even so, it proves that being a husband is a state that makes many men happy.

Marriage is a structure that sets up a lot of power and privilege for men, explained a divorce coach. When they lose it, there's a lot of grief that goes unacknowledged. And that, in turn, partly explains why more divorced men than divorced women remarry, as my ex so quickly did. But arguably, with the ability to move on into new relationships, men live in the present, whereas women have a tendency to get stuck in the past or to project into the future. We are often thinking (and talking) about what we had or what we want, not what we have.

Still, when divorced women start swapping bad-marriage tales like recipes, they are doing more than trying to make themselves feel better. They are disassembling a female fantasy, indulging in reverse wedding mythology. Like Princess Diana, who felt the need to divulge the nature of her troubled marriage through Andrew Morton in his book about her a little more than ten years after her magical wedding to Prince Charles, women want to tell the nightmare of the marriage as eagerly as they once promulgated its fairy tale.

~

"It's a good thing to not be trapped by marriage, if you don't think it's right," writer Sascha Rothchild told me about her starter marriage—a "starter marriage" defined as a union that lasts less than five years and produces no children. In 2008, Rothchild wrote an article called "How to Get Divorced by 30," which quickly morphed into a book deal, and the film rights sold soon after. Married at twenty-seven, she knew she didn't want "status quo mediocrity" as she approached her thirtieth birthday, she wrote. What is admirable is not only her ability to recognize quickly that her marriage was a mistake, but also to act on the intuition and get out. She had decided to lift the bridal veil.

The tradition is all wrong, I now understand—the one in which a bride walks down the aisle to the altar, hidden and demure behind her veil, to be revealed for all to see after the vows have been exchanged and once her groom lifts it from her face. A bride wears a veil after she becomes a wife. Once married, it becomes paramount for the bride and groom to believe, and to show to others, that everything is fine, really, just fine, thank you. "I knew when I was on my honeymoon," many divorced people say about their marriages in retrospect. Nevertheless, they stayed in them. What should have been starter marriages lasted fifteen, twenty years. For many, it's a question of denial, not just of what they want and their un-happiness but also of the characteristics in their mate. I count myself in that group. To some extent, when we become spouses we put on marriage blinkers. We choose to see certain truths and to deny others in the romantic partners we choose to love. The wedding vows should include the words "With this ring, I suspend my disbelief in myself and in you, from this day forward."

Rothchild wasn't thinking about "why I was really doing things," and she acknowledged that "with celebrities who get married and divorced every five minutes, for my genera-tion, [divorce] is not so big a deal." But there's still courage involved in jumping off a train that has already left the station. In fact, she had doubts even before she walked down the aisle. While trying on rings, she chose something non-traditional, "so I could wear it on my right hand after divorce. Of course, I kept this to myself. I was planning my divorce at the same time as I was planning my wedding," she writes.

An engagement is the first step of a very public declaration of love. "It's too late," Lady Diana Spencer's sisters famously told her when she began to doubt the Prince's devotion to her in the months before their wedding. "Your face is on the tea towels." Then comes the wedding, which is the climax of courtship and falling in love, freighted with emotional investment and significant financial outlay, including a dress the price of a fridge. In front of friends and family, you promise to love this person you have chosen until death do you part. If you marry in a religious setting, you are inviting God to watch too. You have spent months planning the details. The bridal showers! The wedding registry! The friends, swooning over the romance of it all! Your mother cries tears of joy.

I remember feeling that an expression of doubt about a decision so profound would disappoint many people, and be an admission—again, very public—that I didn't know myself well enough, that I was naive, at the very time that I was supposed to be stepping fully into my maturity. "One of the first things older men say to a young man who has just married is 'Well done,'" explains a man who has been married and divorced three times. "It's as if you have joined a club of grown-up men." And what woman has not felt that, when she becomes a wife, she is suddenly at a new level of womanhood? Many of Rothchild's friends, who also married in their late twenties and divorced by thirty, felt pressure to marry—she calls the groupthink "matrimania"—despite their good educations and jobs. "It validates you, to have that ring," she said. When a woman marries, she graduates to china, silver and crystal, and begins to think about taking her ovaries out of storage. Social acceptance of a starter marriage may make the permission to quit easier, but it still means you have to accept a demotion.

Therapists like to point out that there is plenty of cultural encouragement to marry, but little support once you are in a marriage. People have to figure out on their own the delicate negotiation of self-assertion and self-sacrifice required in marriage. I didn't know who to ask and was too embarrassed to admit my dilemma. It may be acceptable to admit confusion over other roles we take on, like that of being a new mother— there are uniformed baby nurses to ask and eager grandmothers full of advice!—or a new work responsibility where you feel slightly out of depth. You ask for training and insight. But it's not appropriate to say that that you don't know how to be a wife or husband. You're supposed to know in the same way you're expected to know how to be a member of your sex—or *how* to have sex for that matter. (Somehow that's not as hard to figure out.) And then once part of a couple, you become "an item" in pop-cultural parlance, one being, composed of two halves—and no one helps you figure out how to be whole within your half.

Shortly after I was out on my own, Joy told me that for as long as she had known me—almost ten years at that point—she felt I had been deeply unhappy and conflicted about what to do in my marriage. *That long?* I thought. The first time I ever said anything negative about Eric was to a casual friend in the first year of marriage. The outburst made me feel horribly guilty and disloyal to him. It didn't feel right. But as time went on, I did complain more and more, especially to Joy. It was part of the processing I had to do. We can sometimes unfairly burden our friends, I now think. I needed a professional listener far earlier than I sought one out. Still, I don't consider that time wasted. One thing I have learned is that no one can tell another what his or her heart wants. I didn't listen to mine for the longest time. Not closely, anyway. I was afraid of the truth. Now when it speaks, I take note.

Hormones didn't help to clarify its messages, that much I also know. New love lights up the brain's chemistry like a drug, overruling the calmer wisdom of the heart. So widely accepted now is the hormone hailstorm that there's a T-shirt that reads, "It's the oxytocin, stupid." The bonding hormone has a lot to answer for, if you ask me. What women need is a condom for the brain and the heart.

How is the woman in a new sexual relationship supposed to know if what she's feeling is the real thing? Go celibate for a while to let the oxytocin fade? One relationship therapist told me that the hormone high of being in love—the initial infatuation—doesn't start to wear off until two years have gone by. Two years! A couple could have bought a house together by then. They could have married, had a child. We're wired to bond through sex—a neat little procreation trick. It's astounding to me to think back on my own powerful urge to have babies with Eric. I let nothing dissuade me—not his growing alienation from his girls, not his controlling behaviour with me.

Over time, the denial of unhappiness can also increase with what I think of as marital acclimatization. Even in a dysfunctional environment—and mine was not severe—partners get used to the new temperature, one degree at a time, like a frog in a pan of water that slowly reaches the boiling point. I thought of this when news broke of Josef Fritzl, the seventy-three-year-old Austrian man who confessed to keeping his daughter Elisabeth, then forty-two, in a bunker beneath the family home for twenty-four years. People could not understand how his wife, Rosemarie, did not know. He had fathered seven children with his daughter. Rosemarie had believed him when he brought three of the children upstairs, claiming that Elisabeth had dropped them off, unable to care for them, because she was living in a cult.

Hers was an extreme case of spousal denial—obviously. And he may very well have a psychopathic personality, which criminal psychologists say describes someone who is skilled at deception and compartmentalization. He or she maintains dual realities: seemingly normal in one life, criminal and evil in the other. This explains why it's not uncommon to hear stories about wives of serial killers who say they had no idea what their partners were doing.

Delusion comes in varying degrees. Did Elin Nordegren never suspect the infidelities of her husband, Tiger Woods, before she made the fateful discovery? Did Silda Spitzer never once suspect the behaviour of her husband, former New York governor Eliot Spitzer? He was using high-end prostitutes for several years. Wouldn't she have known? Did she notice some odd behaviour and rationalize it away? Certainly, many ex-spouses will say, when some uncomfortable truth is exposed, that they intuited something was a bit off about their partner's conduct. I know people who discovered, post-divorce, that their spouses were involved in dubious business activities, for example, or had affairs while they were married. But at the time, they were tied up in wanting to believe the best of their partner. They were prisoners of hope. And perhaps some were blinded by status. No one wants to admit, "I am married to a controlling, difficult and mean-spirited man, who probably has affairs with prostitutes because he never wants sex with me." She wants to say, "I am married to the governor of New York." Or: "I am married to the greatest golfer the world has ever known."

When I was embroiled in the heat of married life with Eric, I used to feel that I was in the middle of a complex, dense novel, the plot of which I didn't know. The two pro-tagonists—Eric and me—revealed themselves bit by bit as the story unfolded. How he was as a father was part of it. How I was as a mother was another. What he brought out (or denied) in me, and I in him, was a chapter. Finally, finally, the *Story of Us* came to its conclusion. I could see how I con-tributed to the problems, how I enabled them and why we had them in the first place. I was able to close the book.

"Life can only be understood backward, but it must be lived forward," wrote Søren Kierkegaard. It is only in the fresh air of ex-hood that you can see your former partner for who she or he truly is—and yourself.

Divorce finally lifts the veil.

II.

Emotional Flu

For several years, my divorced friends and I talked a lot about our recovery. "I have wished many times that there would be a hand that would come out of the clouds offering either a pill or a note telling me what to do," my friend Mary Tomlinson, a separated mother of three and a Jungian psychotherapist, said to me at one point. Recovery, she said, is "a matter of both time and conscious self-awareness."

It is our impulse to push past grief, gloss over it, find a fix, seek escape. But the loss of a marriage takes time to get over. Jessica Kerwin quit her job as a fashion reporter for *Vogue* magazine to travel to a leper colony in India following her separation. "Everything I feared most was right in front of me: being old, sick, abandoned, childless, poor," she said of her job giving massages to old women in a leprosy treatment centre in the state of Maharashtra. Travel offers one the chance to get out of oneself, to find new experiences that will provoke unexpected responses—a temporary form of recovery. I remember thinking about moving somewhere new in those early years after the divorce, even though the logistics were impossible at the time, with three children still at home. I knew a woman who took her child for a year-long job in another country, a sojourn her ex agreed to (somewhat reluctantly) in an effort to be supportive. "This place has too much pain, too much disappointment," she explained about the city they knew. "I need new people," she said. One night I talked to a couple who had each endured a divorce. When I explained my desire to bolt the country, the province, the city—anything—the man leaned forward and put his hand on my wrist. "I felt the same way after my divorce," he explained. He did leave the city where he had spent his previous married life. "But you know what I found?" He paused. "I discovered that your problems follow you. They are inside. Nothing on the outside will make a difference."

I know that for parents who lose the custody of their children in divorce, full recovery is a luxury they will never know. I was lucky in that regard. My children needed me, and I funnelled my energy into their well-being—as a cure for my own heartache and a focus that required competency and stability. "You will stay in this house for a long time, won't you?" Luke asked me soon after we moved into our new place. "Yes. Until I'm very old," I replied. Some of my emotional recuperation came out of necessity—I didn't have the luxury of *not* coping—and some was a matter of time passing.

I know the desire to avoid the Miss Havisham syndrome. The character in Charles Dickens's *Great Expectations* hardens her heart after being betrayed in love. Perpetually dressed in her wedding gown and covered in cobwebs, she shuts out the world and remains in a state of mourning.

I have friends who say that recovery from divorce is a matter of calculation. Take the number of years you were married, divide by two, and that's the number of months it will take you to find a new equilibrium. Nine months? Forget it. More like thirty-six.

To achieve self-awareness is painful and takes time. "It's a tough honesty gig," Mary explained. She had "crowbar moments," she said, her term for "when I separate myself from myself, pry that space open a little and really look at who I am."

I found no shortcut. In the years immediately following my divorce, my life was a roller coaster. Some days I felt great, knowing that I was starting a whole new period, filled with possibility, and other days, I was dragged down by despair. What had I done? What would happen to me, to the kids? I would often lie in bed for hours, at night or when the children were at school, thinking through the film of our marriage. And I allowed myself, still, to be sideswiped by news of Eric's behaviour. "Why do you let him pull you into his emotional tornado?" Mary asked me once, when I was telling her about some child-support issue.

My friends helped. But no one could make me better. I had an emotional flu. I just had to wait until it lifted.

As time went on, I gradually found that when I heard news of my ex, I was able to not care. I felt angry when he let down the children—of course. I had some bad nights of revenge fantasies, I assure you. But when I finally allowed myself to step back from the situation, I could dismiss the emotion. His actions were not aimed at me, although at times it felt that way. (I was left to take up the slack, after all.) I phoned him once, years after our divorce, to ask him for help with one of the children, who was acting out. "If you're having problems in your relationship with him, that's your problem. I get along fine with him," he replied. He hadn't seen any of the boys for many, many months. And of course, when he did, they were on their best behaviour, eager to please him. I often envied the happy ex-relationship many of my friends have with their former husbands. If they were worried about the children, they could phone up the dads and talk through the issues. In his memoir, *The Film Club*, about his efforts to help his teenage son, novelist David Gilmour writes about how he and his ex-wife, the mother to his son, went off to the Caribbean together, leaving his current partner to house-sit his ex's place. "To outsiders or to her occasionally unforgiving friends, it must have sounded a tad peculiar," he wrote. "How odd life can be." *And how sweet in a way*, I thought as I read that passage. I know people whose ex and the new partner and stepkids are like a grand, extended family, who visit on special occasions and gather for holiday meals.

Soon, though, I realized that Eric's decisions to be the kind of father he was being were about him. He would have to live with those choices. And it wasn't a matter of feeling sorry for him, either. Pity would suggest superiority on my part, as though I thought I had been vindicated, that I had won something. But what exactly? It was just a hole he had left.

He was and is the master of his own life. He had his reasons for not being more involved as a father, which I cannot know, not fully, anyway. And he had his way of dealing with disappointment. He had a need to survive in his own way. His personality was no longer my issue, as it had been when I was his wife. He was someone else's problem now—and someone else's source of happiness too.

⁓

"If this is what you want, why are you so sad?" my mother asked me one day not long after we had decided to divorce.

"Because even if it was the right thing to do and unavoidable, it's still very difficult," I tried to explain.

My mother can imagine the grief of widows but she doesn't understand that divorce causes bereavement just as intense, only different. My parents knew the horror of the legal proceedings. They helped financially with their grandchildren's education. I was reeling not just from the shock and disbelief of it all but also sad about a lost dream.

"Marriage makes you feel that you have taken care of something in your life," a thirty-one-year-old newly separated man said. "When it's gone, it's like someone has passed you a bad cheque. . . . It's a very unstable time." A spouse loves you out of choice, not out of duty, as parents do. That kind of loss is profound. Someone is now choosing not to love me, because of who I am, what I've become, what I did or what I want. And just as a love affair is mysterious in its inception, so it is in its dissolution. When the marriage of a friend of mine ended after twenty-six years, she endured a lengthy recovery. "I am unpeeling a lifetime together," she said to explain her need to understand what went wrong, and when. The habit of living with a person, however difficult, can be hard to break. Once, in the early days of our trial separation, I called Eric in the country. The day had been awful. I had lost some tapes of recorded interviews. I was stressed. "Come back and make everything okay again," I said. We both knew it was a bad idea, and so he didn't.

During my marriage, I was never prouder than when we went out as a family, the mommy and daddy ducks, with their offspring in tow. This was hubris, sure, that unspoken pride in children who reflect well upon you. But it was so much more.

In the summer of 2007, Anne Mirvish, the widow of Toronto's famous entrepreneur Honest Ed Mirvish, recalled what her husband had told her around the time of their sixty-fifth wedding anniversary, just over a year earlier. "We're a team," he said. "We did it together. We're good for each other."

Marriage is a shared experience, made richer when children are present. You create a unit, a tight little world of love and connection, like a community of people who subscribe to the same newspaper, and read the same words, the same story, at the same time. In a family, all its members witness the same event, live through the same circumstances, use the same shorthand, love or hate or ridicule the same things. "Harpy Easter," my elder sister wrote in an e-mail to me one spring. It was a familiar greeting. Our younger brother had written a handmade card for one of our grandmothers one Easter, when he was small, and misspelled the word.

In a family, we read from the same page of memories.

I have come to understand that women leave marriages for themselves; men leave for other women, from my observation. A family lawyer agreed with me when he said that many of his male clients like to have a woman in the wings. "They swing from one to the other," he said. Call it the trapeze syndrome. They like, need even, to have a safe place to land. Many women leave their marriages for their lovers too. But they also leave simply because marriage itself, its demands and compromises, had become too much of a weight and a restriction.

So we take the risk of leaping into the void. "You have to learn to live with a certain degree of unknowingness," a wise, older woman told me when I was facing the future as a single parent. There is more hope in not knowing what the future might bring than there is in living with the past and present of a difficult marriage you already know. At least you can imagine a difficult possibility. *I will just have to fling myself into the arms of the universe*, I remember thinking.

"You're different," some of my friends would say after time had passed. "You seem more . . . well, light-hearted."

The first step to my recovery came when I changed the identification in my married name back to my maiden name. The background noise of distress about my identity was finally silenced. I had lost myself in being a wife, in a highly romanticized notion of surrendering to love. I had found a new, happy self in motherhood. And despite the difficulty of the marriage and the divorce, it has been an important crucible—a second childhood in a way and an education I would never have had otherwise. My divorce was a bid for authenticity, to reclaim an old me and celebrate an emerging version of her too. At least I was back to being one person.

To honour that passage, one of the first things I bought for my house, several months after I moved in, was a painting I found of a woman in a yellow dress diving into a vast, blue ocean. She was making a leap, and she would have to swim to stay afloat.

~

As sometimes happens, life soon presented me with a surprising exchange that helped me understand how to put my marriage in context and approach mid-life relationships. It happened on a date with Leonard Cohen—okay, a professional date, an interview, a long, long conversation in his house in Montreal, conducted over wine, cherry pie and Greek bread.

"How old are you?" he asks.

I tell him.

"The same age as Anjani." Anjani is his partner.

"It's different for women, being single at this age," I say.

"It's different all the way around," he acknowledges, falling easily into a discussion about later-life love. "I remember telling a friend of mine, an older woman who had a nice boyfriend, I said, 'Listen, darling, don't try to fine-tune this. Just let it come through without too much static. This is not hi-fi. Stay away from the dial. It's good enough as it is.'"

Don't ask how it happens, but sometimes it does. An interview will suddenly turn personal. Lily Tomlin asked me to stay for dinner with her at the Dresden, a popular haunt in the heart of Hollywood, when I was supposed to have only half an hour with her. She drank three martinis (I had one), we ate dinner (I insisted on paying) and then she offered to drive me to my hotel in Hollywood in her white Rolls-Royce. As we sailed down a wide boulevard, just the two of us, she talked to me about going to Palm Springs to visit her mother on the weekend, and I looked at her in profile, wondering how I had got there.

By the next day, celebrities have forgotten about the close encounter, but to the mere mortal, who receives (however briefly) the attention of a cultural god, the moment never fades.

Now, with Leonard, I am seated at a simple, wooden table on the second floor of his Montreal house, which has a higgledy-piggledy quality, as quirky as an imagination, with two front doors leading to the same foyer (side-by-side row houses have been made into one), a hidden staircase that runs between floors, and unexpected rooms—a tiny, cupboard-sized space tucked under the stairs, containing a claw-footed bathtub.

We have turned to the subject of men, and I'm not sure how. But I am not questioning it, not when the poet and songwriter who channelled the despair of heartache and the transcendent nature of sex, whose work woke me up in my private-school-girl tunic at fifteen when I lived up the mountain, where nobody seemed to talk about anything important, is volunteering advice. Who needs to pay for a goddess seminar on healing your heart—it's an industry, in case you haven't noticed—when Leonard is telling you about the nature of love.

"Everybody is an amateur when that feeling of real attraction arises," he is explaining now in his low, rumbling voice. "It sends you off into horrors of rejection and unfulfilled appetite and self-pity and dreams of triumph of working it all out."

He laughs lightly, this gentleman of hip, dressed in a suit jacket, over a shirt and pants, a cap perched jauntily on his snow-white hair. Sex is "a sacrament," he says, and "the interaction between men and women and now between men and men and whatever it is . . . you don't want to even talk about it. Otherwise you soil it. You diminish it. It allows you to become sensitive to the creator, to this curious phenomenon of existence."

He asks about my marriage. I tell him a few sentences: the basic outline.

"Does he continue to support you?"

I briefly recount the nightmare of chasing him for child support and having to negotiate away any spousal income, interim or otherwise.

"Marriages break up, but you can't leave someone in the lurch," he says. He never married, but he has two children with Suzanne Elrod—not the Suzanne of his famous song. "I still support the mother of my children. . . . It's tribal."

I feel somewhat recovered from the divorce, I explain, which is a good thing. I can now see the difficulties so clearly. I had to leave.

"You're not doing anything," he responds. "It's being done through you. It's your destiny to bump into this person. You can't blame yourself. There's no way that you could know. You loved him. You shared a bed with him, and you brought forth beautiful children."

"But it's hard to scrape away scar tissue from your heart."

"You just need to find someone to go to dinner with, to sleep with from time to time, to telephone every day and write. I mean, you know, it's what you set up that is defeating. . . . A little goes a long way at a certain point," he says, laughing gently again.

"Maybe I should go younger," I suggest playfully.

"It's a good idea," he says. "At a certain point in someone's life, it's very refreshing. There are a lot of young men who like older women, and really want that experience and that kindness that only childbearing and the real abrasive education of life can give somebody. They just feel like being with someone who's been around the block a few times."

I laugh. Leonard Cohen is giving me romantic advice, right into my trusty tape recorder. "Well, if you know anyone, send him my way," I joke.

"Okay." He smiles. "I have friends who are going out with younger men. I remember when I met Marguerite Duras, she had a young boyfriend. He was about forty years younger. He was in his thirties, and she was in her seventies. I think it's completely legit. That's one of the things that takes a little bit of courage, but it's worth cultivating. Just to say, 'Screw you, I don't care about your opinions,' whether it's your children's opinion, your peers' opinion, your colleagues' opinion. You should just think, 'This is really nice for me.' So, think, 'Yes, you want to sleep with me? Lovely. You're eighteen? Okay, that's maybe too young. Okay, twenty-four. Lovely, how lovely.' You don't have to tell anybody. You don't need anyone's permission. Give yourself permission to make a few mistakes. You know, blow it a bit. Have a few drinks. Fall into bed with somebody. It doesn't have to be the final thing. In fact, there is no final thing after a certain period when your childbearing years are finished. It's different for a woman who hasn't had a child. There's biological tyranny, and she has to choose the guy who touches her heart but he's got to be able to provide. There are so many aspects to the choice. It's bewildering for a woman who's got that clock ticking."

He had explained earlier that most relationships between a woman and a man, when younger, descend into "the old horror story . . . I'll give you this if you give me that. You know, seal the deal. What do I get? What do you get? It's a contract." But his long-term relationship with Anjani is perfect, he tells me. Their relationship "gets deeper and deeper." But they are separate, too. He likes to wake up alone. He has a flat upstairs. This is her floor. Still, he has made it clear to her that they are together. "As you get older, you want to accommodate, and say, 'Yeah, we're living together. This is for real. I'm not looking for anyone else. You're the woman in my life.' . . . You want to make those minor adjustments, moment by moment, so we feel good, so we validate each other," he says. Companionship matters. "We're both incredibly 'solitudinous' people at this stage in the game." She has been married and divorced. "And I've had a few wrecked things myself. It's just a pleasure to have someone who's not judging you every moment.

"Have modest expectations," he advises, his hands folded on the table in front of him. He looks out from under his cap. "Start off with dinner."

I leave a short while later, but not before he gives me a small tour. The bathtub under the stairs looks inviting, I tell him, like a cocoon. "Come back anytime," he says in his casually friendly manner. We go downstairs to the front door. Standing in the foyer, he doesn't think I am dressed warmly enough. The Montreal spring is wet and cold. "Here, let me . . . ," he says, handing me an old navy sweatshirt and a grey wool scarf.

Later, when I am back in Toronto, I e-mail Leonard to thank him for the generous amount of time he gave to me and to the newspaper.

"Don't forget the promise of the bath," I write as a postscript.

"I'll get the towels ready," he writes back.

"And the candles, Leonard?"

"Will have to check with the fire department" comes his reply.

A few weeks later, I send an e-mail to let him know when the piece will be published in the paper. And I remind him that I still have his sweater and scarf. I will return them by post, I suggest. But he has forgotten that he ever gave them to me. Never mind, he says. Keep them.

They remain in my closet, unwashed.

I have told my friends his advice many times. He offered a way of being at mid-life. And I feel it. The profound desire to marry, to want something permanent, only makes us vulnerable. We are freed of that now.

12.

Tulips in the Spring Are More Reliable

There are many examples of Wife. Sure, some aren't very helpful, but at least there's a cornucopia to choose from. But the Ex-Wife? Hmm. Let's see. There's Wallis Simpson, the twice-divorced American who stole the heart of King Edward VIII, causing him to abdicate his throne in 1936. Invariably described as a hard-headed go-getter, including of new husbands, she reputedly had naughty sex tricks up her Schiaparelli sleeves. She fit the cliché, in other words. When I was married, I remember seeing divorced women and not wanting that persona. I assumed they were desperate, something a bit pitiable. (Oh yes, married women— even conflicted ones, like me at the time—can be cruelly judgmental. We're smug, even when we're miserable.) The cultural foil to the demure bride is the vampy divorcee.

She sports prodigious cleavage and too-short skirts, not to mention spiky heels. She's always on the make. Well, I didn't want to be her.

What I've found is that you just make it up as you go along. And one rather helpful thing that seems to come with the territory is wry observation. Wallis Simpson had it—a certain ironic distance from the social whirl that allows you to see it all clearly. That's because you have been passed to and from the married and unmarried spheres, and you know that neither is exactly how the other perceives it to be. You develop what I think of as the divorced MLW attitude— laconic, breezy, straight-shooting.

Here's a starting point. Single-single means you live alone, and don't have a romantic partner. Single-double means you live alone, but have a lover who lives in his or her own place. The guy is around when you want him—and when he wants you—but not when you need to have your own space.

"I am happy to see him go home," a mid-life woman once explained about her single-double life. "We have a great time together and a great time apart."

The arrangement is best described as Dessert with a capital D. That was the name my friend Julie and I had for her lover. I was married at the time. Then in her mid-forties, she was divorced. But with children still at home, she didn't want to integrate her new boyfriend fully into her life. Her children might get the idea that she was introducing a new father figure. And she needed and enjoyed her independence as she recovered from a long, difficult marriage. She didn't want any domestic squabbles, or comments from her boyfriend on how she was managing her life. Everything about her relationship with him was a pleasure, a lovely indulgence in intimacy. A single, mid-life man who had no children, he wanted to be more involved in her daily life, but she kept him at a distance, and he was understanding of her wishes. He became someone she enjoyed after the main course of her life as a divorced, working woman with bills to pay and children to protect.

"What did you do last night?" I would ask her on the phone.

"Oh, not much. Fed the kids. Watched some TV." Pause. "Then, I went out and had a little Dessert."

"Any good?"

"Oh, yes, very," she would say. "Delicious. Just what I needed."

I got a taste of that life with Paul, a man I dated, on and off, for close to two years after my divorce. (I later referred to him as my "transition" man. You know you're with one if you spend a lot of your time with him discussing the adjustment to your divorce.) He suggested at one point that we should think about living together. "I'm not sure why," I explained to him as gently as I could. "But that doesn't feel right."

To be honest, I think it didn't feel right because I was in the process of turning alpha. I was feeling like one of those plucky animals in a children's fable who finds out she had nice wings of her own all along. They had just been tucked away. I didn't need a man anymore—not in the way I used to, anyway. I was making enough money. I had learned how to change a tire. I put out the garbage. I could saw off a tree limb that was hanging over into my garden. I had come home at midnight to find a leak from a toilet that had soaked through to the floor below, and, without panicking, called an emergency plumber. (I was leaving on assignment the next morning.) As one of my divorced girlfriends observed, "This is the stuff my husband used to do. But now that I have to do some of it, I think, 'What's the big deal? Is this all there is to it?'" We are all Rosie the Riveter with a screwdriver in our tool kit and highlights in our hair.

Many women this age have the self-possession and authority of a sans-serif monogram, a sort of this-is-who-I-am assertion. Over the course of our lives we all shed and acquire identities: from girl to woman, innocent to experienced, young to old, smooth-skinned to wrinkled, pretty to handsome. (Yes, age is identity too. And so is physical appearance, especially for women.) But when the cloak of wife is donned, and then, on top of that, the identity of mother, a woman inhabits aspects of self she may not even have known she had. Later, when the children grow up and become independent, the mother identity loosens. It can be hung on a peg in a closet from time to time. And if she divorces, the wife identity falls to the floor. What is left is a self, shaped by time and experience, but stripped of any convenient cover-up. The divorced MLW is nakedly herself. Authentic. Unapologetic. Frank.

Soon after I had moved into my post-divorce house, one of my girlfriends, Lisa, who had separated from her partner after ten years, came over for supper. A wry wit, she speaks with the humour of a latter-day Mae West, minus the platinum-blond curls and red lipstick.

"Well, it's great for men," she said, when I showed her the wall-to-wall mirror behind the toilet in my small bathroom, which I hated and wanted to remove. "When they pee, they can admire their dicks."

Back in the kitchen, I offered her a stool.

"Any boy news?" she asked over the rim of her wineglass.

I filled her in. There was the divorced man almost twenty years my senior.

"Forget him." Lisa waved her hand in the air, swatting away the romantic possibility like a fly.

"And there's Mr. Merlot," I said. I had met him at a party in a restaurant a few months earlier. Lisa had been my wingman that night. He and I were standing near the bar, waiting to fight our way to the bartender, and had started talking. Lisa came up behind him for a moment and motioned to me that I should get his contact information and offer mine. She was mouthing with exaggerated lip movements the words *Get his card*, and air-signing on an imaginary piece of paper.

"Do you have a business card?" I finally asked him, summoning my best show of nonchalance. "Just in case I want to follow up with you." We had been talking about the banking industry. (Listen, it helps being a journalist. A girl always needs sources.)

"Sure," he said, as he pulled out his wallet. "And do you have one?"

I didn't, not on me, anyway.

Lisa was rolling her eyes over my dating incompetence. She promptly took control of the situation by telling him my e-mail address and writing it down for him on the back of one of his extra cards.

I didn't take the initiative to contact him. He was nice, a fiftysomething professional. But a lot of people are nice. Besides, Lisa had told me not to. It would look too needy, she said. A week later, he e-mailed me, asking if there was any banking information that I might need. We went for drinks, and no, we didn't talk about the interest rate.

"I saw him again last week," I reported to Lisa. "Drinks, again. And just like the last time, he said he had somewhere to go after about an hour and a half. It was a birthday party for someone this time. Last time, it was a friend he had to meet."

Lisa frowned.

I knew that these signs were bad. He was engaging in what a longtime-single male friend of mine explained is a "very legitimate practice": serial dating. It's not a matter of his not wanting to commit to a woman once in a relationship: he doesn't want to commit to a relationship, period. Or he is in the interview phase, perhaps, auditioning prospective girlfriends in one-hour go-sees. I am an item on his electronic calendar, filed in between other appointments, all of which he presumably clicks and drags and dumps into new slots at will. When we meet, he makes me feel like I'm a pool he only wants to dip his toe into. During a conversation, he won't even wade in up to the ankle.

"Ah, men with little black books," Lisa said, waving her hand in the air again.

"The whole process makes me feel like sabotaging my own chances. I want to pick my nose or something."

"They're players," Lisa said with a sigh. "They think they are so eligible, they have to protect themselves."

"But they can come off as insecure, too eager to impress. Remember Mr. Map Room?"

He was a fortysomething divorced father who was known to invite women back to his nicely appointed house on the second, if not the first, date. Not for sex. Just for a preview of what they might be able to share with him if they achieved the position of girlfriend. He liked to give tours, to show them his small library, which featured a few framed antique maps on the walls, his newly renovated backyard, the master bedroom and ensuite with a huge Jacuzzi bathtub. He also had a habit, over a flute of champagne, to pull out a little model of a palatial-looking cottage he was planning to build on a lake up north. "I hope to share it with my soulmate one day," he would say, a tad mournfully. Mr. Map Room, needless to say, had become an urban legend among women of a certain age.

"Too weird," said Lisa.

"I think someone should tell him he has it all wrong."

"Why bother?"

"Because he seems to think women our age care about that stuff."

"Well, that would be because many do," Lisa said, popping an olive into her mouth.

"What about you?" I asked, changing tack.

She calls her potential lovers "prospects," which I love. Single MLWs do their own kind of date interviews, to be truthful. A mid-life woman knows that when she is "with someone," she has to move into his head a little bit, see what kind of mental furniture he has, how comfortable it is, how accommodating, and whether it will work with hers. We all have well-defined mental furniture at this stage, sofas of preferences and dressers of immovable habits.

"There are a few prospects," she said. One is a younger man in his early thirties, someone she had met at a party. She told me his name, occupation, what he looked like. "But do you think it's a problem if he doesn't know what arugula is?" she asked, poking her cheek with the manicured fingertip of her index finger, an expression of mock consternation on her face.

"No. You can educate him."

"Ha," she offered.

"But can you be with someone who doesn't get cultural references to—I don't know—*Gilligan's Island*? The professor and Mary Ann?" I said, and sang a line from the song.

"He is very cute," she continued, smiling to herself and ignoring me.

The week before, she had told me her sexuality "feels fluid." I have several friends who could have stepped from the pages of Gail Sheehy's *Sex and the Seasoned Woman*. They know who they are. They know what they want. They are more comfortable with their sexuality than ever before. A forty-something divorced friend of mine, who at the time was dating a younger man, once called me to tell me about the "profundity of his erection."

This is how my divorced friends and I began talking about men when we had sufficiently recuperated from our marriages to entertain the possibility of them again. We issue bulletins from Boys News Daily, charting the blips of romantic possibilities like the ups and downs of the stock market. And each, like a company, has a Mr. code. We keep it all at an ironic distance most of the time. It's a soothing distraction from our work lives.

"Come on, do you really want a man frying up his eggs in the morning on your nice stove?" Lisa asked, when we lapse into wistfulness about the shared live-in life.

"Well, not unless he's handy with a hammer," I tossed back as a joke.

"Do you know many marriages that you would like to have?" we remind each other.

I even have a name for some marriages I know, the ones in which one partner is isolated and lonely. That union is a double-single. One spouse is often away on business or so deeply ensconced in work that he is spiritually if not physically absent. The other is raising the children virtually as a single parent. Or if the children have grown up and left home, the husband and wife have disappeared into separate interests and eased into a deadened state that gives them security, but little pleasure.

A fiftysomething married woman I know once cried while watching the movie *Frida*, starring Salma Hayek, about the Mexican artist Frida Kahlo. "Her life was so passionate," she said later, to explain her tears. Her own life wasn't—had never been, she felt. Some people would use the insight of the teary moment to bolt from double-single to single-single— the departure of children from the nest is often the catalyst for late-life divorce—but she remained with her husband, too ashamed to be in the world as a divorcee. It wasn't that she and her husband fought or that he was mean. They had moved through their married life with a great display of competency as successful people with three charming children. People congratulated them as they reached their thirtieth wedding anniversary. But to her, it felt like a corporate partnership. Secure as a positive balance sheet, and just as dry.

Isolation in double-single unions can come from mismatched sexual libidos—when one partner wants sex more than the other. Husbands are often the ones who complain about a drop-off in sexual activity in marriage. More than one woman I know has confessed that her former husband accused her of being gay when their sex life stalled and she began routinely turning down his advances. (Invariably, and sadly, the accusation caused her to doubt her own ability to be a good partner.)

Openly claiming the strength of one's libido has become part of the marital discussion—at least in books. Like the 1960s feminist encouragement to get housewives out of their aprons, it is the latest instalment in the renegotiation of domestic expectation.

Duty sex is not acceptable, says Joan Sewell, author of *I'd Rather Eat Chocolate.* "This is your body. There is nothing more personal," she told me in conversation. "When you don't have desire, it's not merely sexual, it's invasive." Her husband, Kip, wanted sex five or six days a week whereas her preference was once or twice a month. He was feeling emotionally isolated; she was simply angry. They managed to fix their double-single imbalance by working out an agreement. Orgasm became optional. She could take breaks. And they discussed how they were feeling in the moment.

Resentment breeds sexual isolation, of course. Many women describe double-single marriages that developed with unhappiness over their husband's behaviour. "I couldn't have sex with him, not when he was so mean to me," explains a friend. "I just blocked it out. I learned to live without it. For ten years before we divorced, we had no sex. I call it being a member of the dead-from-the-neck-down club." They had remained together because of the children.

It's not just women with low libido who threaten the health of their marriages. From readers, I discovered that there are many wives who are dissatisfied with sexually underperforming husbands. "One of the most common things I hear from my pregnant friends is that their husband has no interest in having sex while she's pregnant, despite her huge sexual appetite," one woman reported. Others complain about sexual technique. "He was not my first sexual partner," explains another mid-life woman. "I had had maybe two lovers before him. But I was his first. He didn't know what to do. He really wasn't able to satisfy me, and he wouldn't talk about it." They remained married for four years. "I tried for about two or three years, but it got to the point that when he expressed interest in sex, I just said, 'No thanks. Unless you're going to help me out and not just roll over, then forget it.' Finally, I told him, 'You're not good in bed.' It was a huge blow to his ego. I regret saying those words," she adds. "But I don't regret [saying] how I felt. It was completely valid."

Our culture tends to view sexual activity as the litmus test for the health of a relationship. But even about that, I have learned not to make assumptions. In early 2009, *Good Morning America* reported that more than 20 million Americans live in sexless marriages, which means they are intimate fewer than ten times a year.

But are all of those unions unhappy?

"I have been called anti-feminist and pre-Victorian," Sewell confides about her claim-my-low-sex-drive marital stance. But she believes that women are fed unrealistic images of abundant female libido. The early feminists, after all, fixated on the patriarchy's repression of female sexuality, but they neglected to acknowledge that not all women see ultimate self-expression through their bodies and the pursuit of the big O. Lack of desire is the new taboo in today's sexually explicit culture, Sewell suggests.

A woman I know, who has been married for almost twenty-four years, describes her sexless relationship as perfectly satisfying. She passionately defends it, even though they sleep in separate rooms. "We are true companions. Is it not wonderful when someone brings you flowers from the garden, when he deeply cares for you, when you share all your thoughts and feelings?" Some might call that kind of marriage—one that works in all ways except in the sack—the double-double-single life.

Romantic relationships are fragile chemistry experiments, and it's hard to know the governing principles that will accurately predict when and if some pairings will bond, bubble, ignite or implode. But frankly, all the work they entail to stay intact can feel like marriage muck. The divorced know that what initially attracts two people—that lovely, fiery chemistry—is not necessarily what makes for a healthy, long-term partnership.

When the feminists finally turned their attention to home, after realizing that it's just as much a part of a woman's life as her desire occasionally to escape it, the equitable marriage, they believed, would be the next stage in the revolution. My term for that? The state of being double-double: you do many things together, can laugh about your family life, share in the household tasks and are still in love and having good sex on a happily synced basis. It's the Holy Grail of shared life. But it's rare.

And so when my girlfriends and I are disappointed that dates don't work out or the men we liked turn out to be wrong for us or we for them, we shrug off any sadness and console ourselves with the knowledge that it's good to be on our own.

While I am interested in men, I have little patience for the drama or games of looking for love. Anticipating the appearance of my tulips in the spring or watching the progress of my garden through the summer gives me more pleasure. At least I can rely on the flowers to show up as planned.

"I would rather be single than in a difficult relationship" is the refrain of the divorced MLW. Or as sixty-one-year-old May Musk, a dietitian and model in New York City who has been a divorced mother since her early thirties, said, "What's the point of being in a relationship if it doesn't make my life better?"

"Let's not forget," my friends and I tell each other when we need an extra boost. "We could still be in our marriages."

13.

The Dating Pool Is Very Shallow

My friend Pam has developed a MANtra. Oh, I know that sounds ridiculous. But let me remind you, in case you haven't discovered this for yourself: women of a certain age never lose a certain adolescent goofiness especially when it comes to prospective or new boyfriends. At heart, we are all still in high school. Pam and I have known each other for almost ten years, and we used to talk in a guarded way about our lives, about our children, their academic progress, about our family holidays, the nuisance of our dogs. We were married then, you see. Both the same age, we first met as wives and mothers at the school our children attended. But one night, I met her by chance when we were out walking said pets in a local park. She told me about trouble in her marriage—her husband had temporarily moved out. I told her some of our struggles. We parted half an hour later, our friendship irrevocably altered. Under cover of darkness, unable to see the expressions on each other's faces, we had confessed sins of marital love, as if to an anonymous priest. Once we were both on the labyrinthine path to Marriage Exit, we talked frequently—and nothing was off limits.

It's astonishing what the floodgates of female conversation can usher in, once unbolted. And so there I was, listening with rapt attention as Pam explained that she had been reading about the law of attraction.

"You're going to think I've gone all woo-woo," she said, giving me a wary glance.

"Oh no," I replied. "Are you kidding?"

I can be woo-woo with the best of the New Agers, if I let myself. And when I do, it feels like an indulgence—a Hershey bar for the soul. She then told me that every morning and night, she repeated aloud (in the privacy of her bedroom, mind you) her desire to meet a man with the attributes she admired, all of which she listed—kind, gentle, curious, not penniless. Within three weeks of starting it, she had met her kind, gentle, curious, not-penniless fiftysomething boyfriend through a friend. *Poof!* He appeared out of thin air!

She said I should try it.

"And what if we're both single at the same time and I want the same kind of man you do, and our MANtras are the same?" I jokingly asked her. Yes, she was with her new man, but who knew how long that would last? She was sampling love à la carte. Just getting back in the flow of being single, she was rediscovering non-marital, spicy sex—and variety. "We might attract the same guy. The universe might deliver him at the same time for both of us! Then what?"

Well, she said, we would just have to discuss the issue dip-
lomatically. Which is big of her, and why I like her so much.

The truth of the matter is that navigating the landscape as
a recycled singleton in modern times is not easy. You need
your girlfriends, in order to survive and to deconstruct what
the heck that guy you sort of liked meant in his e-mail. Can
anyone tell me what a man wants or thinks when he signs off
with "hugs"? And just as every woman approaches motherhood in her own way, finding her specific balance between
baking cookies and pursuing goals outside the home, she can
also decide how best to approach the challenge of finding a
man—or not.

The first, rather shocking, realization is that the landscape has changed since the last time your wedding-ring
finger was naked, and so has your sexual allure. Newly separated, we think available men will appear, magically, like
the sun every morning, just the way they did when we were
younger. But the dating pool for mid-life women shrinks.
"I have always been cute. I am fit," says Joan Price, a sixtysomething California-based fitness instructor and dance
teacher. "But in my late forties, early fifties, all of a sudden,
men were not seeing me. They were looking over my head
to see younger, perky-breasted women. I was crushed by
that. Men seem hard-wired to go for fertile women."

Some are, yes. But I have come to see that men, poor
things, can be bewildered by the choices. At mid-life, they
can go fishing for someone ten, sometimes twenty years
younger, the same age, or older, and they will often, if not
always, come up with a willing partner. Single, divorced men
will tell you: the female fish, especially those long in the gill,

are practically throwing themselves into their boat. "It's not going to come out right no matter how I say it," one fifty-four-year-old divorced man confides. "But the most difficult part of being single at this stage for men is wondering whether you have made the right choice. There are so many attractive older women who are divorced out there. And they are eager," he continues, bugging his eyes slightly, trying his best to look sheepish about the embarrassment of riches available to him. "And I *like* older women," he adds limply for emphasis, saying that all his male friends have been urging him to "go younger."

It's understandable that some women choose to bow out of the game. "It was nice to be through with all that nonsense," says one woman, now in her seventies, who has been single since she divorced in her early fifties. Or, as another woman in her late fifties put it: "A sexually transmitted disease is not worth an orgasm."

But many are not willing to give up. Oh no. They lean over their cleavage and say, "Just shoot me, shoot me, if I ever start talking about not being interested in men." They take on the job as CEO of the Dating Game and tackle the challenges of meeting a man the way they would go after a promotion. A divorced mother I met at a party explained that she posted a profile on several dating sites, and in the last six months had thirty face-to-face encounters with prospective boyfriends, and more than one date with eighteen of them. "I'm a go-getter!" she cried. "I'm not waiting around for them to come to me!" She was pleased with her result—a guy who left his toothbrush in her bathroom after the fourth date.

I have known otherwise sensible, nice women who turn into Ladies of the Casserole, barely able to suppress their gleeful hope when they hear news of a fresh widower and begin plotting when to arrive bearing condolences and a hot supper at his door. Many divorced MLWs develop creative methods to meet available men. "I have a new dating technique!" exclaimed one divorced mother in her late forties. "Check out the parent list at your kid's school to find out which couples live separately! Figure out who the single dads are. Then, at parent/teacher night . . ." Her voice trailed off and she gave a wicked smile.

Pam and I have talked about the dangers of getting too comfortable with your single life. "You can get all oh-single-life-is-great," she said. "You get used to it. And start liking it. And you get resigned to it." A few months earlier, she and I had gone to see *Last Chance Harvey*, a "crinkly sex" flick, as I like to call love stories with older women. We turned to each other in the darkness of the theatre over the accuracy of the line that the mid-life woman, played by Emma Thompson, says to brush off her disappointment that Dustin Hoffman's character hadn't shown up as planned. "I'm just more comfortable with being disappointed," she said.

I have a few thoughts on the matter of mid-life dating. I have heard many valuable tips, and in the interest of solidarity, I will pass them along. Most important? Humour goes a long way to cure disappointments.

Remember that wine on a Friday night by yourself does not qualify as a cozy date, no matter how nice it feels.

"Unhelpful," Pam said one day when she was describing a night spent on her own the weekend before.

"Pathetic," I added. (I had done the same thing.)

"Very."

"And bad for the meno-pot." That's our name for the persistent tummy of the MLW.

"Oh, I know."

"Wine becomes a comfort, don't you think?"

"It does," she said. "You don't have a partner, and it becomes this thing you look forward to at the end of the day."

"Like a hug."

"Yes," she said, forlorn.

Well, here's the good part. If you can self-medicate, you can also self-diagnose. Consider it mid-life wisdom.

Beware the Delusional Projection. This is an affliction in the dating world that infects both women and men. You think that every person who strikes up a conversation with you is making a pass. This is not true. He might very well just need to know where the nearest bus stop is. And in the same category is the assumption he and others will have that you are single for a suspicious reason. "The question always comes up," confides Julie Hannaford, a fiftysomething family lawyer, head of her own firm, who has never been married. "They think, 'What's wrong with her? Is she a lesbian? Too picky?'" Once, when she was on a third date with a man who asked why such an attractive, accomplished woman was single, she decided to try a different kind of answer. "'Well,' I said casually over my glass of wine. 'It's just that three years ago I was a man, and it took a long time for the sex operations, and I wasn't ready to start dating until now.'"

Know that single women can get a bad rap. Men often assume desperation, even if you are content with your status. Which is why less is often more. "It was in broad daylight," a man in his fifties said with shock when recalling an encounter with a single MLW. He was in a casual restaurant with a male friend, also in his fifties, when a woman plunked herself down at their table. One of the men made an innocent remark about a tattoo on her finger, and within minutes, she had dropped her jeans to show them another tattoo, this one on her waxed pubis. "I'm the queen of hearts," she purred as she indicated the two-inch crown just above her, um, vault.

Men really do like interesting, independent women. "Do not underestimate your confidence," a man advises. "You are the sum of your experiences, and should be proud of them," he says. That feeling you have that your experiences add rather than detract from your appeal? It's right. But remember that the empowerment a woman feels in her advancing years can work to her disadvantage. Be careful not to scare him. It is amusing to your girlfriends but perhaps not to your lover or prospective ones to openly discuss the unsatisfying sex you just had. Imagine for a moment how you would feel if you were the hapless lover who sat beside his woman in her bed as she tried to increase his understanding of the English language. (The poor man was a bad French lover, if that's possible.) "Let's conjugate the verb *to come*," she instructed from her pillow. "I come. I came. I will come. I will have come," she said, adding how he could get her to the future imperfect. (Or should that be future perfect?) Avoid the Feminazi persona. There's a fine line between a super-confident woman and one who makes a man think that she doesn't need him— or that she might crush him.

Best to see a man as icing to your cake. Not the cake—which you can bake yourself. Many older men like a woman who knows how to look after herself and doesn't see him as the solution to her life. They are no longer on the roller coaster of female expectation. "It's quite liberating," says a fifty-seven-year-old divorced man who is dating a fifty-three-year-old divorced woman. "I feel she is attracted to me for who I am rather than for what I can provide materially." But, again, tread carefully. "An erection has no conscience," admits a man whose girlfriend told him that she doesn't want to have an exclusive relationship in her post-divorce life. "But I don't want to be hurt," he says, adding in a defensive assertion that "I'm not needy." They want to be wanted. Who doesn't? Don't channel Maureen Dowd, the *New York Times* columnist who wrote the book *Are Men Necessary?* They are. They might just require a little help understanding how you feel. Be kind. It's important to explain, for example, that even though a woman is strong and independent, she might still want to be swept off her feet now and then.

While searching for The One, enjoy The Many. Flirt. Do not think in absolutes of total love or utter rejection. Enjoy nuance. Dwell not on happy endings and closure. Be comfortable with emotional subtleties and ambiguity. Hold your cards close to your chest. Be willing to accept experience that doesn't necessarily go anywhere. There are men who can be just friends, or "walkers" as women in my mother's generation called male companions they took as escorts to events. There are men to keep simply as lovers.

Here's Pam on another one of our walks.

"I missed my period," she told me.

"What did your doctor say?" We know the state of our perimenopausal bodies the way our children bemoan the sorry state of their beloved sports teams.

"Oh, you know, wonky cycle."

"Maybe you're pregnant." I raised an eyebrow at her. She had been talking about her MANtra-produced man she had yet to introduce to her friends or her children.

"Couldn't be."

"You sure?"

"I had my tubes tied after the last pregnancy," she said. "Wait." She turned to me with a mischievous grin. "Do you think he was so passionate, he caused them to, like, unknot themselves?"

We had to stop walking we were laughing so hard.

A good lover is cheaper than going to the spa for a skin treatment, massage and mani/pedi. And the results are the same. You look refreshed and feel like a million bucks. Besides, an older woman often has a voracious sexual appetite, which has something to do with the fact that when the womb begins to go dark, the body starts screaming at her to try to make use of it before the last good egg escapes her ovaries. And for post-menopausal women, there's no longer the fear of getting pregnant.

It's a brave new world of clipped and waxed romance. Many are going metrosexual and hairless, even your newly single Aunt Alice.

There is more on the sexual menu. If you don't know what he's talking about, demur for a day, and look it up on the Internet. It's all there. With photographs.

Don't be Afraid to Get Naked. There is often shyness about the aging body. But let's shed some soft, cinematic light on the subject.

Imagine René Russo and her new man, a Pierce Brosnan type. They are undressing in haste for the first time. Much kissing. Much heavy breathing. He removes her blouse, her bra, her shoes, her pantyhose, her panties. But when his hand reaches for the button on the waistband of her skirt, she pushes it away. "The skirt stays," she whispers in his ear.

He stops kissing her for a moment, pulling his face back to give her a quizzical look.

"My Caesarean-scar tummy," the mother-of-two murmurs, apologetically shaking her head. "It's better that you don't see it."

Poor René has forgotten that a man is attracted to a woman for who she is, not necessarily for the shape of her breasts or her stomach. And she is not considering the fact that this handsome older man, despite his smooth demeanour and easy smile, may have gone through a rather extended dry spell himself. Who knows? It may have been a while since he last saw a woman's breasts.

But never mind. The truly honest conversations take a while to spill forth. And so, they carry on with their skirted intercourse for at least two months. Eventually, with gentle encouragement, René ditches the cover-up and bares her stomach. And when she does, he whispers sweetly, "You are beautiful in every way."

Men have frailties of their own, after all. Even though many treat erectile dysfunction like a sore throat, carrying a tablet or two of Viagra in their back pocket, just in case, some don't want to take the drug or can't. Which requires a whole different kind of communication. "When I was younger these were just not the kind of conversations I had to think about or know how to have," confides a woman in her fifties about dealing with her boyfriend's occasional impotence. "We worked it out," she adds. "It requires a certain acceptance, because you realize it's not going to change, and you have to decide if you can live with that. But the sex was amazing. You realize that you are here to make love, not screw your brains out." Think of sex as a kindness the mid-life body still allows. When young, the naked body is about vanity. But as you age, it's about vulnerability, which is far more attractive, really.

Beware the married men who come knocking on your door. While it is tempting—and arguably perfect in the first year post-divorce when the idea of commitment can be scary, making an unavailable man very attractive—the situation rarely leads to happiness. You might become hopeful that he will leave his wife. You might suppress the ethical dilemma, forgetting that people would get hurt, especially if children are involved. And he might start promising that he will leave, just as soon as his wife gets through menopause or the children leave home or the house renovation is complete or whatever it is that causes him hesitation. He is with you when he can be, but not when you need him, not on Christmas, not on your birthday and not when you have to go to the emergency room. You become a hope addict. He sends you a Valentine's Day present, and you are convinced all over again that he really loves you, that he means it when he says he can't live without you, even though he is, of course, living with her. You are his refuge, but he is your prison.

Feel free to be vague about your age. If he says, "You don't look old enough to have children in their twenties," allow a digni-fied smile. "You must have been a child bride," he might say. No correction is needed. Having said that, it's good to act your age. Younger women have their youth. You have your humanity. Use your wrinkles as a screening device. If he is interested simply in the surface, let him have that with someone else. "If you're not most human at forty, forty-five, fifty, you will never be human," observes a man in his fifties. "Younger women are sperm foraging. With older women, you hope for a heart. You hope that they have been disillusioned by power, as you have been, if you are self-aware. To meet an older woman with those attributes is like sitting in a broken-in seat in a car. New leather is slippery. But a broken-in seat, well, there's nothing more comfortable and there's nothing more personal."

Okay, so being thought of as a "broken-in seat" is not the most wonderful image. (He was rather cute as he said it, though.) Men are not perfect, and neither are you. Allow yourself to see past their corny language. Maybe he was nervous.

Regale your friends with stories of your forays into the online dating world. Think of it as a way to do something positive with the experience. Sure, it will make your married friends glad they're not single. They will cringe, wince even, as they take in updates about your romantic life. They will treat your messy dating business like a tragedy, a fatal disease. Best cure: Laugh. (Men like a sense of humour, anyway.) The hilarity might just keep you registered on dating sites until you find a nice person. Much weeding is involved. If it feels like a job, that's because it is. Expect many "interviews" over coffee. You have to look good. Leave the yoga pants at home. Put on some lipstick. Say just the right thing. Pitch the product of yourself, minus the tendency to drool in your sleep. Love is out there, experts say. You just have to keep looking.

Tell your girlfriends about the man who noted on his profile that he was a landscape planner. In fact, he paved driveways. Never mind, you thought at the time. You may be a successful designer in your forties, pretty and fit, but you have to keep an open mind and heart. And when the irony of the female mid-life situation gets on your nerves—just as you reach the top of your game, you are encouraged to relax your standards on men—recall that life is full of paradox. (If unconvinced, read the Bible. That Jesus had to die in order to live forever is just a start.) Love comes in all kinds of packages. And so you agree to a second date, and over dessert, you learn that he works for his uncle. Still, trying to stay positive, you agree to a third date, and that's when you discover that he lives with his mother. He was short on the first date, shorter than you, actually, which is something you had to get used to. "I'm not used to being the big person," you confess to your friends. But with each date, "he just got shorter and shorter."

Give your friends the details of the guy who carved eagles with a chainsaw, and tell them about the hospital orderly who was a garage sales addict. "Even he knew it was going nowhere when I could not control my reaction to his purchase of a package of bread yeast that was past its best-before date," you write to your girlfriend in an e-mail.

Resist the Boyfriend Daydream. Oh come on, we all do it. You meet a guy for a movie. It's your first date. And he's nice. You talk. You have a drink afterwards. Off you go home, and before you know it, you are imagining him with your mother, in your kitchen, in your bed on Saturday morning, and watching a movie with your kids. You're seeing how he fits in the film of your life before you even know if he lives with his mother or not.

Talk about your kids, but not too much. If you have a man you like seated across a table from you, try not to interrogate him—not too firmly, anyway—which many women do in an effort to protect their hearts. But go ahead, talk about your children. "Hello? I have them, too," says a divorced dad. "It's important to have the trust and comfort level with someone to talk about your kids. They are a huge part of life," he says. But avoid slipping into mom mode, endlessly talking about your worries, challenges and triumphs as a parent.

Let go of anger or bitterness from past relationships. "Smile, smile, smile," says Susan Kates, who runs a dating service called Dinnerworks. She often sees women of all ages show up for dinner events with glum expressions and attitudes to match. Avoid complaints about the ex. The most you should say on the first or second date is that the relationship didn't work out. Dating is not therapy.

Be careful not to slip into spouse mode. You are accustomed to intimacy, to saying what you think and feel to a man. But in dating, you must learn self-containment, if you haven't already. "We got to talking about this and that," explains a fifty-three-year-old writer about the time he was introduced to an attractive woman his own age. "And I mentioned that my work is not as romantic as people think, that it is stressful. And then she said that her work was stressful too, so stressful that she has IBS. I mean, it's great to be brave and spontaneous and unselfconscious, but did I need to learn within ninety seconds of meeting that she has irritable bowel syndrome?"

Pay attention to what they do, not what they say. Trust your intuition. That's one of the good things about getting older. You have heard that little voice for many years now. Just listen to it. You know when something doesn't feel right. Remember that guy who put Barry White on in his car after he took you out for dinner? He slapped in the CD as he pulled his BMW from the parking lot. You gave him the benefit of the doubt even though a part of you knew there was nothing ironic about his gesture. Which would have been funny, if there were. As Barry moaned, your date asked you to come to his house for a nightcap. You agreed, but as soon as you got in the front door, he mentioned that it was the third date. "And you know what that means," he said. The creep-o-meter gauge started going off the scale. It's not that you didn't like the guy. You thought you did—until that moment. So you said that you would love to have a quick cognac, but that, really, you must get home to your son who is waiting up for you. (Children can be a graceful exit strategy.)

Finally, refrain from derogatory comments about a middle-aged man's younger girlfriend or trophy wife. That would be mean. We have our humanity, remember? Let him have what his heart desires. Why not? You can too—in Greece, perhaps, or Cuba. Do not, under any circumstance, let him hear you sound resentful of his lovely young companion with the perfect breasts, impossibly tiny waist and gorgeous long hair. Bitterness, ladies, is strictly for girlfriend talk.

Whether we're looking for a lasting relationship or not, dating is an amusing leisure pursuit. It's best to see it that way. Men can be fun and relaxing—sort of like shopping on a Saturday.

14.

Living Happily with My Bitch Wrinkle

Dating in mid-life can deflate the hard-won confidence of the divorced MLW. Which is why mature dating sites are festooned with advertisements for cosmetic improvements. The realization that the body isn't what it once was is disturbing for anyone, but especially for those who are back on the singles market. We want to start over again, when we're halfway through our lives. Just as you wake up to the New You (or rediscover the Forgotten You from the pre-marriage days), you find yourself in a deteriorating body, or a wrinkly one.

Well, yes. But who wants to feel the need to "remake" herself for the benefit of others, especially when she's been a wife. I am through with feeling compelled to be "a better Sarah" for someone else, thank you very much. I think aging just requires an attitude adjustment, frankly. I was surprised recently to feel delighted when Dr. Fresco liked my eyeballs. In fact, he thought they were superb, the backs of them, I mean.

He is my optometrist, and I had gone to his office for a routine exam.

"Did you play a lot of sports when you were a child?" he asked, as he peered at the photo he had taken a moment earlier of the interior of my eyes.

"I don't know. The average amount," I replied casually.

He let me have a look. "Your veins are very well developed," he said in the sort of voice a boyfriend uses to compliment your tits. "See?" Dr. Fresco said, pointing to snake-like things in my eyeballs.

"Wow." I was impressed too. "You're right."

And I realized how I had shifted—in a healthy way—my appreciation for my body. You take compliments about it anywhere you can. My vision may be failing. I may have to wear contact lenses, and reading glasses to see the fine print. But, hey, my retinas are still attached! My optic nerve is a nice bright dot! My veins are fat and juicy! What more could a girl want?

When the dental hygienist told me I had great gums that didn't bleed too much despite her vigorous attention to the plaque she had blasted off my teeth, I felt weirdly pleased. It's like finding out that the foundations of the old house you bought are still sound. No repairs needed there! The walls are crumbling, the paint peeling and the floorboards lifting, but, hey, what's underneath is holding up, even though no one can see it. Too bad you can't flash your foundations. "My bones are still very dense," you could say in a husky voice to a potential suitor. The knowledge that a part of you is as it always has been is enough to make you justify another glass of wine with dinner. Toast the parts that haven't yet let you down, that haven't yet betrayed you without warning.

It's always without warning, of course. Aging sneaks up on you, when you aren't looking, like a mischievous kid with a BB gun. Pow, got you in the jowls! And now in the knees! Someone else is doing it to you, playing a prank on you— that's what it feels like, anyway. And you are a little annoyed, wounded even, because this is not something you would do to yourself. You're sure you had nothing to do with it.

I often feel that I have passed through a time warp or that I am an astronaut who has been up in space, flying around for what seemed like a day or two, only to come down to Earth and find that a decade has passed since I was last here. Since when did I have the crease between my eyebrows? And the wattles? When did they appear? And wasn't it just yesterday I could slip on my jeans without having to hide my muffin top? Don't ask about the grey hairs. One was cute at thirty-four. Who isn't willing to admit to it, then? It's a strategic juxtaposition, like a crumb on the lip of a supermodel that only serves to draw attention to her beauty. More than a few grey hairs? Only CNN's wonder-boy reporter, Anderson Cooper, is cute with a silver head of hair. Along with the crease between his eyebrows, it gives his boyishness a certain gravitas. He stood in the disaster of Hurricane Katrina, windblown and concerned. If you ask bitter old me, that crease made his career.

I sometimes feel that I am living the inverse of the inside-outside duality I knew in my youth. In my twenties, I could dress up like the best of them. After my paternal grandmother died, I was given the Oleg Cassini dress she wore for her formal portrait. Her daughter discovered it in the bottom of a trunk, perfectly preserved. It fit me beautifully, and I wore the black silk satin dress several times, which always felt like an exercise in wicked duplicity. From the outside, I looked perfect. On the inside, I was wobbly as Jell-O.

Now, I feel great on the inside, as pulled together as a perfectly tailored outfit from Prada, certain of self. But on the outside? What MLW hasn't caught a glimpse of herself in a mirror or a shop window, and thought, *Who the heck is she?* But I resent being made to feel bad about a process that happens to all of us. I've earned every line. Still, to check out my options, I went to a doctor who diagnoses aging like an illness.

"Frown," commanded Dr. Verbeeten, a general practitioner who has started to do some "cosmetic enhancement procedures" to meet the demands of her patients, who are mostly women.

I frowned for her.

"You have strong muscles," she said clinically, pressing my eyebrows.

Strong is not good. Middle-aged men get Viagra to feel young again. Middle-aged women have Botox. One stiffens. The other loosens.

To neutralize my muscles, I would need a few injections. Total: $400, plus taxes. (And that's a summer special sale price.) I would have to commit to top-ups for two years ($200 a session every four months), if I wanted the best results for the investment. In the years ahead, I would have to keep it up, otherwise everything would return to its natural state. Maintenance is a "finger in the dike," as Nora Ephron wrote.

"If you don't start now, they will get worse," Dr. Verbeeten said. "And at a certain point, the creases get deeper, to the layer below the dermis, and that makes it harder for the Botox to have a positive result."

"Hmm." I poked the muscles on my brows.

"We could also lift the eyebrows a bit," she continued, still scrutinizing. "Here, look straight at yourself. You'll see," she said, handing me her little mirror. "You don't have any eyelids."

What? It felt dire—life-threatening, even.

"The skin droops. And it's flat here," she continued, indicating the area below my brow line. "Men have that. For women, you look more youthful if you open the eyes a bit."

I felt like I had a fatal disease. I have eyelids like a man's? God, give me a pill, an injection, a facelift, whatever.

She pushed at the corners of my eyebrows a bit, to show me the effect of lifting them.

"You do that with Botox?"

"Oh, yes, people put Botox everywhere. The jowls, the forehead, the neck, the upper lip, the lines on the chest," she said, pointing at her cleavage area beneath her white coat. "The lines at the side of the eyes." She paused momentarily. "Where else?" she said, turning to her assistant, a young woman with a perfect body.

"The bunny lines!" the assistant added helpfully.

Bunny lines?

"The little lines here," she explained, indicating the area on the inside of the bridge of the nose, near the tear duct of the eyes. Mine were underground—invisible for now.

"We could just start with Botox for the Chapter 11," Dr. Verbeteen suggested soothingly.

"Chapter 11?"

She wiggled two fingers at the area between the brows where the two vertical lines appear, one beside the other: an eleven.

"Oh." I nodded.

Chapter 11: the American term for bankruptcy, an unfortunate metaphor.

"I just don't know if I want to put toxins in my face."

She nodded knowingly. "That's what divides people. Some people don't care, and some people do."

The doctor smiled. Her face was as smooth as a baby's bottom. "Think about it," she said with a shrug, before heading out the door to her next appointment. "It's up to you. No pressure."

Beauty treatments for women of a certain age are often framed in feminist language. "Clarins—The Right to Choose" reads an ad promoting a variety of "super-restorative" and "regenerative" creams. Control (or the illusion of it) over the diminishment of physical beauty is positioned as empowering because some women feel they are compromised, put at a disadvantage, by their loss of youth.

Later that day, when I was talking to Joy, I mentioned the consultation about Chapter 11.

"Ah, the bitch wrinkle," she said in a singsong voice.

"That's what people call it?" Reaching mid-life is an education. "Have you thought about it?"

"I did, a few years ago. But then I thought, why would I want to have anything neutralized?"

I was reminded of the time I asked actor Ted Danson why he was no longer dyeing his white hair brown. "Just the feeling that I've earned the right not to," the sixty-year-old said flatly.

If men feel free to embrace their authenticity as they age, women are encouraged to see their right, their freedom even, to cover up their age and the natural changes of their bodies. L'Oréal reminds women to colour their hair or use wrinkle cream "Because I'm Worth It." Just as we are coming into our own, learning about our authentic selves and celebrating them, we are being encouraged to deny the years of experience that brought us here.

There may be power in age-defiance. But it is also just a different form of self-subjugation. I remain un-Botoxed with a man's eyelid-less eyes.

⁓

I have a little theory about the body: that we think of it as a crucial, but mysterious, machine. We obsess about its details. In puberty class, when I was about twelve, I loved the diagrams they put up on the blackboard and the little booklet passed out to the girls about the mechanics of menstruation and conception. They were like blueprints—this is the hose that runs from the testicle down the length of the penis and in this drawing is the ovarian piston, which fires its little emission every month, whether you want it to or not.

As the machine of the body ages, it begins to develop unwanted problems. It grows puffies—my mother's word for wobbly bits. "I was shocked. I thought, where did these things come from?" a skinny friend of mine said, mortified, when we were on a power walk through a ravine in the city. She was referring to the appearance of small saddlebags on the outer tops of her thighs. Joy had a similar reaction when she discovered that her back was giving her trouble as she set off on a shoot with all her camera equipment. "Shit," she said with the surprised disappointment of someone who has just discovered that there's no gas left in the car when she turns it on.

As a woman ages, the machinery tends to go a little haywire. The temperature gauge breaks down. I have heated up like a faulty radiator in the middle of a serene dinner party. The engine splutters every once in a while, causing momentary forgetfulness as it struggles to retrieve things from the memory bank. The hormone levels swish around like gas in a tank. Too high or low and they can make you want to run over the guy on the crosswalk who is taking too long to get to the other side. Tears appear when you least expect them. A few years ago, I took Luke to see the musical *Lord of the Rings*, and there was a scene at the end of one of the acts, when the music swelled and little bits of ribbon were flown out on a wave of air toward the audience. I started to cry. Luke looked over at me, and sunk a little bit into his seat, shaking his head. "It's just so beautiful," I tried to explain from behind my tissue.

Divorced women scrutinize their parts unfairly, I think, out of a belief that to be attractive to men, they must look as they did at twenty. They note the shape of their breasts. They employ the technical-sounding names for issues that arise, such as cankles (thick ankles). The gludgeons are the loose skin in the flabby armpit. They note how the armpit, once a sculpted thing, as beautiful as the arcing vault in a cathedral's apse, is reduced to a lumpy pillow. The loose skin flaps under the upper arms are bingo wings or Dinner Lady Arms. They remind each other of the woman who said, "Never wave goodbye on a beach if you are over fifty." The flesh on the upper arm can swing and jiggle alarmingly. And the Alluvial Fan is a description of the upper-chest creases. They look like the small tributaries in the delta of a river mouth. A divorced, single woman I know says she moisturizes the area liberally each night and never allows herself to sleep on her side.

But why be so hard on ourselves? Why let our age diminish our sense of self? I think about the body-as-machine often when I am seated in my ten-year-old car that reads about 94,000 kilometres on the odometer. I have had to replace some parts. The clutch, twice. And the radiator, brake pads, tires, exhaust pipe. (As of yet, my body runs on its original parts.) But I do not worry about the age of my car. She is my vehicle. I have lived in her, and she has served me well. Many important conversations with my children have occurred on road trips and rides to the grocery store. They are captives, and it is easy to start and stop a discussion, to let them fill a silence or not, as the world whooshes by. They have talked about their school work, their girlfriends, their plans. And when we were in the early stages of divorce, I remember allowing them to let it all out, their disappointment when it arose, and their anxiety, their anger. The car would contain all of it, and so I would try to tie up the big looseness of their thoughts and worries by acknowledging their feelings, by letting them just be, by saying that we would travel through the storm together.

Let us accept ourselves for who we are and how far we've come—through love, hardship, hurt and now into the serenity we once could only imagine. Here is the MLW's Creed for Aging (sort of) Gracefully:

We will not automatically cut our hair short in the shape of a helmet. We will do our best to avoid hairspray, which makes us look hard and fear open car windows. We will remember the joy of hair blowing in the wind. We will think of Meryl Streep in *Mamma Mia!* And we will forget what a male colleague once said when we happened to mention, in a discussion about age, that we colour our hair. "Oh really?" he responded as if we had just pointed out to him that the sky is blue.

We like to think that men cannot tell, that they don't notice such things. We would rather they not know how we manage to look so good. Crediting vegetables, swimming and superior genes is a much breezier response to a compliment. Who wants to thank Clairol, even though, please, we're not fools. We know that fifty is the new thirty only because of chemicals. Still, even if men do notice the dye job, we don't care. Sure, we colour religiously in part because we will not forget what a hairdresser once whispered into our ear as he was applying the offending goop on our grey roots. "Women with grey hair do not get laid," he said *sotto voce* in the manner of a butler delivering some unwanted bit of news to his employer—the unexpected arrival of a guest at the door, say. But we do it for ourselves too. It makes us feel better. We will continue to do the maintenance job—it must be kept up like cleaning the eavestroughs in the fall—because there is something about covering grey that feels like fixing a slip that has fallen beneath the hem of a dress. And hair is resilient. It may turn wiry as it greys but it doesn't sag. It doesn't wrinkle. It can look forever young, just like our nails, the maintenance of which is a bit like keeping up the curb appeal of a house.

We will make changes with the advice of a good colourist and the opinions of our girlfriends, who will not lie. We remain grateful to the hairdresser who put down her scissors and began to wave her arms in the air when the subject of leaving a few grey streaks came under discussion.

"No!" she cried. "Never works. You'll look like Cruella De Vil! Cruella De Vil! Not good." She was unstoppable. "Do you want to look sixty or forty?" she asked pointedly.

"Forty-ish," we replied, chastened.

"Well?" she said, hands on her hips.

We are not so defiant that we won't sometimes do as we were told. Sometimes, I repeat. Not always. Defiance is our right at this stage. We will make our own rules much of the time. And if that means streaking our hair with blue or pink or bright orange, so be it. Others may consider this colour urge a subconscious compensation for the sadness of becoming invisible to the opposite sex, a plea to "look at me!" but we know better. We do it because we want to.

We know we can turn all formidable and hefty, like a figurehead on the prow of a ship, a considerable bosom leading the way, with wafting, loose clothes like sails. Get out of our way, if you have a problem with it. If we are Hillary Rodham Clinton in a pantsuit, losing our sexuality in polyester, pastels and sensible pumps, maybe it's because we want to be. Who said being invisible is all bad? There's a relief to being out from under the male gaze. We entered it at puberty, and now we're leaving it. It was just a stretch of highway on a long journey. And now we have passed through the toll booth on the far end. There is no more payment required. Besides, we can get so much more done when fewer people are watching.

We have said goodbye to short shorts. We will not wear animal prints, unless ironically. We will wear skirts no higher than the knee to show off a good turn of calf. We will think of the scene in Palm Springs, the land of fruitful senior dating in the desert. In the afternoon, white-haired gentlemen loitered like high school teenagers (albeit in a golf store) talking about their "lady friends." And in an outdoor restaurant, a woman who looked to be in her seventies took to the dance floor by herself, twisting and moving around to the beat of a jazz band playing behind her. Slim, with white, feathery hair in a stylish bob, she wore a fitted dress, a belt at her waist. Her legs in medium-sized heels were fantastic, and she knew it. Up near the bar, a group of Walter Matthau look-alikes, seated on stools, watched her every move, like she was a tennis ball in a match.

We will bear our cleavage without shyness à la Helen Mirren and Susan Sarandon. We will give into our sway. And if our meno-pot bulges at certain times, we might do as my friend Pam did, when we were walking. "I figure if I just let it out, people will think I'm pregnant," she said after confessing that the effort to hold it in was just about killing her. She turned to me with a winsome, pasted-on smile and assumed the pregnant lady pose: back swayed, hands folded over the top of her bun. "They'll look at me, and go, 'Oh, what a nice pregnant lady!'" She smiled beatifically and even gave a little wave of her hand to the imaginary sympathetic onlookers as she walked along the sidewalk with an exaggerated waddle.

We understand what Evie Gorenstein, head of the personal shopping service at Loehmann's, a New York designer discount store, tells her clients: "If you're fifty and trying to look thirty, you're going to look older than fifty." Leave the low-rise jeans and sheer blouses on the rack. "It's okay to be a little girl dressing up as Mommy, but the reverse isn't okay, especially if you want to be taken seriously," she says. We will remember Nora Ephron's words: "You have to cut open a redwood tree to know how old it is, but you wouldn't have to if it had a neck." Hello, turtlenecks. We will listen to Jeanne Beker, who says that older women have the advantage of knowing their signature style. "The older you get, the more honest you become with yourself," she says. "There is tolerance. You are no longer delusional with yourself." Many women have come to know the one key thing that defines them: their hands, their nails, a mane of hair, a great eye for unusual jewellery. They edit themselves, Beker says. "For as many things about ourselves [that] we hate, there's something we love."

We will consider channelling Mireille Guiliano, celebrated author of *French Women Don't Get Fat*, a colossus of graceful aging in a size-zero dress. We will think of her particular brand of street and designer fashion, which she makes seem as effortless as her weight maintenance. "This?" she said, when complimented on a green suede jacket she was wearing. She held the edge of the sleeve between her thumb and forefinger, as if she had just found it crumpled up on the floor. "It's nothing. I bought it at a flea market." Her next bestseller should be *French Women Don't Wear Muumuus*.

Giuliano exudes a look of *bien dans sa peau*, the French phrase for being comfortable in one's skin. With the former chairwoman of Clicquot Inc., the American subsidiary of Champagne Veuve Clicquot, we have only one bone to pick, or rather, cork to pop. The now sixtysomething dynamo is able to maintain her weight of 112 pounds at five-foot-three by eschewing prepared food, but enjoying her indulgences, a croissant every morning and champagne when she feels like it. But here's what we cannot abide. She says French women never drink wine on its own, only with meals. Well, we cannot be French in this regard, not consistently. Wine is as essential as the Spanx support garments in our scented underwear drawer.

We will go to the gym as much for our health as our derrière. We will remember that a fiftysomething man said that men who like MLWs "don't want fake boobs, lots of plastic surgery or a woman who is wearing clothes for a much younger age group. . . . The key is she is making the effort to work out and feel good. The results are not that important." We will see it not as a duty to work out but as a pleasure, a treat at the end of the day or at the beginning, something we do for ourselves. We will take up the suggestion of hiring a cute trainer who is paid to direct and admire our perfect squats. And we will do as Guiliano does. She walks everywhere. Walking is our meditation. You can see us in groups on weekend mornings. It's a social exercise. We process our problems as we walk. We talk. We stride through whatever crosses the path of our life: a lover, a break-up, the ex, an issue with our children, our mother, our boss.

We will remember to celebrate the wrinkles we have earned. They start out vertical, and then they go horizontal. "Like a quilting pattern," observed one lady at sixty with a laugh. "If I pursued perfection, I'd have a facelift," Jane Fonda snapped, annoyed at the question about how she deals with aging in her sixties. People she sees in Hollywood who have had plastic surgery don't look like themselves, she said. (She has since admitted to having some.) Margaret Trudeau, also a celebrated beauty in her youth, would never go under the knife. "I want my grandchildren to recognize me," she said, laughing. "Like everything else, aging is a matter of accepting it," she observed. And it's a matter of being in the right light. As Shirley MacLaine said to me once in an interview, "I would rather have a good chimera light than a man."

We will remember that makeup can betray us, rather than enhance us, if used too liberally. Beware the hazards of wrinkles around the lips. As Diana Athill wrote, some senior women in scarlet lipstick can end up looking "like a vampire bat disturbed in mid-dinner." We will consider wearing blue-tinted eyeglasses indoors, as Diane Keaton does. Very cool, and better than eyeliner. We will stand up to the pressure to Botoxize ourselves. In our hesitation over whether to do it, we will think of better uses for the money. A trip to Venice to see Tintoretto, perhaps? And we will console ourselves with the knowledge that women who get the repeated injections tend to look like members of an identifiable alien race. Be kind to the Flappy-Lipped People with the immovable foreheads, but you do not have to be one of them.

We will realize that mid-life is a time when it is good not to have been a great beauty. Youthful beauty isn't always valued simply for its worth in the male gaze, although that is considerable. It can be a prized and pleasing possession for its owner, a source of identity. She has something everyone wants, yet she didn't have to do anything to get it. With its loss, and the irreversible decline of the body, there is a narrowing of possibilities. No more easy power over men. No more unearned attention. A loss of self. It is far easier to have been average. Those of us who do not have to mourn the loss of beauty are lucky. We are freer. The playing field levels out. Everyone ages, but the beautiful have further to fall. Brigitte Bardot is most remarkable now for how her beauty has decayed. We look at her out of morbid curiosity. We can relax into the realization that to be attractive in youth is a cinch. It doesn't take much to look fantastic. To age well is an art, requiring grace.

When our son looks at a picture of us, taken when we were younger, and then shifts his glance from it to us and back again, slightly bewildered as if trying to see where our younger self resides within the older one, we will not whack him across the behind. We will ride out certain comments. "No wonder Dad fell in love with you. You were hot," he says. We will smile. We will kiss him on the cheek. We will figure he is doing his subconscious best to prepare for his imminent departure from home. The frontal cortex, where the capacity for empathy resides, doesn't fully mature until the early twenties, we will have read. We will tell a friend, "My seventeen-year-old daughter reminded me that I was the same age as Susan Boyle." We will cringe at the middle-aged image of the forty-seven-year-old spinster in a mother-of-the-bride frock and the unibrow who stunned the judges and the audience with her beautiful singing voice on *Britain's Got Talent*.

But, ah, we will laugh because we can. We will remember

that however humbling it is to be fifty, we will be fifty-five, sixty—older, if we're lucky. And from that new height, we will look back and reminisce about being younger, a spry fifty. Best to enjoy the age you are. Which doesn't mean that we will allow someone to photograph us from a low angle (not good for the jowls). Neither does it mean that we will not act upon the advice of one beautiful older woman who said that after a certain age, one should not be on top in the lovemaking position.

It will stay with us that a hint of unbecoming vanity, some level of it, always underlies the use of cosmetic enhancement. Nora Ephron was forced to offer a defensive answer when asked, at sixty-eight, why she goes to the trouble of having Restylane and fat injections. "Do you think you're a great beauty?" the *New York Times* reporter asked. "No. Oh, God, no. . . . I thought I was attractive enough. I didn't think anyone was ever going to look across the room and say, 'Get me her!' But I thought that once they met me, I probably would be all right." Vanity is axiomatic in youth, but with age, its insistence suggests a weakness, an inability to value the complexity of the self beyond its mere physical presentation. Still, some form of it, a healthy version, can remain. "It's because of my vanity and my pride that I don't want to have my skin drawn tight across my face. I don't want to have big lips," fifty-ish British actress Kristin Scott Thomas has said. "Isn't perfection really about being able to wear your years in a way that is still agreeable to look at?" There is beauty in the fragility that comes with age. The aged body is like Venice, where past glory is present still, and made more poignant as it fades.

We can know that the best wrinkle-diminishing device is

forgiveness. Anger is aging. So is resentment. "You will live longer," our lawyer might say to us, when we decide to drop the chase for support from our ex or we sign a legal agreement knowing that he could very well have money put away somewhere that we did not know about. We will now talk about our exes as The Wasband. It puts them in the past, not completely forgotten, but vastly diminished. And that, we know, is the best way to avoid Chapter 11, both on the face and in the bank account. We will fight for positive, empowering things that we really want and need for ourselves and our children.

In the pursuit of that, and that only, we will happily deepen the Bitch Wrinkle.

As I age, I understand the respect I must give the vehicle of my body. I must keep it in good shape. I am more aware of its machinery working hard, the shock absorbers in the knees and back that are not what they used to be, the heart running a little fast, thudding under the hood. I try to give it good fuel. Cleanse it with a detox. Polish it with lotions. I want it to take me farther along the road.

At no other time was this brought home to me as forcibly as on a trip I took in the year following my divorce. I was commissioned by a magazine to write about a hiking trip to Devon Island in the High Arctic, between Baffin Island and Ellesmere Island, within a thousand miles of the North Pole.

Muskoxen roam the marshy meadows that are exposed in the Arctic summer, which lasts for about a month from mid-July until mid-August. I went there as a kind of healing exercise—my little foray into penance travel—to a place that is barren and beautiful, to contemplate being alone, and the loss of my marriage. I was drawn by the name of the place where we would land in the small propeller plane that brought our group of twelve to the island for the ten-day hike. It was called Truelove Lowlands.

Part of me harboured the romantic fantasy that on the Truelove Lowlands, I might find the real thing. My mother had the same thought. "Oh, that's wonderful," she enthused when I told her of my plans. "Maybe you'll meet your next husband." But I was more apprehensive than excited, because I had just injured my back. "Oh, don't worry too much," she said, when I expressed concern to my shrink. I wondered if I was being foolish about going to the top of the world with a bad back to trek with a sixty-pound backpack for ten days over hill and dale and rocky incline. "If you're badly injured, you will just have to be rescued by some cute Ranger in a helicopter," she counselled. (Who says women come up with rescue fantasies on their own?)

The trip passed without crisis, if you don't count a freak snow blizzard at the end of July. My back endured. My tent-mate was a lovely woman named Gisela, a fifty-seven-year-old who was strong and as thin as a flagpole. She had been married for a long time with two grown sons, but her husband didn't like adventure travel. So, she stayed at her middle-management office job, even though her husband had retired, to save her money so she could go on trips with her friends, male or female. She and her husband had reached a happy compromise over how they managed their leisure time—some of it, they spent together, and during the rest, they pursued their own interests.

She and I talked in our small tent at night about our children and our marriages. She was a seasoned adventurer. One late afternoon, after we had pitched our tent, we sat outside on the gravel, watching the sea, where the ice pack was breaking up, groaning as it split. Devon is the largest uninhabited island on the planet and so remote and otherworldly that NASA has an ongoing Mars experiment there. Astronauts get to walk around and pretend they are on another planet. It is unlike anything you would ever see in everyday latitudes. Humans don't belong there and would not thrive for long without assistance. Still, your body will bring you to the edge of towering blue glaciers that cover two-thirds of the island, to see walruses roll in the frigid waters off the coast and polar bears lumber across the ice.

I looked over at Gisela. She had propped herself up against her backpack, her legs stretched out, hiking boots unlaced. We had been hiking for close to eight hours that day.

"Amazing, isn't it?" I said. The landscape shrinks you in its vastness. We are alone, all of us, always, a spirit in a body on a planet, temporary witnesses.

"Yes." Gisela sighed. "I am just so glad to be alive."

PART FOUR

Your disappointments will become your stepping stones.

15.

Vows of an Ex-Wife

"Just follow the 404," my instructor tells me as I fly the Cessna 150. Since telling my mother about my desire to fly, I have been in the classroom called Ground School. It's fun—well, sort of, if you like technical material. Now, in the hands-on flying lessons, we go through a series of manoeuvres to see how all that theory applies. Today, I have to stall the aircraft and then practise recovery from the rapid descent. Let it go too long without adjusting the pitch of the plane to re-establish the flow of air over the wings and we will go into a spiral. Perfect Sunday morning adventure.

The world tilts away from me, the horizon line cutting through the plane's windshield at thirty degrees; I feel the force of the turn, the aircraft's strain, the organs in my body shifting, the Earth pulling, and I am in control. I can hold on to my courage. Let me say that again: I am in control!

I can see the lights, houses, churches, the human traffic far below, shiny beetles skimming across concrete ribbons, and I imagine what everyone is doing, where they might be going, what they're talking about. I feel selfishly triumphant, as if I have somehow managed to elude concerns. "For a brief period, one seems to escape the limits of one's own species, the prison-bonds of a human body, as if one had shed a skin and become another creature with other senses and powers," Anne Morrow Lindbergh wrote in her journal about piloting a plane. I understand this now. I am a shadow, a shape, passing over their heads. Over my shoulder, I can see the needle of the CN Tower far in the distance—I had been to the tip of that with the children when they were small—and over there is a lake Eric and I once visited, and look, there's the forested area I cross-country ski through with my aunt in the winter. She and I sometimes hear the engines of the small planes as we slip along the snowy trails, past a hush of pines.

I see it all, laid out beneath me, in front of me, behind. I am passing over my own life.

"What did you do today?" my mother asks me later.

"Nothing much. Out with friends," I reply.

"Not flying, I hope."

"No, Mom. Of course not."

⁓

"We'll fly over some farmers' fields, up over there," my instructor tells me now through our headsets. "Just in case," she adds, turning to me with a smile.

"Okay."

If there is any concern in her eyes, I can't see it. This tiny twentysomething woman is wearing tinted aviators. If we crash, we will be killing only ourselves, and maybe a cow or two.

"Relax your grip," she says, glancing over at my hands.

I am white-knuckling the column. I reduce the speed as she has shown me to do; the stall horn whines in the cockpit. My heart lurches.

"There's the stall," she says calmly, my indication to make the right move. I pitch the nose steeply down to gather speed.

"Good," she says, as the plane gets proper airflow over its wings. "Level out."

I level out. The fear goes, not because I have overcome it and not because my instructor is here, although she is mightily reassuring for someone so small. It goes because something else takes its place—an appreciation, a trust, in the physics of flight. It is an invisible thing to fix my faith on, but I do.

In the middle of the blur years of being a parent, when the boys were ten, nine and six, I remember telling Eric that I wanted to learn how to fly. I longed for the easy escape of airports. You board; you leave. Within hours, you can be anywhere. He thought I was crazy. How could I justify the time and the expense? He was right, of course. But the desire to fly reflected a longing for a temporary exit from the overwhelming demands of my life at the time.

Now I am drawn to it again and I think that some of the appeal is that an aviatrix is a nonconformist. Beryl Markham, a flying pioneer in the 1920s, was impetuous, single-minded, beautiful. Her unconcealed affair in 1929 with the Duke of Gloucester, the son of George V, led her husband's brother, Sir Charles Markham, to threaten the British Royal Family with naming the prince in an embarrassing divorce suit. The Windsors promptly put an end to the romance. She was paid off with £15,000 from the Duke's trust. And Amelia Earhart's view of marriage was ahead of her time. "Please let us not interfere with the other's work or play," she wrote to her fiancé, George. "In this connection I may have to keep some place where I can go to be myself now and then, for I cannot guarantee to endure at all times the confinement of even an attractive cave."

Divorce forces a rethinking of the myths, the expectations, that brought us to the crisis point. It clears the mind of ideas we once had about how our lives should be lived. We see how willingly we failed ourselves by trying to fulfill the fantasy. Like other difficult events—a health problem, a job crisis, the death of a loved one—it invites a hard, critical look at who we are. I found myself making vows to myself as an ex-wife.

I shed parts of my feminine psychology, unconscious or not, that had been unhelpful. I roused myself from the financial nap I had been taking. I had grown up with the expectation that men in my life would take care of me: first my father, then my husband. When I spoke to Barbara Stanny, daughter of H&R Block co-founder Richard Bloch, she explained that she had been raised with a similar assumption. "My father's message to me, which was very much the message of his generation, was 'Don't worry!'" When she married, she let her husband handle the finances, only to discover that he was a gambler. Her divorce forced her to take charge. "We women devalue ourselves. We give away our time, our knowledge and our expertise," she said. Author of *Prince Charming Isn't Coming*, Stanny now advises women on negotiating what they want in the workplace. For many women, only a crisis such as divorce, or the death of the husband, will make them pay attention to their finances, she says. That was the case for me.

I allowed myself to slip out of that "nice girl" identity I had learned in my youth. Nice girls don't talk about money. They aren't bossy. They don't make demands. In many households, boys are encouraged to do tasks for money, whereas girls, despite feminism and the influence of working mothers, are simply expected to help without compensation, financial coaches report. Boys learn that they work for money. Girls learn that they work for love. I faced my ignorance about dealing with money. I thought of what an older woman who recently divorced told me when she had to arrange for car insurance. "I had never done it before. But you know what? I suddenly looked around and thought, 'Not everybody driving a car is a genius. They must do car insurance for dummies!' And so I found an agent and simply said, 'I know nothing about this. Please tell me what I need to know.'"

Instead of going to an avuncular Bernie Madoff type, who would make me feel that I could relax, put things in his hands and not be involved, I sought out a female financial planner. We sat at a table, like a pair of girlfriends, holding nothing back, as we discussed all the financial vulnerabilities and possibilities of my situation. I asked many, many questions. It was sobering. I had been one of those people who would rather not open her bank and credit card statements. But the process of divorce requires disclosure of assets and debts—family lawyers get to see their client strip financially—and the next step for me was to put myself on a good regime. Let me stand financially naked all the time—fine— but I wanted to look good. I would have to work hard to afford what I wanted for me and my children.

Gradually, I could see how much of my own security and happiness I had put in other people's control. And while I could never completely change my personality, I was not going to abdicate my responsibility to myself, as I had done for years. I would not do what others thought I should do. I would not behave according to someone else's plan. I would risk not being liked if I wanted something others didn't. I would say what was on my mind.

Of all the ways I chose to assert myself, one of the most significant was my decision to write about marriage and divorce, including my own, in the *Globe*. (Talk about making lemonade from lemons.) Divorce is usually something a person only talks about with others who have gone through the same thing. We are survivors of a major, life-altering explosion, after all. But it always irked me that the demise of a marriage is not easily discussed at a party with Smug Marrieds, say, those who are living in their beautifully appointed houses and sending out Christmas cards with Dad smiling over the shoulder of his beloved wife and the wee children spread out at their feet like presents. First of all, husbands and wives rarely think divorce will happen to them, and many people are not interested in the quotidian unglamorous struggle of others: what it means to be old when you are still young, what it means to be lonely when you live in a richly peopled life, what it means to be single again when you are still married.

Sometimes, I think that's because life is too big, too varied, to share in its entirety. We need common experience to bind us. Maybe empathy has limits out of necessity. One person cannot identify with the whole world. We need the comfort of close circles because so much of life is unknown and sometimes frightening. But in mid-life, post-divorce, looking over where I have been, it seems a waste not to express it, not to chart it somehow for myself and for others.

We can defuse the power marriage holds over us by discussing what lies inside it. Strip away its fantasy illusions, and we can enter it for the first or subsequent time with clarity and purpose, with humility.

⌒

"I don't think you will be able to cope," Eric said to me when we made the decision to divorce. He did not say it out of genuine concern. I knew that. Consciously or unconsciously, he was aiming to provoke my fear. I had been dependent as a wife, looked after. I had found comfort in life at home, as mother, curtain-measurer, nest-fluffer. It had been easier on some level than to face the cut-and-thrust of the full-time work world. At times, I willingly disappeared into the domestic realm as a respite. I succumbed to the comfort of its forgiving purpose. Being a mother is a job from which you can never be fired even when you don't like it. Only if you're really bad at it—and someone finds out—can the responsibility be taken away. I often referred to my freelance writing, which never provided a secure living, as my "sidecar" career. The driving force was my life as a mother.

Upon divorce, I didn't have the luxury to not be in the driver's seat. I knew I could rely on my parents, if I needed to, but I didn't want to. I was an adult. I would figure it out. My work had been a useful foil to the wife and mother identities, a way to keep a part of myself for myself and a reminder to my children that I was someone beyond chief spaghetti-maker. Once Eric and I separated, I felt lucky I had a professional foundation, however small, that I could build on.

During my marriage, work had often been a place to go emotionally and intellectually when we argued. The problems with my husband disappeared when I entered it. But as peripheral as my work was, it gave me confidence to leave, something many wives in earlier generations did not have. Their husbands were their only source of identity and income. If Eric's comment about my lack of self-sufficiency was meant to make me feel vulnerable, it didn't work—not for long, anyway. I was beginning to feel the familiarity of an old steely determination and defiance, the kind an adolescent feels when told by his parents that he can't do something. *Oh yeah?* I thought. *Just watch me.*

Every year after we separated, I made more money by taking on more freelance work and expanding the range of what I did. In 2007, I came on staff at the *Globe*. The children were growing up, leaving the nest in the foreseeable future— even more reason to fill up my work life. I know many momaholics who flounder, deprived of their fix, when their children leave. They haven't worked outside the home for twenty years, and are not able to recoup their former careers. Or, they don't want to. They face a more drastic reinvention. Mine was not so difficult. I thought of my work as a long-neglected partner, now the latest recipient of my devoted attention. For twenty years, he used to have to get by with only a fraction of it. Now, it was his turn, and I was glad he was there, that he had been waiting for when I had more time.

I found that my life experiences—having had children, having faced the realities of my doomed marriage—brought value to the workplace. "I didn't know how much your heart is expanded as a mother," Rosanne Cash, the singer/songwriter and daughter of Johnny Cash, once told me in an interview. She and her second husband, John Leventhal, have five children between them: three from her first marriage, one from his, and one from their union. "Once you get a glimpse of the fragility of life and the beauty of it and how precious every life is, there's no going back," she said, explaining that the compassion she feels informs her music. For me, it is not only motherhood but also the disappointment of divorce that have made me more interested in other people—a good thing as an interviewer. More than ever I am interested in the unfolding of a human life. I had become aware that we all have different paths, none of them perfect, few of them straight.

"Alimony is like being married," explained Jessica Cherniak, a forty-four-year-old divorced mother. She stayed at home with her four children (aged nineteen, seventeen, fifteen and twelve), working part-time as a birth coach, during the seventeen years of her marriage. After her divorce, she developed her birth-coaching service into a full-time occupation. "Basically I got nothing. He didn't have any money. I got my equity out of our house and bought one that needed fixing up. I took a government course about how to start a small business. But I'm glad that I never got support, not even child support, because it forced me to get on with it," she explains. At one point, she was juggling three jobs to make ends meet. Every divorced woman she knows who still depends on an ex-husband's support spends too much time worrying about the safety of the ex's job and whether he will be able to keep paying her. "They are living a step down from their life before, but they don't work. They don't grow," Cherniak says. "They are still talking about issues with the ex." Spousal support can be a golden handcuff.

In Canada, there are rules about property division following divorce and legislated guidelines for child support. But spousal support is discretionary. There is a complex calculation based on, among other facts, length of the marriage, age of the children, and age of the spouse to be supported. But the guidelines are not law, and therefore subject to argument. In 1992, a landmark Supreme Court of Canada case introduced another reason to argue—the notion of compensatory support. If, for example, a woman had adjusted her work habits to accommodate the care of the couple's children, she could argue for a payment from her ex that was indefinite in endurance. Even when the children left home, even if she remarried, and even if she re-entered the workforce full-time, she could get support to make up for her diminished lifetime income resulting from a decision years earlier to shift her work-life priorities in favour of caring for the children.

The decision is a victory for women's choices—and recognition of their obligations. Many women who might have preferred to maintain full-time work after they had children make some adjustment to their schedule to accommodate the added responsibilities that fall into their laps. Guilt alone forces many to spend more time at home. It is hard to escape the feeling that a woman is judged by how she measures up as a mother. A successful business career means nothing if her children are screwed up. And some stay at home because they want to. They give up everything to be the primary caregiver, and when the divorce happens, their job prospects at an advanced age are slim at best. One mother I know moved several times to support her husband's career, which made it difficult for her to establish one of her own.

But some women abuse the system. They argue for spousal support because they want to fight for everything they can get. Many divorced men complain about having to support an ex-wife who finds a reason—emotional, medical or circumstantial—to not work. "There are cases where women cry wolf to try to get themselves off the hook for having to work," a family lawyer said. They still want to be taken care of, like wives, on some level. They "see [support] as a sense of entitlement," he added. Or, they see it as a form of emotional compensation. One man wrote to me about having to pay spousal and child support to his ex-wife, who was living with a boyfriend in comfortable circumstances. Meanwhile, he was barely scraping by. "I am paying for her fancy holidays with her boyfriend," he fumed. A doctor told me that his ex-wife, also a physician, was taking him to court for hefty, indefinite spousal support because she had reduced her practice to four days a week after they had two children. Throughout those years, they also had a live-in nanny. He didn't understand why she was spending thousands of dollars to get additional support when she had a lucrative career she had never fully given up.

Money can be a substitute for many things—a fight over inheritance among family members is often a redistribution of the love they did or did not receive from the deceased— but it rarely, if ever, satisfies. Women I know who received handsome divorce settlements struggle often in the same way that children of wealthy parents do. They float along in their privileged lives, uncertain what to do with themselves. "Work is what we're made for," Ruth Reichl told me. The food author and editor never stopped working after she had her son. Her maternity leave from a newspaper where she worked at the time was a matter of weeks. "Indolence breeds unhappiness," she observed.

Besides, in mid-life, there is often a new impetus to see what we are capable of. (And when you see how you were hiding some parts of yourself in your marriage, there's curiosity to know what other aspects of your personality can be brought into the light.) Margaret MacMillan published her first book, *Women of the Raj*, when she was forty-five. Her first bestseller, *Paris 1919*, was published in 2002 when she was fifty-nine. Isabella Rossellini went back to school in her mid-fifties to develop a series of short films, Green Porno, about the mating rituals of animals. "This is a time in life when a lot of things have lifted . . . the big aha about growing older is the mental freedom. When you're young, you give yourself obligations, to be financially independent, to prove yourself in your career.

I've had ideas throughout my life, and I reached the age where all of a sudden I wanted to be a filmmaker."

In Washington, there is talk of the powerful posse of empty-nester women, professionals who managed the work–life balance and now, with their children grown, are reaching new heights in their careers. Among them are Desirée Rogers, White House social secretary; Hillary Rodham Clinton, secretary of state; Valerie Jarrett, senior adviser to President Obama; and Nancy Pelosi, the first female speaker of the House of Representatives.

Whenever I see older women I admire, I think of something journalist Barbara Amiel said. Until the age of forty, a woman's power is physical beauty. Over forty, it is intelligence and engagement with the world. Over sixty, it is money or self-sufficiency. Work is not just something that gives you an identity, an income, a purpose. It is a beauty treatment. I realize that I like myself more now than I ever did, even when I was in my physical prime and wrinkle-free.

And if I used to think that the institution of marriage was the foundation of adult life, I now see that I have something far more solid and secure. I am my own institution, and I have built it myself.

16.

Neighbouring Solitudes

Earlier in my post-divorce life, I thought marriage would never happen again for me. Having exited a painful one, I had no desire to enter another. Why would anyone want to repeat a difficult experience? Many widows and widowers, by contrast, are often keen to remarry. They did not choose their loss and want to replace what was taken away. They are luckier than the divorced in some ways because while every marriage has moments of imperfection at least the widowed are left with untainted memories of what they had—love and companionship, a traditional family unit. They don't have the layer of divorce. They don't have to wonder why they couldn't sustain their marital happiness. They don't have to bear any culpability for making their spouse leave.

For me, I felt that my heart would never be as trusting as it once was. I had lost my faith in marriage. I wasn't sure it was the best custodian of love. And I still feared how the wife identity could sabotage me. I was content to sit to the side and let others have their turn at giving the institution a whirl.

Now I see that age (and divorce) can alter the approach to marriage in a positive way.

For some, the psychological obstacles that prevented earlier marriage have vanished with age. Joe, a friend who didn't marry for the first time until age fifty-five, explains that he couldn't commit in previous relationships due to a "fear of expectation." When he was younger, he thought women would see him as a Provider, a role that would limit career flexibility. He might want to stop being a financial services manager but wouldn't be able to because he was supporting a family. "And what if I wanted to take off for Australia or something?" he explained. He saw marriage as a relationship of set roles. Meeting great women wasn't the problem. He had dated plenty of them.

Then, at age fifty-five, after a year of dating a divorced woman his own age whom he had met online, he proposed. "I realized it doesn't matter anymore who you are or who you think you are or what you do for a living. I am just myself. And I realized that to make a relationship work, you have to decide to make it work. It's a matter of making a decision," he said, as if mystified that it had taken him so long to figure it out. "That's all! I didn't want her to have more disappointments in her life. She had been through some. I wanted to work things out with her; I wanted things to work for us."

Gloria Steinem married at sixty-six—a decision that surprised not only observers. "We shocked ourselves," the iconic feminist admitted once in an interview about her marriage to human rights activist David Bale, actor Christian Bale's father. "Neither one of us thought that we wanted to get married." The certainty of self in mid-life made the prospect of melding two lives in marriage less threatening. "It was something about me," Ms. Steinem replied when asked what it was about her husband that made her decide to do what she once had considered diminishing to women. "I was sixty-six. I was who I was. I no longer felt that I would have to give myself up in a way." It is a sentiment I have heard from many mid-life women. "I'm ready finally to marry," says a forty-eight-year-old single woman who never married out of fear of losing her identity. "I have done what I needed to do on my own, to carve out my career and figure out who I am." She never wanted children. "Now I can see myself sharing my life with someone else permanently."

Maturity also clarifies what you need in a partner. Rosanne Cash told me about her remarriage to John Leventhal in an interview several years ago. "John is very rational. Very like *this*," she said, smoothing the air with the palm of her hand. "He is always cheerful." And her ex wasn't? "No," she replied flatly. "Rodney and I were too similar to stay together. John has provided this incredible emotional stability for me. And I really needed that." She met Leventhal through her ex, as both are involved in the music business. "John is very much in the world," she told me, without prompting. "He has brought me to the surface. My tendency was to go too much inside, too obsessive, down too many dark paths in the service of writing, and it would spill over into my life, and it was not good for me."

With that certainty of self, honest communication becomes easier—communication about how to create "interdependence"—which is how fiftysomething Linda describes her new marriage to Peter. "As a woman who has gone through divorce and has been happy being single, I wanted interdependence," she says. "There are some things we look to each other for, but we maintain a level of independence. That may mean that we like to spend time alone, so we talk about that." Peter, who has been married and divorced twice, had to make adjustments, especially after they married. "I found I still had traditional behaviours that were hard to break," he explained. "I had developed them from being in dependent marriages before, and Linda didn't appreciate them. I wanted to be helpful in areas where she was competent. I didn't do it because I thought she was incompetent. But I was sending signals that I am a man; you are a woman; I should do this. And she had come from a place where she was accustomed to doing stuff by herself." She was alpha woman, capable of doing what are traditionally seen as men's tasks. "She didn't need help, and she didn't ask for it," Peter says, recalling the time he tried to take over the lighting of a fire on one of their early dates. "Even if I volunteered help, it could be seen as a statement of me thinking she is not competent."

They custom-designed their marriage to suit them in a way that echoes what Rainer Maria Rilke wrote: "All companionship can consist only in the strengthening of two neighbouring solitudes." They keep separate bank accounts—a non-negotiable for her. "We just divide up the bills," he explains. They do not use the terms *husband* and *wife*. "We say we are each other's spouse or partner," he says. "Spouse connotes a more equal footing than the word *wife*." For six years they dated before they decided to marry, and never lived together. "Our relationship developed at a speed that allowed this interdependence to form," he says. Still, the decision to marry was not an easy one for her, mostly because her experience as a wife had not been happy or easy. "But I didn't want to be alone," she confesses. The catalyst was September 11. Peter was in New York the day the Twin Towers fell. For a time, she wasn't sure where he was. Finally he called; he was okay. "When that happened, I just thought, 'What am I doing? I love this guy. I want to be with him.' All this worry about marriage seemed silly." In the spring, they married.

Awareness of one's mortality can drive an urge to march up the aisle again. "You may have twenty good years left at this stage, if you are lucky," my friends and I say when talking about the desire to have love in our lives. And if there is a stage of life that marriage seems to usher in when we are younger, it is also true of the decision to wed at a later age. "We certainly didn't get married to have children," quips Marlene Hore, a legend in the Canadian advertising world. After her first husband died, she spent twenty years on her own. Then she met, or rather met again, Bill McLaughlin. They had known each other as friends when they were both married. His marriage had ended in divorce. In 2006, on Valentine's Day, they wed. "We are trying to achieve other milestones" as a married couple, she says. "It wasn't for security. It was for the relationship." They each have grand-children. "It seemed that we were a family."

The possibility of physical frailty in late life is a deterrent to some: "Why would I want to take on an old goat?" one older woman said about men her own age. But it is also more reason to love, fully, in the moment. Joan Price was fifty-seven when she met sixty-four-year-old Robert Rice. "This dashing, silver-haired man walked into my line-dancing class, fastened his ocean-blue eyes on me, and I tried to remember to breathe," she recalls. They were friends for nine months before their romantic relationship began, quickly turning into a passionate love affair. Five years later, they married. He had been diagnosed with leukemia and lymphoma. Initially, he wanted to give her the opportunity to cut loose so she wouldn't have to endure what lay ahead. "We'll still be friends," he told her. Her response was unequivocal. "We're in this together. The only thing I couldn't stand is if you distanced yourself and didn't let me share this with you." He died in August 2008. "I was deeply saddened over the loss," Price says. "But I was also deeply in joy for what he gave me."

The same was true for Steinem, who lost her husband after only three years of marriage. "Even if I knew what was going to happen, I would have chosen to go through with it." When love is present, it doesn't matter how long a marriage lasts. Gratitude is what people feel for however much time they had together. When Harold Pinter, the celebrated playwright, died in December 2008 at the age of seventy-eight, Antonia Fraser, renowned historical biographer and novelist, said something that resonated for many happily married people. She and Pinter had married in mid-life after their previous unions ended in divorce. "He was a great," she said of her soulmate. "And it was a privilege to live with him for over thirty-three years."

⌒

"Somewhere in the back of my head is [the idea] that you can't get married again," Joe Flaherty, the *SCTV* veteran and renowned comedian, told me several years ago. The divorced father of two children was explaining his hesitation over remarriage. "Why is that?" I asked. "Because you had your chance at it," he replied with a weak smile. Marriage may have been diminished by the ease with which many people seem to enter and leave it, but it is a psychic threshold some refuse to cross again. A friend of mine recounted a dream about her ex. "I put my hand on his back, and I said, 'If it makes you feel any better, I don't plan on getting remarried.' I didn't want him to feel bad," she said. In her dream, her ex was apologizing for some of his long-term behavioural issues that had undermined their marriage. But that didn't make her want to reconcile. She just wanted to give him something—her vow of non-marriage—to acknowledge their bond. Would she be happy if he remarried? I asked. "Oh yes," she answered without hesitation. "I was the one who said we were through. It would make me happy that he had found someone to love." His remarriage might assuage some of her guilt, she confessed.

But if some hesitate about a return down the aisle, others have no qualms about trying it again. The divorce culture negates the notion of lasting love but many remarry in an attempt to find it. Such is the power of the institution, and the hope and certainty it suggests, that nearly half of divorced Canadians remarry. Even the failure rate—about 20 percent of second marriages end before the eight-year mark—does not deter them. There are some who say that the failure rate is due to the challenges inherent in the blended family; others put it down to self-denial about difficult personality issues they have.

A friend of mine always stifles a little laugh when the subject of remarriage comes up. His father married five times. All except his last, which still endures, ended in divorce. His father's first marriage was to his mother. His father loves marriage, but he never fully resolved his own issues that contributed to their demise. His mother attended her ex's subsequent weddings, out of affection but also out of curiosity. "My mother would always introduce herself to the new bride," my friend explains. "But it's not just about being friendly to the stepmother. She wonders if the poor girl has any idea what she's getting herself into."

There are those who would never understand Barbara de Angelis, author and love guru, who says that "the purpose of a relationship is not to make you happy. It's to make you grow." They see marriage as their right to be happy, even if they never figure out their own sabotaging behaviour. It's their go-to cure. "I think you're finally better from a divorce when you are in love again," a man said to me once. I think there's truth in that comment. Remarriage has a way of whitewashing the past. It makes those who are entering into it again feel that they have the chance to make things right, to be redeemed.

Consider the photo shoot of Chris Evert, the former tennis champion and symbol of all things good about America, posing as a gushing bride-to-be in a recent issue of *Vogue*. Disregard for a moment that the marriage she was preparing for lasted a little over a year. The point is, at fifty-three she had aced the age-defiant boomer culture simply by being in that white dress. Her two previous marriages had ended in divorce, as would her third, but there she was, looking like a mermaid, standing poolside at her South Florida home, with her three teenaged boys at her feet in the water. Dressed in a strapless Nina Ricci gown, her body was slim and toned like that of a thirty-five-year-old. Her fiancé, Greg Norman, golfing legend and hunk, also fifty-three, calls her "Beautiful" and she calls him "Handsome," she explained. The ring on her finger? An Asscher-cut diamond. (No carat size reported.) When talking about her upcoming nuptials, she confided, "I asked Greg if he wanted me to wear an off-white evening gown, and he says no, he wanted me to wear a wedding dress." The message? You can still be a bride, on the cusp of happiness, even though you're more than half-way through your life.

A remarriage transports people to the positive from the negative: they are no longer just someone's ex; they are a new spouse. The bid for transformation is evident in celebrity culture. Stars divorce and remarry frequently, as if a new union is as alluring as a good screenplay in which they see themselves starring. It is a reinvention, a new skin, or feels like one, anyway. And for some, re-couplings add to their social resumé. Exes left behind enhance their appeal. I think of it as "the positive ex quotient"—the magic fairy-dusting a person receives when he or she is the former lover or spouse of someone famous or socially prominent.

A number of years ago, I interviewed reclusive poet and classics scholar Anne Carson. Enormously talented and fascinating, the Canadian writer had just won a prestigious MacArthur Foundation "genius" award, worth US$500,000. I asked about her life because little was known about it. Was she married? "I think I was, a long time ago. I don't remember," said the author of the acclaimed *Beauty of the Husband*, a philosophical exploration of desire. She looked at me in a mysteriously obtuse manner and did not name him. The next weekend, when the story was published in the newspaper, a man approached me on a soccer pitch where our children were playing. I knew him—he was a writer and an ad guy. But I had no idea that he had once been her husband. "I see you interviewed my ex," he said, and mentioned her name. "Isn't she wonderful?" I agreed, and as I watched him retreat in his baseball cap and dad jeans, I had a whole new appreciation for his intellect and creativity—even if she had dumped him for being a bad husband.

It is not unusual on the social circuit for people to let it be known who their ex is, if he or she is someone noteworthy. Recently, at a cocktail party, a man made a point of mentioning his by name. She is well known—in Toronto at least. She didn't have to be there for him to ascend to her lofty social level, despite the fact that it was a party well below her station. And consider the decision of the late Pamela Churchill Hayward Harriman to have her married surnames follow her everywhere, like a train on a beautiful dress, swishing in her wake as she moves through the corridors of social and political power. The important and powerful men who were her husbands and lovers largely defined the U.S. ambassador to France, and Washington insider. After her divorce from Randolph Churchill, son of Winston Churchill, she had affairs with a roster of A-list men: Aly Khan, Gianni Agnelli, Baron Elie de Rothschild and shipping magnate Stavros Niarchos, among others. Her second husband was Leland Hayward, a legendary Broadway producer. And her third was Averell Harriman, a railway tycoon. Significantly, even though she was from a noteworthy family in Britain (her father was the eleventh Baron Digby), she dropped her own last name for those of her husbands—a nod to her desirability, her worth as a partner, and the power matches that boosted her social and political agency. At the end of her life, she was known simply as Pamela Churchill Harriman. She had dropped Hayward from her name, perhaps for convenience sake. But she always hung on to the Churchill connection—understandably. It had the greatest social clout.

The positive ex-factor also helps explain our obsession with Jennifer Aniston. In 2009, she graced the cover of *GQ* magazine, nude but for a tie. For the photo shoot on the inside pages of the magazine, she reclined on men as though they were furniture. Were we intrigued because she was on the cusp of forty with a beautiful body? Okay, partly. Or because at the time she was dating John Mayer, a pop singer eight years her junior? Sure, celebrity hook-ups are fun to speculate about. (Hey, maybe he serenades her in bed.) The interest in her is not based on her being the most gifted actress on the planet. In almost every film she has made, she is a variation on Rachel, the bubbly, fun-loving character from *Friends*, the long-running sitcom that made her famous. No, we focus on her because Brad Pitt was once her husband. He may have dumped her for the more sublime and gorgeous Angelina Jolie, the Veronica-archetype to her Betty. But the point is, they once loved each other enough to marry. The connection, even severed, helps her image—and maybe even her career. Former lovers help Pattie Boyd, the sixty-four-year-old who was profiled in many magazines and newspapers in 2008 for her photographic exhibition. She is a talented photographer, but more important, she is the ex of George Harrison and Eric Clapton, not to mention the subject of some of their most famous songs: Harrison's "Something" and Clapton's "Layla" and "Wonderful Tonight."

The social cachet that comes with having a well-known ex could also be called the Larry Fortensky Factor. He was the dude (and former Teamster) who met Elizabeth Taylor at the Betty Ford Center, when both were battling alcoholic addiction. They married in 1991. He was her seventh husband, and five years later, her seventh ex. But that didn't matter. In the weird and wonderful world of exes, the construction worker was suddenly on a par with, among others, a famous actor (Richard Burton), a U.S. senator (John Warner) and an heir to a fortune (Conrad "Nicky" Hilton). They all have a striking commonality: a marriage, however brief, to Liz Taylor. Perhaps, for the duration of their marriage and even now, the connection enhances Fortensky. Hey, he could be more than his mullet suggests.

Recently, at a special family gathering, my younger brother, Harry, got up at the end of dinner to remark on how delightful it was to have everyone in one place. He wondered when the next occasion might be. A marriage? he speculated. He had married young at twenty-four, he pointed out. My younger sister was twenty-eight. And on he went through the rest of his siblings and our parents. Over dinner, he and some of the grandchildren had made casual bets on whom would be the next to marry.

"Any thoughts?" he jokingly asked the rest of us.

Several people suggested some of the older cousins, including my sons.

"Sarah!" piped up my father.

Harry turned to me, and raised his wineglass. "Ah yes," he said slowly, smiling, amused at his oversight. "The dark horse."

We laughed. And I raised my glass too. "Never say never."

17.

Lessons in Love

Soon after my divorce, I remember standing on my own in the middle of a party, when an overwhelming sadness came over me. And then I realized what it was: *I am not a wife*, I thought. It's never easy, never straightforward, the shift from one identity to another. But now I don't miss the "status" of wife. (Having said that, I should admit that I always feel like a second-class citizen when I have to tick the box that describes me as "divorced" on those government forms. I mean, do they have to call it my "status"? Why not something less loaded with a sense of worth? I know! Ask me to name my "state of being.")

I have lived as a non-wife for several years and I like the distance it has given me from the way I once approached love and marriage. If I were to marry again, I would not be the kind of wife I once was. I have lost my bride innocence, my marital virginity, if you will. I have broken the marriage code so I can do it a different way the next time.

"I haven't ruled out the hope that the marital experiment might yield a better result the second time around," Daphne Merkin wrote in an essay titled "Memoirs of an Ex-Bride," in which she describes the challenges of divorced life and her understanding of what went wrong the first time. Being a spouse is significant. It has meaning, even when stripped of all the freighted retrograde ones. Simply put: someone desires you and you desire him.

In mid-life, having achieved some of the goals set in youth, there is an opportunity to love another not out of neediness—for what he or she can give you—but simply because you want to share what you already have. And part of allowing yourself to consider the possibility again, especially when a previous marriage has been unpleasant, is to realize that each relationship is unique.

I once told my divorce lawyer, who is now in his third marriage after two divorces, that dissolution is always there as a possibility, as a shadow to the light of happiness.

"No," he replied. "You are wrong. Happy marriage is possible to find."

Recently, a reader of my column wrote to me, saying that he didn't understand why everybody always says that love requires work. He had lost his wife to cancer after nearly thirty-one years of marriage. "I am sure that there are many people who, like me, found marriage to be wonderful and no trouble at all. In fact, I can honestly say that I never, ever, thought it was hard work. Quite the contrary—it gave me and us strength, comfort and joy. I wanted to do things for her. And she wanted to do things for me," said the father of two grown children.

I now see that while I might find the same traits as my ex-husband in someone else, and want to avoid being attracted to them, they would never appear in quite the same combination, with the same weighting, the same shadings, nor would they rub against the grain in just the same way. A relationship will always involve emotional risk—and possibility. And as I have changed, so have my docking-points in a new relationship.

At mid-life, nothing can be forced. People are, at least to some extent, set in their ways. Their life has a shape; its narrative is sure of its voice. You cannot convince someone to love you, and vice versa: you cannot convince yourself to love another. Perhaps you were capable of that at a younger age, when your ideas and your life were more malleable, when you would willingly subsume a part of yourself for the sake of compatibility, or ignore it, because you weren't yet sure how important a piece of yourself it was. "I married the man I married because I liked his version of myself better than my own," wrote Lynn Darling in an essay in *Esquire* about her marriage at thirty-four. "I suppose I was pleased by the person I saw reflected in his eyes," she continued. But in mid-life, the self does not have the luxury of depending on what others think. Like a sculptor, chipping away at a great slab of stone to uncover the form that lies within, life's knocks, both big and small, whittle out the person. And as a result, the real test for love in later life is not how much thinking its negotiation requires, how much compromise. It is the absence of thought that marks a good union. It works. Or it does not. You fit like jagged, well-formed pieces of a puzzle, or you do not.

Business author and veteran columnist Diane Francis, who is in her fifties, was attending a dinner at the Fraser Institute in Toronto, simply minding her rubber chicken, when fate intervened. There were seven hundred guests at the function, but the only available seat happened to be next to hers, and that's where construction baron John Beck sat down. By the end of the evening, they were smitten with each other. Three months later, they married. "When it's right you just know it," she explained about the speed of their courtship. "We were happily single but are now happily married." With experience and age, the right love is as easy to recognize as a suitable business opportunity. You do not hesitate. You seize it.

⁓

I have also discovered that being divorced makes me think about marital sex—not wistfully, you understand, but how it could have been better if we had taken the time to understand how the other was feeling. Let me suggest the complexity of the issues—and perhaps some solutions—through an imagined conversation between Husband and Wife.

The Husband is sitting on the edge of the bed, his head hung low. In bed, he had turned to the Wife, putting his arms around her body, feeling for her breasts. She had promptly rolled away from him.

"I cannot beg. Don't make me beg," he says quietly.

"I'm tired," she says. "The kids. Work."

"But you're always tired."

Glum silence.

"Can I be honest?" says the Wife as she props herself up on her pillow.

"Sure. Why not?"

"You know Sue. Married to Ed?"

He nods.

"Anyway, she was telling me how she feels sometimes about her day. 'I work, I come home, I do the laundry, I do dinner for everyone. And then I have to "do" Ed. That's what it feels like.'"

The Husband winces.

"It's harsh, I know. But I laughed. It is kinda funny. And honestly? It's the way I feel sometimes." She pauses. "They say communication, even bad stuff, is important," she adds in a small voice.

"Okay."

"I do love you, you know."

"I know. I love you too." He runs a hand over his hair. "Want to hear mine, then?"

"Go ahead."

"I have feelings too. Men do, you know. And sometimes we feel that we have been sold a bill of goods about sex. I mean, when we were first together, it was, like . . ."—he gestures and makes the sound of fireworks—"and so we think, 'Well, gee, was she like that simply to get me to marry her?' We feel cheated."

"It's just that other things take over," she says quietly, apologetically. "And after kids . . . I just feel that everyone wants a piece of me—at work, and then when I come in the door, the kids. Everyone's always in my space. I have no time for myself, and when I get into bed, it's finally quiet, it's finally still. I can rest. I need rest."

"You have your friends, though."

"So?"

"And I don't. I have you. You are the only person I really talk to."

"We do talk," she says, then adds, "sometimes."

"But part of the way I communicate is by making love to you." He turns to look at her.

She offers a small, sardonic smile. "Been watching *Oprah*, have we?"

He laughs. "One day last week, when I was sick, remember?"

"Uh-huh." She folds her arms across her chest.

"Men express themselves that way."

She says nothing.

"Look, it's hard for me to talk about this stuff," he says, filling the silence. "Men don't do relationship talk very well."

"Go on. It's okay. I'm listening."

"Vulnerability, tenderness, need get expressed through sex," he says, looking away from her again.

"Now your penis is your pen," she says, giggling.

He laughs too, and turns back to her. "A big, long pen, baby," he says in a low, gravelly voice.

She is laughing now, uncontrollably. She throws a pillow at him.

"And it's not healthy for that to be denied," he explains as he catches the pillow. "It makes me feel bad about my urges," he says, his tone sober again.

They are both quiet for a few minutes.

"I get it," says the Wife. "But really? Sometimes, I don't feel like it no matter what you want or need. I guess I don't want to be the paper." She shrugs. "I feel it's not about me so much as your need for, well, expression . . ." She makes the sound of fireworks this time. "I could be anybody with breasts and a vagina. It feels routine—like you're scratching an itch."

"What do *you* need, then?"

"For you to talk to me," she says, leaning forward, eager now to have her turn. "For you to want to know me, always, each day, for me not to feel that somehow I owe you sex because you're my husband."

"And?"

"And, well, to remember that your picking up a dishtowel can be an aphrodisiac. Or a mop. Even a feather duster, now that I think about it."

"Men don't see dust." He shrugs.

"Pretend if you have to. When you offer to help without being asked, when you acknowledge that I have more on my plate than you do."

"Like now?"

"Like now."

"Would it help if we talked about it more?"

"No," she says, beckoning him to come closer. "We have talked enough."

⌒

I don't think there is anyone who doesn't question the nature of love when they have endured divorce. If nothing else, as it did for me, it shows you what you cannot fix, and when it is dangerous not just for you but for the other person, too, to keep insisting on love, to keep enabling an unhealthy dynamic.

Sometimes, people see where they went wrong. "Being a husband is a title," explains a man, now fifty, who has been divorced several times. "It's what you become when you marry someone. But it shouldn't be a preset role. It should be about being in love. I let the institution of marriage and the role of husband and father be enough. You fall into these roles, and all that men and women really want is the person they fell in love with." I have learned that love sometimes comes with expectations that are wrong and unfair. It can be contractual. "Darling," you might say if you dared to be honest. "When I look deeply into your eyes, I see my new Audi." Sigmund Freud, in his 1914 paper "On Narcissism," mused that falling in love is a self-sustaining redeployment of energy. It's about giving in order to get. Love, he said, was an extension of erotic energy (or, he said, libido) to another person, an action that depletes the narcissistic investment in one's own ego. Having love returned, however, restores one's self-regard. I have felt that, too, when Eric and I were in concert as loving parents, when we wanted so much to get pregnant and then discovered we were, when we were planning our house renovation to accommodate our growing family. We had this symbiotic exchange of energy.

I have often asked people to tell me what they think love is, as if I were a student on an anthropological study. "Authentic love is when a person puts himself or herself in the place of the other person," explained Canon Milton Barry, who has been married for thirty-eight years. "I'm learning to see marriage, loving another person, as a call to serve that person,"

says Phil Reinders, pastor at First Church, a Christian
Reformed Church in Calgary. A forty-four-year-old father of
two, he has been married for twenty years. "I think when I got
married, I was mostly thinking, 'What am I going to get out
of the deal?' instead of, 'How am I called to give myself self-
lessly?' or 'How can I serve my spouse instead of first thinking about how she can serve me and my agenda?' I got married
with some incredibly self-absorbed notions. And in marriage,
I have experienced the end of my self-absorbed thought."

My greatest lesson in love, though, has been taught through
my children. When they grow to become fascinating young
adults, you see how gentle love is, how kind, how curious. It
has something to do with being an engaged witness.

There was the incident of the Horrible Tattoo.

"Mom," said Tait. "I have something to tell you." I was
standing in the kitchen, the place where many things seem to
get announced. He was twenty. It was the day before we were
about to meet my parents and siblings for a beach holiday.

"What is it?"

"I wanted to tell you before you would see it," he began.

"See what?"

"I got a tattoo," he explained, and started to lift up his
T-shirt to expose his midriff.

"Don't!" I squawked. "I can't look!"

"But it's my own design," he said a little dejectedly.

"I don't care."

"It's meaningful to me," he countered.

"I don't want to hear," I said, putting up a hand to silence
him. "And if you needed to commemorate something, why
not, like, buy a poster or something. Something cool to wear?"

"Forget it, Mom," he responded, disappointed that I didn't understand.

By that point, I was on my way to my bathtub, to soak in lavender oil. *What had I done wrong?* I thought to myself. *I breast-fed him! I made his baby food. I helped him learn to read. I practised multiplication tables with him! And he does this?* I was up to my chin in warm bathwater. I sank down to my nose.

The next morning, I said nothing to him on our trip. Later in the afternoon, on the beach, I saw his body art. (I peeked at it from behind my William Boyd novel.) The abstract design covers one side of his ribcage. I watched as my mother, whom the children call Babu, poked at it with the tip of her finger, teasing him. "Ooh, Tait," she cooed. "Does it rub off?" she asked, intrigued.

"See, Mom?" Tait said later to me, pleased at the acceptance everyone had given him. "Babu doesn't care. She even likes it."

"Well, that's easy for her," I explained. "She's not your mother."

Eventually, of course, I accepted it. What else could I do? I told him there is such a thing as "tattoo regret" and that it would be wise not to get any more.

"I was thinking about having 'I Love My Mommy' tattooed across my forehead," he said by way of an answer.

"Very funny, Tait."

Children teach us about love in a way few other people can. They may not follow the career path you have envisioned for them. They make mistakes. Sometimes, they embarrass you. But you adore them through it all. You discover that love is about allowing that person to become the individual he or she needs to be.

18.

In the Ring of My Own Light

In the summer of 2008, my youngest, Luke, graduated from high school, and together we had decided that he should take a year off to volunteer, work and travel through Europe. He had deferred his offer of acceptance to university until the following September. He didn't feel ready to settle into more studying right away. The year off would give him time to mature.

"Got everything?" I said to him as we were driving to the airport.

"Stop asking," he shot back, eyes forward.

I offered a comment about the sunny weather, meteorology having become a benign conversational silence-filler during the reign of teenage muteness. In the rear-view mirror, I could see his enormous hockey bag stuffed with his belongings, a bulky reminder of his imminent absence.

"I'll figure it out," he had been telling me, when I expressed worry about his year away from home, much of which had been planned.

"I know you will," I always replied.

"You should get back in touch with Paul," he said suddenly, apropos of nothing, as we rounded a bend in the road approaching the airport. He placed a hand on my forearm and squeezed it tenderly. "He was a nice guy." He was the only boyfriend I had ever introduced to Luke. I was aware how quickly children think (and worry) that a new romantic partner in a single parent's life might become their next mother or father figure.

"Yes," I replied. "He was."

"Why did you break up with him?"

I gave a brief explanation.

"Well, you should call him."

This was not about Paul. Luke was thinking, *Mom is alone and I am the last one to leave.* Five years ago, when Nick was entering university, Luke did the math about when each brother would be gone. Tait, the middle child, would leave in two years. "And when I go, you'll probably be married again," he projected.

"I'll be fine, Luke," I told him as we neared the airport. What else could I say? I'm dreading the empty nest?

I parked the car, and we went into the terminal together, his bag heaved onto a cart. He walked slightly ahead of me, blissfully motherless.

"I'll walk with you to security," I suggested, once he had checked in.

"No, here." He looked around, checking to see who might

be watching. This was to be the location for the Embarrassing Final Mom Hug.

I reached around his tall, lean body, my head resting briefly on his shoulder. "I love you. Be good. Have fun. And I want e-mails."

"I love you, too," he replied, giving me a big hug. He kissed the top of my head. "Okay, Mom, okay," he said, releasing the embrace. "See you," he said jauntily. Then, he waved good-bye, and turned to walk away.

I watched him disappear. I would not see him until Christmas—six months, the longest we have ever been apart.

⁓

She rides a bicycle, this woman I sometimes see. Sitting tall, head high, feet on the pedals, long legs gently propelling her through the streets of my neighbourhood. Once, I saw her on her way downtown, and her manner was the same, despite the chaos of morning traffic. A small smile played about her face. She wore a skirt and blouse, makeup. Her purse and a few bags sat in a basket attached to the front of her bicycle. There is never anything about her that suggests unpleasant exertion. Her shoes have heels.

I'm not telling you about her because I know her. I don't. Not her name. Not if she is single. Or divorced. Or a mother. It's just that she is how I see myself now that I have found a way to be comfortable on my own. She is not in an anxious state, my bicycle lady. I never get the feeling that she is hoping for a man on a white horse to whisk her off her ride. It is her life, and it is good. I am like her. I am threading my way through life, work, adult children, friends—male and female. And the route is interesting.

My life has changed, as so much does. My house is no longer full of people and demands. There are no more running shoes blocking the hall by the front door. The mountains of laundry have flattened. My cupboards are not stocked with Kraft Dinner and my fridge no longer contains huge cartons of milk and juice. Outside the window of my home office, the outline of trees has disappeared against the darkening sky. It is dark inside too, except for the light from the lamp encircling me. I can hear the whir of the dishwasher downstairs, a car going by on the street. But nothing else. And I let the stillness of my house rise around me like its chaos once did. It is different. That's all.

When I lived in chaotic Boyland, I used to have to leave my house to find peace on a walk in a ravine, or calm in a café with a friend. I would drive home and wonder what state I would find the house in. Often, before I opened the front door, I would take a deep breath, steeling myself, in preparation for a bounding dog, hungry children, complaints, a disagreement that needed a fair resolution, homework questions, a scattering of Lego and socks. But now it is the reverse. Outside is where I find the hurly-burly of life. Except when I have very loud dinner parties that go to all hours of the night. I can bring it on, as and when I please—a nice reverse to my former life.

Soon after a post-divorce relationship ended, my friend Lisa told me to enjoy the time alone. "It will be good for you," she advised. She knew how to be single, having spent her twenties on her own. After the break-up with her live-in partner, she picked up where she had left off. And she knew that being happy alone was an important part of preparing herself for her next, good relationship. Other women have said the same thing. "I wanted a clear perspective on myself if I ever met someone again," said Karen Ott, whose ten-year marriage ended in divorce after three children. For four years, she refused to date anyone. "It had to be this time for me. I had to figure out a lot about myself. Too many people fall into the same pattern, and I thought, 'I can't go there. I can't bring myself down to that place again.'"

I had never been on my own for an extended period, not completely. I lived in dorms at university. And I had house-mates in the apartments I rented when I was working. I had a place of my own for mere months before I moved in with Eric. And sometimes I even think that my discomfort with being alone in Halifax in a lonely apartment propelled me into his arms. I didn't know what to do with myself on weekends, and when I returned home after work, I hated being alone. I was rattling around inside my own head.

But now I enjoy the complete responsibility for myself. No one acts as gatekeeper, suggesting that perhaps I should not have that extra glass of wine. I have to be one for myself—should I want a gatekeeper that night, that is. I tell myself to rest, when I need to.

When I prepare supper for myself in my kitchen, I like the ritual. It wasn't always so. I have eaten leftover pasta from a Tupperware container, standing beside the fridge. Even M.F.K. Fisher, the legendary food writer, once admitted that "it took me several years of such periods of being alone to learn how to care for myself, at least at the table." At the start

of my single, empty-nest living, when I went out to buy groceries, I would sometimes feel that I was watching myself,
like a movie camera with a wide-angle lens following a
woman, all by herself. *There she goes, our plucky heroine, smiling
bravely through her request for one portion of halibut, please.* I think I
was just trying to place myself in the social context, not as
married woman, not as mother who had a brood at home to
feed. (I often felt a funny sort of pride when the children
were small and onlookers commented on the heaping contents of my shopping cart. *That's quite a load!* they would marvel.
Yes, three growing boys to feed! I clucked, throwing in a look of
mock exasperation.) But I have learned to prepare food for
myself with care. I kick off my shoes when I step through my
door, put on some comfortable clothes, listen to Joni Mitchell.
I have a single friend who bought a headset for her kitchen
phone, so her hands could be free to chop vegetables while
she chatted to friends for companionship. But I don't mind
when it's quiet. People say food is our communion with
others, an expression of love. And it is—even for oneself.
A present. And a meal in low light at a stool by your kitchen
bar can be a sacred close to the day.

I once felt that I needed a love relationship not just to complete me, but to help manage myself. I could give him some of
my thoughts—not to mention a few anxieties—and he could
relieve me of them. They could be his for a bit, and it made me
feel better, that holiday. Or maybe I just wanted to spill all
this stuff out, so he could mop it up. Sharing things with a
man was a good head cleanse. But I rather like being as self-
contained as an unbroken egg—or trying to be. I accept my
own power to change my mood. I jolly myself along when I

am sad. And sometimes, I just sit with a glum mood and try to ignore him—that sullen little package of a man—for as long as he wants to stick around. He always leaves eventually.

I counsel myself not to think too much. I take myself for a walk. Without the interference of others' input, I can see my thoughts arise, their pattern, how they save me, and sometimes, how they defeat me. After years of giving so much of myself to others, of being fragmented, trying to balance all the needs of home, husband, children and career, it feels like a luxury to have only myself to know. I no longer think that the only way to be known to exist purposefully is to be loved by someone else.

Being single forces a challenging encounter with the self. Many of us can go a whole lifetime knowing more about other people than we do about the person we live with every day— ourselves. We spend a lot of time striving against loneliness. We read a book, watch TV, go to a movie, anything to avoid the self. When people ask Pema Chodron how she got involved in Buddhism, "I always say it was because I was angry with my husband," she writes in her beautiful, meditative book *When Things Fall Apart*. He had come home one day, when they were living in New Mexico, and announced that he was having an affair and wanted a divorce. "The truth is that he saved my life," she writes. "When the marriage fell apart, I tried hard— very, very hard—to go back to some kind of comfort, some kind of security, some kind of familiar resting place. Fortunately for me, I could never pull it off. Instinctively I knew that annihilation of my old dependent, clinging self was the only way to go." Later in the book, she writes that in order to stay in a sweat lodge and experience all the good and bad it brings, one should not sit near the exit. If you are sitting near the exit, you will find a way to use it.

"It is a very selfish time," Shirley MacLaine said, when I asked her in an interview how she enjoyed her life as a single woman at seventy-four. (Just for the record, we also talked about the aliens and spaceships she claims to have seen.) She has a platoon of female friends. "All my friends are over their marriages, and they live alone too. I think a lot of people think they shouldn't be alone. They think they should be afraid, that they are missing being the other half of something. I think that has been promulgated through the culture, and I don't think it's true." She and her friends often joke about hiring a nurse and living in a big house together in their dotage. She feels no need for a romantic relationship, and has found that her menopausal disengagement from the need to mate has increased her appreciation of men. "You start to look at what sex is for. It really just satisfies the hormones raging," she said. "I'm having a wonderful time in my life now with my platonic relationships, because when that sexual tension is off the requirement of the interplay, then you get to see who the people really are and to see yourself."

Leonard Cohen also spoke of the beauty of being alone. I had asked him if the longing for others ever completely disappears. "Whatever version of that longing there is, you know, of completion. Everybody is involved in that activity. It is what we are supposed to be doing, apparently. And there are many versions of it. It can be spiritual, romantic, erotic." When he was on Mount Baldy, during his meditations, the typical man–woman fantasies would "cease to have charge. They bore themselves into non-existence," he said. "You see them as diversions from another kind of intimacy that you become more interested in. That is, I guess, Socrates—'Know thyself.'"

I am not saying that being single is a state to celebrate. Whenever I read about "Women Rule" parties, in which newly single women drink martinis and dance around to music, I always think that they are overcompensating, which does more to highlight their disappointment than their happiness. We all want companionship. Few people choose to be alone. While there is always a passive suggestion that a person is somehow responsible for his or her single status—"You have an Occupied sign on your head," some people will say. "You are not open"—the truth is that romance is often simply a result of fate, a matter of place and timing, of love finding you rather than you pursuing it. Dating sites and matchmakers do well because we don't want to leave to chance something we deem so crucial. Posting a profile is a tiny protest against the random nature of the universe.

But if it's a state we shouldn't necessarily celebrate, it is not to be feared, either. It brings so much freedom. "If I want my toothbrush just so on my bathroom counter, it is just so," says Gail Vaz-Oxlade, a financial author who has three failed marriages behind her. "If I want to go to sleep with my underwear on the floor, I go to bed with my underwear on the floor. I am through with compromise!" the mother of two exclaims. I too enjoy the ability to live as I wish.

Some believe that being in a relationship is a mark of mental health. I disagree. A relationship can often be a safe haven, a shelter from the challenge of being alone, a crutch.

"A lot of people don't have the emotional grit, the spiritual grit to face the existential abyss of being alone," observes lawyer Julie Hannaford. Assertiveness in the dating trenches often speaks to insecurity about being alone rather than confidence. If some younger women are eager to couple up by their thirties, driven by their ticking biological clocks, some women in their forties and fifties become anxious about finding a mate because of a perceived best-before date. "It's easier to find someone at forty-seven than it will be at sixty," a mid-life woman worried. And there is fear for their financial security as they age. Women outlive men. Even married women can suffer from the bag lady syndrome, the pervasive fear over their financial future. "Think of your retirement," some women tell each other when they are considering the type of men they should date or whether they should accept their boyfriend's suggestion of living together. But shouldn't we be through with insecurity and wanting a man to improve our lifestyle? I don't mean to underestimate the financial hardship that comes with divorce. It is a great force of impoverishment for both men and women, especially the latter. Many single mothers have difficulty re-entering the workplace, if they opted out, or of balancing their responsibilities at home and office without support of a husband. But fortuitously, I find that the consumer drive of my earlier years has waned. I don't want as much; nor do I need things to accommodate a growing family. A surfeit of possessions feels like an encumbrance I'd rather shuck. In this state of unwanting, I am freer, no longer comparing myself with the Joneses—something many married couples do as they accumulate the accessories of the modern family.

Being alone is a skill worth cultivating. Many married women end up as widows. I have decided that the anxiety about meeting a partner is a distraction. There's so much else that responds to desire in a way you can control. I can work hard, and make more money. I can exercise and get fit. I can love my children, and receive theirs in return. "I realized that all the energy I was putting into finding a partner, and worrying about it, was really just a way for me to avoid thinking about what I had to do for my own future and career," confessed a divorced forty-seven-year-old mother of one. When they let themselves ease out of the lifestyle of having a partner—the hubby habit, I like to call it—many mid-life women find themselves feeling the way men did in their twenties—less sure about commitment, focused on their career trajectory and making more money. Many women, at that earlier stage, wanted a relationship that led to marriage. Ironically—who said life isn't weird—it is mid-life men who often want the comfort of a permanent relationship. Near the end of their career, after having been at it for thirty or forty years, they want and deserve an exit. Women are a connection many men crave. Not as skilled at maintaining and developing social networks as women are, mid-life men are often willing to invest a lot in their romantic relationship.

Which brings me to friends—virtual and real. I once posted on my Facebook update that my children think I should get a dog. Ketchup had died, and they thought I could use the companionship. Well, I got several unsolicited suggestions of breeds and a lot of encouragement to take my children's advice. I still haven't—a dog is like a child you need to return home to at the end of the day, and I prefer a lack of domestic obligations. But I appreciated the input. Facebook, I discovered, is always listening. In fact, you have to be careful what you post, lest you worry your friends unnecessarily.

As I expanded my social networks following divorce, I realized how isolating marriage can be, how exclusionary. I believed that a husband had to be everything to me, a dozen friends in one. Eric also didn't like many of my girlfriends, especially those who he felt encouraged me to turn against him and our marriage.

My friends, male and female, have become a community who fulfill what Lynn Darling once called "the terrible necessity of other people." Some of my single girlfriends have disappeared inside new relationships and are no longer accessible in the way they once were when they were vulnerable following a break-up or divorce. But most, the true ones, have been consistently present. Joy and I still speak to each other almost every day, regardless of whether we have men in our lives. When I am due home from a trip, she checks in to see that I have arrived. I do the same for her. I have friends I exercise with, diet with, some I prefer to travel with, others I talk to about my children, a few I call when I am sick and need help, and one or two who slip easily into a spiritual discussion when I need one. I live with a plurality of kindness.

It is connection we crave, the desire to be known and supported, all of which effortlessly comes with friends who are in your life not because they're fulfilling an expectation, like a boyfriend or husband often does, but out of genuine generosity.

And then there are my children. When they were younger and we were in the throes of divorce, I tried to avoid turning to them for support. It happens. Many divorced parents make their children their best friends well before they are old enough to handle the complexity of an adult life. They become surrogate partners. But as my boys have matured into young men, they volunteer advice when they know I am stressed about something.

"Tell me what you're worried about," Nick, my eldest at twenty-four, said to me recently on the phone. I told him. He made suggestions on how to handle each.

"One thing at a time, Mom," he counselled.

"You're right," I replied.

"It's what you taught us."

"Candle therapy?" I say in a teasing voice. When any one of the boys was overwhelmed with assignments in high school, I would bring a candle into his room, dim the lights and sit on the floor with him to calmly prioritize the workload. They would roll their eyes, but it always helped reduce the stress.

"Yes, Mom," Nick says, laughing. "Candle therapy."

I think of a line I say to my friends when we talk about our single-mom family lives: *Husbands come and go; children are forever.*

When I was deep in deliberation about what to do about my marriage, I drove to Lily Dale with two girlfriends. A spiritualist community three hours south of Toronto across the border in upstate New York, the small town is home to many psychics. The woman we visited in a pink clapboard house invited each of us separately into her back room, where she asked questions and claimed to see the spirits of those who act as our guardians. (Her prediction, incidentally, was that my marriage was over, a pronouncement that didn't make it any easier to pull the plug.) I determined from her description that one of the people she saw was my maternal grandmother, the one who we had visited on her farm as children.

I think of her often. In my house, I have a picture of her, at age three or four, and her younger sister, Bunny, with their mother on the steps of their stone house. It was taken by the society photographer William Notman in the early 1900s. She wears a bow in her ringlets, a frilly dress and shoes with tiny buttons up the side. Her mother, my great-grandmother, wears a full-length dress, with lace trimmings, her long dark hair in a bun, shaped like a mushroom cloud. She is a portrait of serene motherhood, reading to her daughters from a large book that's spread across her lap. But my grandmother's life was far less elaborate as an adult than it had been as a child.

Her husband died when I was barely two, and she lived into her nineties, spending over forty years on her own. Shortly after he died, my grandmother moved into the Glen Eagles, a dark, Victorian-era apartment building on the edge of Westmount that sits on the crest of Côte-des-Neiges, near the top of Mount Royal. Busy thoroughfares to Montreal's downtown surround the building on all sides like a moat too dangerous to cross casually on foot. When she wanted fresh air or to get out for brisk exercise, she would "walk the ramparts," as she called the small walkway around the property.

I do not know if she was lonely. I was too young to realize that people could be, and I didn't know enough to ask. I came to visit her often after school, a few blocks away. She would greet me at the door with a smile and a hug, scented with L'air du Temps perfume. Her apartment was small. In her tiny kitchen, she liked to stand at the counter, with a crisp apron on, using a large silver knife to cut into the Sara Lee cake she always bought for my visits. We sat at the small table, drinking tea from enormous china cups with dainty teaspoons to stir the lumps of sugar she set out in a silver dish.

Her life had not been easy. There had been an illness in the family and her husband was away during the war years, serving in Europe. When she was widowed, she got a job selling real estate.

In the 1970s, when she sold the farm in St. Andrew's East, she bought a small cottage in Métis-sur-Mer, a summer outpost of Montreal Anglos on the Gaspé Peninsula, at the edge of the St. Lawrence River, where it is wide like a sea. Her last summer there, the year before she died, she fell and broke her hip, which required her to move into a seniors' home. But up until then, she had never changed. Birthday presents would arrive right on time with cards inscribed with her careful, looping handwriting. When my mother and father went to visit her, they would often take her out, but sometimes, she insisted on serving them a small supper in her apartment. There was no dining room, just her kitchen table, so she would set up a card table in her living room, place a linen tablecloth over it and lay out formal place settings with her good silver and crystal.

When I grew up and moved away from Montreal, I would call her on weekends. She always inquired about the boys, about Eric, about my life. And she would tell me about hers. She just had her hair done. Yesterday, she ordered a nice roast beef from her favourite butcher on Sherbrooke Street. Her son, Jim, was coming to visit. She started a new carton of du Maurier cigarettes earlier today. Oh, how perfect, I have caught her just as she finished reading the *Gazette*, she would tell me. What a good read it was! And those Montreal Canadiens! Did I see the hockey game last night? There's nothing better than the fights, when the gloves fly off, and the men leap off the bench over the boards!

I imagined her in her floral-patterned chair in her yellow kitchen, the handle of the rotary phone to her ear as she puffed away on her cig. Often, at the end of the conversation, she would tell me: "If anyone ever asks, Sarah, tell them I loved life."

When she died, she bequeathed all her diaries to me. There was a thick notebook from the year she went off to Europe on a boat as a young, chaperoned, single woman. The diaries got slimmer as time went on, but still, she kept them religiously. Every day, she would make notes: about the weather ("Windy. Showers. Clearing"), what she ate ("Steak. Mashed potatoes. Carrots & Gravy. Good!"), what she did ("Got a Parking Ticket!") and what happened ("Joan here for tea. Good cake!! Then drove her to Gay's for night").

Beside every item in her day, she put a neat checkmark. The lesson is simple: No matter what your life includes— divorce, marriage, widowhood, lots of money or little—take special note of its content.

19.

Playing My Cards

From the window of my bedroom on the second floor of my parents' house in Sussex, I can see the dormant winter garden, a high beech hedge with a slice cut out to allow a view of the fields beyond, where horses graze, and in the distance, the South Downs, a chalky ridge that runs across the south coast of England. Pillowy and quilted with rows of winter crop, hedges and fields of green next to brown, the landscape is soft under a diffused light, like a watercolour illustration in a children's book. I retire often in the afternoons for naps. "I think it's because you're home," says my mother of my sleeping habits. "Someone is looking after you."

Rather than spend the Christmas holidays in Toronto, I have come here to be with family. It is my favourite season in Sussex. Holly bushes in the forest have produced their berries.

On Christmas Eve, we sip mulled wine and sing carols outside the pub, the only place of business in the hamlet. Later on, just before midnight, residents file through the gates of the churchyard, past the swooping arms of giant monkey puzzle trees and crooked, moss-covered gravestones, to hear the vicar deliver a sermon in the cool interior of a medieval church.

My other siblings and their families are elsewhere. Tait is in Alberta spending time with his girlfriend's family. Nick and Luke are here.

Nick came over from Ireland. Just before he left for his sojourn in India in November the year before, he had applied to medical schools in Ireland—ignoring the Canadian ones— as many of his friends had too. He found out that he was accepted when he was in Thailand in the spring. Having arranged the financing on his own, he had started in the fall.

Luke has been working in a restaurant in London since September, after a summer spent in Italy. In a soccer camp in Porto San Giorgio in the Marche region on the Adriatic coast, run by a British man and his wife, he helped young children with their English. Then, through World Wide Opportunities on Organic Farms (WWOOF), he lived for a month with an Italian family a little farther down the coast, volunteering on their land, harvesting lavender to be distilled into oils and made into soap. "Your favourite!" he told me. He knew no Italian when he started, and the family spoke only rudimentary English, but he had managed well. I haven't seen him in six months, since I saw him off at the airport in Toronto.

"You've grown, Luke," I say, looking up at him in the kitchen of my parents' house, where he had been staying. Another inch. "Is that possible?"

He laughs, then wraps me in his arms.

"I missed you, Ma. What have you been up to?"

"The usual. Writing. Working."

"Yeah?" He holds me at arm's length to get a better look at my face. "You okay?"

"I am."

"Good, good," he says, patting me on the back.

Luke and I have had an intense mother–son relationship. The divorce happened when he was thirteen, so he endured more of his adolescence with a single mom than the other boys did.

"I'm not your boyfriend," he liked to say to me, when I would ask him to come to the table for supper.

"No, but I'm your mother, and I would like us to eat dinner together as a family," I would respond. The request didn't always work.

When they were home, his brothers were his surrogate fathers, but for much of the time, it was just the two of us. I had to teach him how to shave, sticking out my chin and stretching my neck to demonstrate how to avoid nicking his skin.

We went away together. I took him cross-country skiing in the Gatineau Hills. We went on road trips together to see Nick at university. For his seventeenth birthday, I took him and a friend of his out west to ski. The day they got out of school for their spring break, he and his friend went to the barber to get a mohawk haircut—their way of celebrating a holiday. His friend's mother promptly ordered her son to shave his off. Initially horrified when Luke walked in the door with it, I told him he could keep his, but said it would have to go before school started again. On the plane, my six-foot-four teenager sat beside me, and at one point in the long flight, put his head on my shoulder to sleep.

I have never told him that after I dropped him at the airport on his way to Italy last spring, I came home and went straight to his empty room and just sat there for a while. I had done the same thing in Tait's room when he left home the first time. (Nick had lost his bedroom when we moved from the marital home.) When Tait later moved out for good to his own apartment, I converted his room to a guest room—a welcome opportunity to carve out more adult space. But Luke's room would remain as is. "Don't touch it," he had warned before he left. My sons decided it would be the designated Boys' Room that any one of them could occupy if he lived at home again. On that evening, I sat there, thinking about their childhoods, which had once taken over my life, colonized my brain, and that were now—suddenly, it seemed—reduced to one too-tidy room.

My parents' place in Sussex is one of layers: of time, of stories and of people who have tilled the land for centuries, who have walked the public footpaths across fields and through forests and who filled the houses, silent shelters for the passing pageant of each new generation. During summers, my boys have played with other children down the lane. At all ages, they have thrown sticks over the parapet of a small stone bridge my mother calls "Pooh Bridge." If their sticks float through to the other side, wishes come true. We have sat in the low-beamed houses of neighbours, listening to tales of ghosts who share their living space. The present feels like a small scratch on the surface of what's gone before.

In their house, it is the same. Possessions and furniture from my grandparents are juxtaposed with things collected in our childhood—like that mangy wind-up monkey who can no longer clash his cymbals under the Christmas tree—and beside them, items from more recent years, after my siblings and I had left home. Everything—a small dish, a chair, a table, a box, a wooden plaque, a spoon, a plate—is tied to a specific time, person, place, memory. Past and present seem woven together, like my parents' marriage, the strands of their personalities having grown and twisted around each other to form a fabric with no loose ends.

"You're both Virgos," I say to my mother one day. It had only recently occurred to me that their birth signs are considered incompatible.

"My mother never thought it would last." She laughs.

"Virgos like orderliness. Which is good. Because if one didn't, you'd drive the other batty."

"We had to be organized," my mother says defensively. "We had five children."

"Yes, you did." I lay out the acknowledgment like a blanket, calming her. My mother can get prickly, and none of us likes to upset her. After a moment's pause, I say, "It's hard to imagine, really. All those kids."

I think of a photograph taken of my mother and all the children in 1967, the summer of Expo in Montreal, when we had returned from our year in Switzerland and just before we moved to Vancouver. Aunt Mabel had paid for the formal portrait. The photographer positioned us all, dressed in our good clothes, in the living room of our house, arrayed around our mother, who was only thirty-four at the time. My father was not included. (The photo was about the domestic realm.) My younger brother, Harry, and younger sister, Aimée, who was born in Switzerland (hence her French name, meaning "loved"), were toddlers, barefoot and dressed in white clothes. Harry perched on the upholstered arm of the large wingback chair in which my mother sat. Aimée was on her lap. Geoffrey stood behind. Daphne and I were seated on a small bench to her left. My mother's arms lay on either side of her lap, extended, palms upturned. She has always said she hated the pose, that the photographer should have caught the awkwardness of it before he took the shot. But it was perfect, in a way, a comment on her life at the time: her arms open like that, giving, surrendered to her role, a hint of helplessness about her, despite her bourgeois perfection; the smile, the smooth coiffure, tweed skirt, blouse; her legs, uncrossed, positioned demurely to one side in their low-heeled pumps.

"I remember wanting you all to grow up," my mother says to me now, with a sigh, from her position by the kitchen counter.

"And we did."

She looks over at me. "Yes, you did."

⟞⟝

The last time we were here for Christmas was five years ago. The boys and I had moved into our new post-divorce house earlier that fall, and my father suggested we all come to Sussex for the holiday. He had airline points he could spare, he said. It was a welcome invitation. I could not have coped on my own.

I had worked right up to the day of our departure, banking columns with the paper so I would get paid while I took time off. My back was so painful, I had not been able to do much Christmas shopping. I arrived exhausted.

On that Christmas morning, when the children opened their stockings, they said nothing, but their disappointment was obvious. I had grabbed whatever I could at the grocery store while on a food run—toothbrushes, toothpaste, razors, soap, shampoo, a chocolate bar, gum. I hadn't bought any other presents.

"I can't do it all myself," I cried, breaking down into sobs as we all sat around the living room. "It's not fair. I can't do it."

My poor mother dissolved in tears herself over my distress.

My children looked at me with big questioning eyes. "It's okay, Mom. It's okay," one of them said.

But it wasn't. It was a Christmas no one would want to remember, not me, not the children, and not my parents, who were unsure how to react.

The children's expectations had changed with our circumstances over the intervening years. At home, we had created new rituals. We all got stockings. The boys always filled one for me. But presents were minimal and modest. They always expressed dismay about their father's lack of involvement. A discussion about him never failed to arise with sadness and confusion. But we had found things we loved to do in our new unit. We went for a walk in the city streets after Christmas dinner. And we always watched a movie or began a season of some television series that one of them had requested as a present. There had been many years of marathon *CSI*-watching.

Forging new family rituals is an important part of coping with divorce, experts say. Many parents decide on an alternating schedule prescribing where the children spend the big day, which means that some years, a mother or father is alone. To get through her first Christmas without her three children, then aged eight, six and one, Karen Stewart, a divorce lawyer I know, spent the day working on a photo album with all the pictures from the family's seven years together. "There was a lot of crying that day," she says. "I'm sure I snipped my husband out of a few pictures," she says, laughing ruefully now, almost eight years after their acrimonious separation. But she also selected some photographs that she thought her ex would want and put them into a box for him. "I found pictures that didn't have me in them, because I thought he wouldn't want that." When the children came home, she showed them the albums, and she handed her ex his collection of their children's earlier years. "The first few years are tough, but after that, you adapt," she says. There's no scientific evidence that Santa comes on the twenty-fifth of December, for example. If you're child-focused, you don't care so much about having them on that specific day because you realize that you can make the next day—or whenever you have them next—your Christmas with them.

Since the divorce, I had changed as a parent, becoming the head of a matriarchal household—a new model. I stopped trying to replicate what the boys once knew and created new expectations. My family was not broken, just realigned. The description of "fatherless homes" is often used as a pejorative, the suggestion being that mothers don't discipline their children effectively so they grow up to have problems with authority. But there are numerous examples of matriarchal success. Look at Sonia Sotomayor, the first Hispanic (and third female) to be appointed to the Supreme Court of the United States. Her father died when she was nine. Her mother raised her on her own. And I laughed a bit when I heard Jermaine Jackson tell Larry King on CNN that his mother, Katherine, was the one who would make the decision about what to do with his famous brother's body after he died. She makes all the decisions, he said sheepishly, shrugging. A mother of ten, one of whom died in infancy, she has superceded her husband, Joe, who once ruled the family. In her autobiography, *My Family, the Jacksons*, she described how he was often unfaithful to her. She defended her children through their tribulations, especially Michael, who named her guardian of his children in his will. It appears that her softer approach of loving support has won out over her husband's legendary iron fist.

I had to be tough with my boys, when required, which took some adjustment. I had always left that to their father. He had been the one to ground them when they did something wrong, while I had been more lenient, more forgiving—we were the classic good-cop, bad-cop parenting team. The boys were in their most difficult phase as teenagers when we divorced. They would argue their point of view about why they should stay out late, for example, knowing that if they kept at it, I would eventually give in—at least to some degree. At first I was doing what many divorced parents do—trying to compensate for divorce by being generous, by giving them what they wanted. But I soon smartened up. Children need structure, especially when a new situation is uncertain. I learned to say no to a request I didn't agree with, and then, if need be, I would walk out of the room and out the front door, saying I had something I had to do. I would not entertain their rebuttal. "No" is so simple, if you stick to it. The boys wanted to please me—most children do—and I let them know how they could.

I also had to become the provider, strict about what I could do financially and honest about what I couldn't. For the first time, I understood the pressure that some men feel as husbands and fathers. The children complained, saying that they had been able to have more things when their father and I were together, and I agreed, but that's the way it was now. If they liked to have money to do things such as buy video games and other non-essentials, they would have to make it by shovelling neighbours' driveways and doing other chores. All I can say is that when it snows, the boys probably still see dollars falling from the sky.

Despite the hardships, I found I enjoyed the opportunity to be the parent I wanted to be. In a marriage, differences in parenting style often create conflict, and this was certainly true in ours. I would rather talk calmly through issues, not argue. Eric was more confrontational. My boys had to adjust to my style as the only one that mattered now. I wouldn't listen to them if they raised their voices to make their point or confronted me with anger about something. *Talk to me when you're calm*, I would say. *Make a proposal for why I should pay for something, and how you will help.* Eventually, I even received praise from Eric. Four years after our separation, he had flown in for Nick's graduation— the first time he had come to see his son at school.

At Tait's graduation from high school, which came the year after Eric remarried, we sat apart. His new wife was present, and there was a tacit avoidance of possible awkwardness. But for this milestone event, as he would a few years later for Luke's high school graduation, he came alone and we sat together. I told him that I had booked a restaurant for lunch following the commencement ceremony and that if he wanted to join us, that would be fine. If he wanted to take the boys on his own for a drink beforehand, that was fine too. He decided on the latter option.

After the children arrived at the restaurant, where I was waiting for them, Nick's cell phone rang. He answered, and passed the phone to me.

It was Eric. "I just wanted to say what a wonderful job you have done with the boys," he said.

"That's so nice," I said after a stunned silence.

"I mean it."

I looked at the three young men before me, dressed in their formal clothes, and felt tears threaten. "Thanks, Eric." I don't know why he did that. Guilt? Sadness? He had lost touch with his boys. At that moment, I felt sorry for him. He was missing the return on emotional investment in parenthood.

⌒

I was not always happy with the calm formality of my family. I remember wishing that someone would stand up and have the balls to pitch a screaming fit, just to rattle its well-established sense of place—one that had been given, not sought, not earned, not won. It would have been interesting if there had been some spectacular dysfunction, some debauchery, some sense of entitlement to bad behaviour, but there wasn't.

But now, the differences between us no longer irritate, smoothed over by a gentle forbearance we all seem to have for one another. It was a temporary and necessary gulf, that period in adolescence and young adulthood when parents serve as examples of what you don't think you are or want to be. But you can't change your parents. So you love them for the things you share and for those things you don't, even for what you may perceive to be their shortcomings. The lens of self is only that—one aperture that cannot see all. You love both despite the differences and because of them.

It's partly a function of the "positivity factor"—a biological change revealed in brain-imaging studies showing that while young and old people process positive emotions in the same way, part of the senior brain lights up less intensely and for shorter intervals when dealing with negative emotions. It affects many kinds of relationships, even the one we have with ourselves. We're more tolerant. And there's a psychological imperative that also encourages a shift in outlook as we age. Time is like an oil supply that's running out, and as it diminishes, it becomes more valuable. We begin to think about how to use it in a way that makes us happy.

Over Christmas in Sussex, we all slide easily into familiar routines. We go for long walks through the countryside to have lunch at the pub. We read in front of the fire. Play Scrabble. I take long baths in the late afternoon before supper. I cook with my mother. On several occasions after dinner, my parents and I sit down at a small card table to play bridge, making a foursome with one of the boys.

"Are you still taking those flying lessons?" my mother asks me one night.

"Well, no. I've put them on hold for the moment," I tell her.

"They're expensive, aren't they?"

"Yes. The recession has clipped my wings," I joke.

"I'm relieved," she says absent-mindedly as she concentrates on her cards.

"Well, I haven't given up," I put in defiantly. "Maybe I'll start again in the summer."

But no one is listening to me.

"Your turn to bid," my mother reminds me.

I turn my attention to my cards.

"You know how to bid, don't you?" she says over her reading glasses. She is my partner.

"Yes, Mom. I know how to bid." I count the points of my face cards silently in my head. "I think," I add.

She shoots me an annoyed look across the table.

I smile at her—I was teasing. She shakes her head a bit, laughing.

20.

Life Is a Carnival

"I thought it would be better when I left Tom," my friend Pam says one day as we're walking. "I thought he was the problem. But it isn't any better. Everything is difficult, still, just difficult in a different way."

"I still feel terribly guilty," says another friend of mine. "The kids never asked for this. They lost their family." Four years ago, she left her thirteen-year marriage, and the children have spent equal time in their parents' two households ever since. They are teenagers now and well adjusted. Neither parent is impoverished. But there's often guilt and regret, even when a parent feels that she or he had good reason to leave the marriage. "I think I will always worry about the possible impact on the children," another friend admitted to me recently. She was referring to concern about how her two girls, both university graduates, will conduct their own romantic relationships. "It is always a pebble in your shoe," says a fifty-seven-year-old father when speaking of his two failed marriages.

Sometimes, the hoped-for catharsis in divorce doesn't come. A 2008 study conducted at the University of Chicago looked at the "divorce assumption"—the belief that a person in a bad marriage had a choice to stay married and miserable or get divorced and become happier—and found evidence that it was wrong. Two-thirds of unhappily married spouses who stayed married reported that their marriages were happy five years later. In no case did those who divorced or separated show higher emotional well-being than those who remained married, and on some measures they showed lower well-being.

Being single can be great, but not always, I will admit. It's hard when you're sick. The joy of it can feel contingent upon good health. And it's hard when something happens you would rather not have to handle on your own. "Divorce sucks when you get a flat tire," a friend told me one night after a harrowing road trip. When something good happens and you have no one to share the news with at home, you have to phone your friends and trumpet it yourself, if you want to tell someone. Travelling alone is both more of an adventure and a reminder of one's vulnerability. I sometimes miss the enterprise of marriage, the feeling that I'm not alone against the world. And while some people know the health issues that can come with the stress of being alone, many are in denial of them, only recognizing the toll of their single status when they're in a new relationship or remarried. A woman I know in her seventies who was widowed had terrible back pain, requiring her to use a cane. When she remarried, the pain subsided and the cane was put away.

⁓

In the backlash against the divorce culture, which has grown in recent years, there is reason for pause about the decision to split. The reflection that provokes regret is healthy, I think. It's good to acknowledge what you've lost, and the opportunities the marriage may have still held, if you had stayed in it. A marriage, when managed well, encourages the participants to be introspective enough to understand how their personality traits may be contributing to problems in the relationship. Often when people divorce, they are choosing to leave because they are unable (and unwilling) to address an aspect of themselves, some experts say. Divorce, in these cases, closes a door on that part of a person as he or she blames the other for all the problems—resulting in a separation that is not about self-expression, as many think, but about self-denial.

It's also normal to feel some sadness for what you once had. That will always be present. I spoke to a woman who told me that unexpected grief ambushed her long after her divorce, when she read the obituary of her former spouse, whom she had not seen in twenty years. They had no children to keep them in touch and had parted amicably. He had remarried. "It's a paradox between the intimacy and the distance I had in his life," she said. "I had been a participant in his life, but then I became an outsider in his life."

And the outsider, such as the ex-wife, often goes unac-knowledged in the obituary. "Just as the victors get to write history, the current spouse gets to write the obituary," she noted ruefully. What she was feeling—"the first cousin of widowhood," she said of her state—is what counsellors call "disenfranchised grief."

Purer is grief when there is deep love between the deceased and those left behind. After divorce we're trying to work out unresolved issues, resentment and guilt can arise, and second-ary emotions can hamper the expression of sorrow. It's why I encourage my boys, now that they're adults, to talk to their father about aspects of his behaviour that may upset them. I don't want them wishing they could have made peace with him should he die before they have the chance. The woman who contacted me about mourning her long-ago ex told me that she had had "a fantasy that one day with perspective, we would sit down over coffee and talk about what happened in our marriage. Part of the pain I feel is that I won't have that opportunity. It's about unfinished conversations." Divorce, she has realized, is "a quick getaway" that leaves many loose emotional ends.

The bond with an ex never completely fades, as much as we might wish it would. Divorce ends a marriage, not a relationship, however distant. It's a psychic bond, even when you didn't have children together. You get a Godiva choco-late and you think, "Oh, Bill used to give me those." Grief counsellors advise people who feel disenfranchised from the mourning rituals to pay some observance of their own, by lighting a candle, writing a note, or attending the gravesite at a later date.

Hard as regret and grief may be, I like to think that if you had not embraced the relationship in the first place, you would be poorer in experience. You might regret never having taken a chance. Being divorced may mean failure, but it also suggests a willingness to take an emotional risk. The decision to marry is always a leap of faith. The clouds don't part to give you a sign from above that this is what you must do. Almost everything we do is a decision, and all carry consequences.

We take a job, and wonder if we should have waited for a better one. We quit one over a disagreement, and regret our rush to judgment. We decide to have children, and make ourselves vulnerable, because if anything happened to them, we would never be the same. When we decide to marry, we invite a collision of emotions. There's no free pass on guilt and regret. Married couples, too, wonder if they've harmed their children with their behaviour. As a mother myself, I can't imagine that any parent doesn't have some doubt about how he or she raised the children. And maybe when one partner has died or when they're old together, entrenched in a dysfunctional pattern, they wish they had put in the effort, earlier, to make their union better. If they stay together and are unhappy, they may regret never having taken the risk to divorce. They may have financial security, but mourn their forfeited happiness. Someone told me that her mother-in-law was having the time of her life at seventy-five, because her husband of fifty years had died. "Their marriage was a disaster, but they stuck it out," she said. "Only now is she really enjoying herself."

I think of Anne Morrow Lindbergh at Smith all those years ago and realize how hard her life must have been. When she met her future husband, Charles Lindbergh, he was "an extraordinary man, not like any man I had met before," she told us. But she did not divulge the secrets of her marriage. Only after her death in 2001 was it revealed that Charles Lindbergh had led a double life. He had fathered seven children by three other women in Europe for a total of thirteen. When she spoke at Smith in 1978, Morrow Lindbergh had been widowed for four years. It is unclear how much she knew of her husband's secret families at that time. There was a great dignity about her, and a certain self-containment. "Woman must come of age by herself . . . she must find her true centre alone," she had written in *Gift from the Sea*, a philosophy she repeated to us that night on campus. Maybe that's how she coped. By keeping whatever she knew or suspected to herself, she alone knew herself and the sacrifices she'd made, the hardships she had endured. She had made her choices.

Similarly, when we divorce, a host of alternative possibilities haunt us. What if we hadn't had children so soon? What if he hadn't taken that job, if we hadn't moved to another city? What if we hadn't bought that house? Would we have avoided the stress that contributed to the end of the marriage? For older single women, the worry about financial well-being in retirement can be frightening, prompting them to wish they had clung to the security of marriage. Deirdre Bair wrote about the "worldwide phenomenon" of divorce in later life. People live longer and are healthier than they were generations ago, she pointed out. Bair documented numerous stories of couples in their sixties who woke up one morning and decided they couldn't go on together. But when I spoke to her, in the spring of 2009, she admitted that many of the women she knew who had divorced after lengthy marriages were expressing doubts now about their decisions. "I don't know that it's real regret," she explained. "But it's 'Gosh, maybe I should have perhaps slowed down and looked at things carefully before I did it.'"

Divorce may bring relief, but we must accept responsibility for the pain we inflict on ourselves and others. Even those parents who divorce when their children have grown, thinking that they're sparing them anguish, are not absolved of guilt. They may pride themselves on having stayed together for the children, but ask any adult child of divorce if he or she didn't feel hurt. The answer will be no. The answer may even be that it was worse. They question their parents' marriage. They wonder what part was real and what part was put on. They have to rethink their childhood.

Like many, I have spent moments thinking about the forks in the road of my life. I have wondered why I didn't hesitate over the decision to leave England, for example, and come back to Canada. I would never have met my husband. Maybe I would be living in a cottage in the Cotswolds or in a London flat with a small stone garden out back. I imagine other futures I could have had. And sometimes I think about when I did meet my husband and how, if I had been a bit more cautious with him, and a bit more sure of myself and what I wanted, I might have chosen not to get romantically involved. I might have said no when he gave me the marriage ultimatum. I might have said, "Let's just see. I can't say yes now." I might have stood firm on my own ground, listened to my inner voice.

These thoughts can feel like tiny, niggling regrets—yes, fine, I admit it. I would be lying if I said I don't sometimes rewind my life and think about what might have happened if I'd made a different choice at a certain point along the way. But the exercise never gives me any pleasure. It makes me feel bad, as though I have wasted my life and what it could have been. And of course, anything I entertain as an alternative married life is only a projection—not real. And in my fanciful mind, it's always better than what I had, not the same, not worse. It's like when I say that I sometimes feel I was born in the wrong era and that I would prefer to have lived in Edwardian times. Yeah, well, that's because I imagine life as a lady in a nice London house with beautiful bustled gowns, my long hair twisted on the top of my head. I never imagine myself as a scullery maid.

Still, I am unafraid to live with these regrets. That's why I mention them. They make me stronger. They make me focus on what was, and is, good. I realize that for all the difficult events my choices have invited into my life, they are outnumbered by the delightful ones that they made possible too. My beautiful children. My awakening. My career.

I have left any anger about Eric and my divorce behind. We all start with it. Anger is a primal, knee-jerk reaction when others hurt us. We feel like victims, and maybe rightly so. But it's a toxic place to stay. Not only is it limiting, precluding other, brighter emotions, it keeps you rooted in the past. Prolonged anger hurts the person who holds on to it more than the one at whom it is directed. I prefer disappointment. Something didn't work out as I thought it would. That's all.

But if I have shed anger, it doesn't mean that I have replaced it with forgiveness. There are some things you cannot forgive, despite the culture's encouragement to do so. We love the idea of pulling the white blanket of forgiveness over other people's wrongdoings, even our own. It's like the grace of that snowfall last year when I stood in my house all alone on New Year's. It erased things. But for it to be cathartic, the people you're hoping to forgive need to listen to your feeling of being hurt. It has to be an intimate act, not just something you hand over because you're told to. It's a gift that must be earned, I suppose.

I think it's quite beautiful, learning to live with disappointment. In mid-life, if we're honest, we all have a bit of it, somewhere. Nothing ever quite works out exactly as you want, not in every way. Sometimes it works out better than you imagined—true. But we spend so much of our lives thinking that it will be perfect when we're just that bit richer, or thinner, or when we're married or when we're divorced. It is not about perfection though. When I am in a retrospective mood, I tell myself that life is a carnival of choices, good and bad, wise and regrettable, designed not to teach us pride in ourselves for engineering whatever successes we may have, but humility in acceptance of how it happened to unfold.

From my window in the seat of mid-life post-divorce, I look out on a landscape of light and dark, a patchwork that makes me glad to have come here.

Epilogue

A plane in mid-flight is like the island in *The Tempest*. Things get resolved there. Sitting in one, as I am now, I fall into charmed suspension. I'm between places. No one can find me here. I'm disconnected. Time is scrambled. Others can only imagine me as I can only imagine them, where they are and what they're doing. And it seems that even if a tragedy occurs, if the plane plummets to the ground, the horror of it will happen just to me and others on the plane, not to those I have left behind. Poof—gone! I am in a place of self-containment, as intimate and private as the breath my yoga teacher reminds me to feel.

It is the start of the year, yet another one. I have left Nick and Luke in Ireland. After Christmas in Sussex, I had taken the two boys to Ireland, so we could spend a week there over

New Year's and now I'm going home. I wanted to see Nick's university, and his living arrangements, which he had organized on his own in the fall. Luke's plans are to stay there for a while and then continue his travels with the money he had made in London. In the summer, he will return to Canada and attend university in the fall. I had researched where to go in Ireland's southwest, never having travelled there myself. I found a bed and breakfast in Dingle Town on the Dingle Peninsula, where we stayed for four days. I was nervous about whether they would want to spend a holiday with their mother, and whether I could make it fun on my limited resources. It was the first holiday we had spent together, on our own, since the divorce.

I needn't have worried. The drive to Dingle Town was beautiful and easy, with the boys taking turns in the front seat to be the navigator and reminding me to drive on the left side and helping me enter and exit the roundabouts. The countryside sped by like a lovely film, a panorama of rugged coastline and wide, steep fields dotted with white sheep and ringed with low stone fences. In town, we went to pubs for lunches, and always at night. The music scene in Dingle Town is raucous, and the boys took easily to playing snooker with the locals.

One night, at a pub that doubles as a hardware store during the day, we were sitting drinking our pints of Guinness, when a man sidled up beside me to strike up a conversation.

He was from Dublin, he said. Dingle Town is the place to be for New Year's, he informed us. I introduced my boys. Twenty minutes later, my sons and I excused ourselves to go down the street to the pub where live musicians were playing.

"He was trying to pick you up, Mom," Nick said.

"Oh, come on."

"He was. He told you within five minutes of the conversation that he was divorced. I heard him," he said.

We laughed. My boys are now my wingmen, my protectors. In the next pub, we settled in a corner.

"Look," Luke said about half an hour later.

"What?"

"That guy from that other place."

The pub was crowded with people standing in the low-ceilinged room. But over by the bar, I spied him too: the man from Dublin. He was behind a newspaper.

"The Lurker. Beware the Lurker, Mom," Luke teased in a spooky voice, bugging his eyes at me in the low light.

On New Year's Eve, we had gone on a similar pub crawl. There are many bars in the town, each with its own peculiar charm. The boys and I drank like the locals, passing beer over the heads of others, squashed into crowds that were made up of young and old. Tait called Nick's cell phone at ten o'clock our time from Alberta to wish us all a happy new year. Nick and Luke thought of their father at one point, wondering where he was and what he might be doing.

"He loves you," I reminded them. "He's just a complicated person."

"Yeah," said Nick. "Very complicated."

We'd been told several days earlier that half an hour before midnight, a band would gather outside one of the pubs by the waterfront. It was tradition: a few locals come out with their drums and flutes to lead a crowd through the narrow streets to the main crossroads, where a digital countdown is projected onto the wall of a building. We joined them in the damp night, bundled up, laughing. Along the streets, people opened their doors or leaned out of their windows to greet the passing revellers. Outside every pub, there was a spill of people, unable to fit inside. On the steps of the church at the top of the hill, the priest and the curate shook the hands of anyone who approached them.

By the time the parade reached the centre of town, the street was blocked with people. We stood crushed together as the countdown started. And at the stroke of midnight, we hugged, kissed on the cheeks. People cheered.

An hour later, I returned to the B&B, leaving the boys in a pub, where they stayed until the wee hours. As I walked home, I saw couples hugging in the darkness, kissing. But this time, this year, when I got back to the room I crawled into my bed, content.

"You can take a back seat now, Mom," Nick had told me a few nights earlier, when I expressed some silly maternal concerns about each one of them. "Don't worry about us. We're all fine. Just relax, and watch what your boys do."

That night, in my bed, I felt optimistic, full of promise. And I think my frame of mind had something to do with witnessing how my children had grown, even in the last year, how their lives had expanded with new people, experiences, opportunities. As they move into what lies ahead and leave me behind, leave me feeling like a long-distance runner who sees those who have been following her come up parallel and then pull ahead, I have to believe in a benevolent future. They are my children. I love them. I have to believe that good things are there for them, waiting. Otherwise, I would be fearful. I would want to hold them back. And if I can believe that for them, then I can believe it for myself too.

A day later, we were driving around the narrow road that circled the outer reaches of the Dingle Peninsula. It was cold, but without rain. "Shall we stop here?"

"Sure," they said.

"Look." I pointed to a beach far below the road. "I think that's it," I said, recognizing the spot from a photograph. Dingle is a place of spare landscapes, lush with magic. We had stopped at several points to gaze at the endless coastline and the living, breathing clouds overhead, skidding across the sky, spitting, gathering, rumbling, and then separating— briefly, suddenly—to let a finger of sunshine touch the skin of the sea.

At our B&B, there was a map showing places of interest for tourists: the ruins of a fortress, prehistoric beehive structures. The location of a movie shot over forty years ago was the most recent. It happened in the last century at least—an indication, should any visitor need a reminder, that not much happens here. Slea Head—its long, sandy beach, the cliffs and the barren landscape—was the backdrop for many scenes in *Ryan's Daughter*, a sweeping saga about marriage and adultery. Directed by David Lean, the film featured the western shore of Ireland as a character almost as captivating as the village idiot, played by John Mills.

We parked. Luke grabbed his camera. The wind was brisk.

"Want to go for a hike?"

We pulled up the collars of our coats and walked toward the sea, away from the beach to the highest and farthest point to the west.

The hill was steep. At the bottom, on the rocks, lay rusted remains of a ship's hull. "Come on, this way," Nick said, climbing over a fence. We walked in the narrow footpath of sheep, who looked up at us curiously. Rabbits leapt from clumps of peat and thick grass. Birds wheeled overhead.

The sea was grey and rough. Around a corner, facing due west, we decided to rest. Just off the land are the Blaskets, a small chain of steep, green islands, abandoned by human inhabitants in the 1950s.

"Remember how we used to have Memory Number One when we were kids?" Nick asked after a few minutes.

It was a tradition I had started when we went to the Caribbean on a family holiday one winter. Nick and Tait were curled up beside me in a hammock under the shade of a tree. They were about five and four years old. Luke, one and a half, was down for a nap. I was reading E.B. White's *Stuart Little* to the older boys, one chapter per sitting. Looking up from the page, I said, "Remember this picture in your mind. Look at the palm tree swaying against the blue sky. The hammock. The book we are reading. Let's call this Memory Number One, and when we're back in Toronto, in the middle of winter, in the snow, we can say, 'Memory Number One,' and we will remember how warm and beautiful it was."

The idea had worked. "What's Memory Number One?" I would ask when they were in the back of the van in their cumbersome snowsuits. And one of them would immediately recall the image. Since then, on other holidays, we had fixed memories in our minds, all of which we can recall to this day.

"Let's say this is Memory Number One from Ireland," Nick said.

He was seated just in front of me, perched on a rock, his coat up around his ears, his hoodie over his head. Luke was behind me, bent into the wind. We all stared out to sea, into the wildness and the beauty.

"Okay," I said. "Memory Number One."

I close my eyes now, high up over the Atlantic, and see the scene again.

Many people, including several of my friends, often tell me that all the well-intentioned philosophy about disappointment is fine and dandy but that it can never take the place of a loving partner. Romantic love is *sine qua non*. Perhaps that's true. As if to underscore that belief, many stories such as this one end with a new love interest. There should be a man, dressed preferably in a thick wool cable-knit sweater, jeans and boots, who walks unexpectedly into the protagonist's life to sweep her off her feet and into a rosy future. (The Lurker, just for the record, was dressed in tweed and wreathed in *eau-de*-Guinness.) It's what we expect. We fetishize marriage—still. It's an organizing principle of society, so we mark how others and ourselves fit based on our marital status. But I am not sure how many of us get to know the kind of monogamous romantic love that we think is our right, that we imagine to be promised to all. It is rare. I think our idea of love is too narrow, too literal—too unimaginative.

Manifestations of love are everywhere, if you're aware of them, many of them more enduring, more pure, more unconditional than the kind we have with a partner; yet all of them undersold.

I rest my head back on the seat, open my eyes again, look out the plane window into air. My mind fills with the faces of the people I know, have loved and love: those who are living, those who have died, and those who have disappeared from my life. I think of people I have yet to love—partners of my children, grandchilren maybe. Words, expressions, gestures, scenes— they're all there, when I conjure them. We're all points in time and space, the connections between us strong, invisible to the eye, building a strange, magical architecture that rises up, grounding us, sheltering us, and holding us aloft.

Prologue

Pg. 6: Least marriageable individuals are MLWs: "Among the divorced, the least marriageable in our society are older women, highly educated who make a good salary." Dr. Francesca Adler-Baeder of the National Resource Centre at Auburn University, quoted in "In Your Fifties, Looking for Love," *The New York Times* (Sept. 12, 2009).

Chapter 1—My Mother Wore Lipstick in the Chevy

Pg. 23: Joan Didion, *The Year of Magical Thinking* (New York: Random House, 2005).

Pg. 26: Imago Relationship Theory. Books, educational and workshop information at site of founder, Harville Hendrix: www.harvillehendrix.com.

Pg. 29: Interview with Helen Gurley Brown, the Hampson Interview, *The Globe and Mail* (Nov. 9, 2002).

Chapter 2—What the Feminists Forgot to Teach Us

Pg. 41: The wife identity: Anne Kingston, *The Meaning of Wife:*

A Provocative Look at Women and Marriage in the Twenty-First Century (New York: HarperCollins, 2004).

Pg. 42: "a lot of unlived woman's life in me": Speech by Anne Morrow Lindberg, Smith College, Northampton, MA (Apr. 1978).

Pg. 43: "What does a woman need to know, to become a self-conscious, self-defining human being?": Speech by Adrienne Rich, Smith College, Northampton, MA (May 1979).

Chapter 3—Love Conquers All, Doesn't It?

Pg. 55: "the disease to please": Interview with Jane Fonda, author of *My Life So Far* (New York: Random House, 2005), the Hampson Interview, *The Globe and Mail* (Apr. 23, 2005).

Chapter 4—Losing and Gaining Selves

Pg. 58: Women always feel the internal pressure to be perfect: Dalma Heyn, *Marriage Shock: The Transformation of Women into Wives* (New York: Bantam Doubleday Dell Publishing Group, 1997).

Pg. 59: "I feel if I had the role of wife . . .": Oprah Winfrey, quoted on *The Tonight Show with Jay Leno* (NBC, Feb. 2003).

Pg. 60: "When you get together with someone and decide to make them . . .": Interview with J.M. Kearns, author of *Better Love Next Time: How the Relationship that Didn't Last Can Lead You to the One that Will* (Toronto: John Wiley & Sons Inc., 2009), Generation Ex, *The Globe and Mail* (Aug. 21, 2009).

Pg. 60: "I am imperfect in many ways . . .": Elizabeth Edwards, *Resilience: Reflections on the Burdens and Gifts of Facing Life's Adversities* (New York: Broadway Books, 2009).

Pg. 62: "My name is my identity": Measha Brueggergosman, quoted in Generation Ex, *The Globe and Mail* (Sept. 20, 2007).

Pg. 62: "I can't rail against oppression I've never experienced": Kelly Grant, *National Post* (Sept. 15, 2007).

Pg. 62: "I never suspected that as a man . . .": Josiah Neufeld, Facts & Arguments, *The Globe and Mail* (July 27, 2009).

Pg. 70: "I found it tremendously satisfying to give completely of oneself . . .": Speech by Anne Morrow Lindberg, Smith College, Northampton, MA (Apr. 1978).

Chapter 5—The Hamlet Years: To Divorce or Not to Divorce?

Pg. 76: How Mike Todd told Evelyn Keyes he wanted a divorce: Evelyn Keyes obituary, *The Globe and Mail* (July 2008).

Pg. 76: "We were making love, and we were in the missionary position . . .": Quoted in Generation Ex, *The Globe and Mail* (May 24, 2007).

Pg. 80: "we can be very strong and very weak . . .": Interview with Jane Fonda, the Hampson Interview, *The Globe and Mail* (Apr. 23, 2005).

Pg. 81: "an expression of rage": Barry Rich, Toronto marriage therapist, quoted in Generation Ex, *The Globe and Mail* (Nov. 8, 2007).

Pg. 87: "All of us are better when we're loved": Alistair MacLeod, *No Great Mischief* (Toronto: McClelland & Stewart Ltd., 2000).

Chapter 6—The Colossus Generation

Pg. 89: "I didn't want to burden them . . .": Quoted in Generation Ex, *The Globe and Mail* (Mar. 19, 2009).

Pg. 90: divorce as an unfortunate outcome of contemporary consumerist culture: Interview with Mark O'Connell, author of *The Marriage Benefit: The Surprising Rewards of Staying Together in Midlife* (New York: Springboard Press, 2008), Generation Ex, *The Globe and Mail* (Oct. 2, 2008).

Pg. 90: "Marriage is a journey . . .": Quoted in Generation Ex, *The Globe and Mail* (Oct. 2, 2008).

Pg. 91: "What you need is a divorce": Quoted in Generation Ex, *The Globe and Mail* (Mar. 19, 2009).

Pg. 91: Husbands are often in a quandary: Interview with Neil Chethik, author of *VoiceMale: What Husbands Really Think About Their Marriages, Their Wives, Sex, Housework and Commitment* (New York: Simon & Schuster, 2006), Generation Ex, *The Globe and Mail* (Sept. 4, 2009).

Pg. 92: "It sure surprised me": Quoted in Generation Ex, *The Globe and Mail* (July 5, 2007).

Pg. 92: becoming a man is a status that requires proof of competency: Interview with Neil Chethik, Generation Ex, *The Globe and Mail* (Sept. 4, 2009).

Pg. 92: the shift has created problems for women too: Interview with Carin Rubenstein, author of *The Superior Wife Syndrome: Why Women Do Everything So Well and Why—For the Sake of Our Marriages—We've Got to Stop* (New York: Simon & Schuster, 2009), Generation Ex, *The Globe and Mail* (Sept. 4, 2009).

Pg. 93: Abuse (physical or verbal) cited as major cause for divorce: Poll results from Gfk Roper Custom Research North America, commissioned for divorce360.com (2007).

Chapter 7—Destination: Splitsville

Pg. 101: A U.S. study of grown children of divorce: Institute for American Values, National Survey of Grown Children of Divorce (2005).

Pg. 101: Pro-marriage advocates argue that while children can rise to the occasion of their parents' divorce, they lose their childhoods: Elizabeth Marquardt, *Between Two Worlds: The*

Inner Lives of Children of Divorce (New York: Three Rivers Press, 2005).

Pg. 102: stepfamilies will soon outnumber any other kind: Interview with Wednesday Martin, author of *Stepmonsters: A New Look at Why Real Stepmothers Think, Feel and Act the Way We Do* (Orlando: Houghton Mifflin Harcourt, 2009), Generation Ex, *The Globe and Mail* (May 28, 2009).

Pg. 102: The conflict during a marriage can impact children as much as divorce: Discussed by E. Mavis Hetherington and John Kelly, *For Better or For Worse: Divorce Reconsidered* (New York: W. W. Norton & Company, 2002).

Pg. 102: "Divorce was one of the best things that happened to me": Max Sindell, author of *The Bright Side: Surviving Your Parents' Divorce* (Deerfield, FL: HCI Books, 2007), quoted in Generation Ex, *The Globe and Mail* (Mar. 20, 2008).

Pg. 103: Children don't need to be told that divorce sucks: Interview with Richard Warshak, author of *Divorce Poison: Protecting the Parent–Child Bond from a Vindictive Ex* (New York: Harper, 2003), Generation Ex, *The Globe and Mail* (Mar. 20, 2008).

Pg. 103: Divorced Kids' Bill of Rights: Sindell, *The Bright Side*.

Pg. 109: "Marital Biography and Health at Mid-life," article about the impact of marriage, divorce, widowhood and remarriage on health, co-authored by Linda Waite, sociologist at the University of Chicago, and Mary Elizabeth Hughes, assistant professor at Johns Hopkins' Bloomberg School of Public Health (July 2009).

Chapter 8—Un-marriage Ceremonies

Pg. 111: "veil brain": Interview with Lou Paget, Generation Ex, *The Globe and Mail* (Jan. 3, 2008).

Pg. 111: Divorce Ceremonies: Celebrant USA Foundation & Institute, www.celebrantinstitute.org.

Pg. 112: Suggestion of songs at divorce parties and gifts: Christine Gallagher, resources on her website: www.divorcepartyplanner.com.

Pg. 112: Cathy Gordon, performance artist, *On My Knees: A Public Divorce Ceremony*, reported on www.cathygordon.com.

Pg. 112: My favourite un-marriage ceremony is that of Shanna Moakler . . . : Mark Gray, "Inside Shanna Moakler's Las Vegas Divorce Party," www.people.com (Nov. 4, 2006).

Pg. 114: Sharon Hay, feng shui specialist, quoted in Generation Ex, *The Globe and Mail* (Aug. 7, 2007).

Pg. 114: "I don't want any of it": Quoted in Generation Ex, *The Globe and Mail* (Aug. 7, 2007).

Chapter 9—Ghost Dad

Pg. 121: "the one who was the single most constant in my life": Barack Obama, Preface, *Dreams from My Father: A Story of Race and Inheritance* (New York: Three Rivers Press, 2004).

Pg. 123: "You know when you love someone . . .": Sam Berns, quoted in Generation Ex, *The Globe and Mail* (July 24, 2009).

Pg. 126: Discussion about fathers remaining involved with children after divorce: The "Binuclear Family Study," a landmark longitudinal study of family relationships after divorce by Constance Ahrons. Used as the basis for her book *The Good Divorce: Keeping Your Family Together When Your Marriage Falls Apart* (New York: Harper, 1995).

Pg. 126: "The kids would come on a Friday night . . .": Ian Harvey, quoted in Generation Ex, *The Globe and Mail* (Feb. 28, 2008).

Pg. 127: "You can't have a conversation with [children] if they're staring at a tiger": Father quoted in Generation Ex, *The Globe and Mail* (Feb. 28, 2008).

Pg. 127: "The child has a deep longing . . .": Eckhart Tolle, *A New Earth: Awakening to Your Life's Purpose* (New York: Dutton Adult, 2005).

Pg. 127: "It's difficult for men to express their hurt": Calvin Sandborn, author of *Becoming the Kind Father: A Son's Journey* (Gabriola Island, BC: New Society Publishers, 2007), quoted in Generation Ex, *The Globe and Mail* (Jan. 17, 2008).

Chapter 10—When the Veil Finally Lifts

Pg. 135: Greg Behrendt and Liz Tuccillo, *He's Just Not That Into You* (New York: Simon & Schuster, 2004).

Pg. 136: Statistics Canada, National Population Health Survey, "Depression in Men After Marriage Break-up" (May 2007).

Pg. 137: "It's a good thing to not be trapped by marriage . . .": Interview with Sascha Rothchild, author of *How to Get Divorced by 30: My Misguided Attempt at a Starter Marriage* (New York: Plume, 2010), Generation Ex, *The Globe and Mail* (Nov. 27, 2008).

Pg. 139: "One of the first things older men say . . .": Quoted in Generation Ex, *The Globe and Mail* (Feb. 19, 2009).

Pg. 141: Now when it [my heart] speaks, I take note: Paraphrase of "When the heart speaks, take notes," a quotation used by Greg Mortenson, co-author (with David Oliver Relin) of *Three Cups of Tea: One Man's Mission to Promote Peace . . . One School at a Time* (New York: Viking, 2006).

Pg. 141: Hormones didn't help to clarify its [the heart's] messages . . . : Louann Brizendine, *The Female Brain* (New York: Random House, 2007).

Pg. 141: "It's the oxytocin, stupid": Carole Radziwill, author of

What Remains: A Memoir of Fate, Friendship and Love (New York: Scribner, 2005), in *The New York Times* (June 2007).

Chapter 11—Emotional Flu

Pg. 144: Jessica Kerwin, "The Magic Touch," *Vogue* (Sept. 2007).

Pg. 146: "It's a tough honesty gig": Mary Tomlinson, quoted in Generation Ex, *The Globe and Mail* (Sept. 13, 2007).

Pg. 147: "To outsiders or to her occasionally unforgiving friends . . .": David Gilmour, *The Film Club: A True Story of a Father and a Son* (Markham, ON: Thomas Allen Publishers, 2007).

Pg. 148: "Marriage makes you feel that you have taken care of something in your life": Quoted in Generation Ex, *The Globe and Mail* (July 19, 2007).

Pg. 149: "We're a team": Anne Mirvish recalling what her late husband, Ed Mirvish, said on their previous anniversary, *Toronto Star* (July 2007).

Pg. 150: "You have to learn to live with a certain degree of unknowingness": Quoted in Generation Ex, *The Globe and Mail* (May 24, 2007).

Pg. 151: Leonard Cohen interview; some material appeared in the *Globe and Mail* (May 26, 2007).

Chapter 12—Tulips in the Spring Are More Reliable

Pg. 164: Gail Sheehy, *Sex and the Seasoned Woman* (New York: Random House, 2006).

Pg. 164: "profundity of his erection": Sarah Hampson, "You Go, Girl," *The Globe and Mail* (May 13, 2006).

Pg. 166: Interview with Joan Sewell, author of *I'd Rather Eat Chocolate: Learning to Love My Low Libido* (New York: Broadway Books, 2007), Generation Ex, *The Globe and Mail* (June 21, 2007).

Pg. 167: "One of the most common things I hear from my pregnant friends . . .": Quotation about married sex lives from reader of Generation Ex. Subsequently quoted in Generation Ex, *The Globe and Mail* (June 21, 2007).

Pg. 167: "I had had maybe two lovers before him . . .": Quotation about married sex from reader of Generation Ex. Subsequently quoted in Generation Ex, *The Globe and Mail* (June 21, 2007).

Pg. 167: more than 20 million Americans live in sexless marriages . . . : Widely quoted survey result, backed by sexologist Bob Berkowitz and writer wife, Susan Yager-Berkowitz, as reported by *Good Morning America* (ABC News, Feb. 2009).

Chapter 13—The Dating Pool Is Very Shallow

Pg. 172: "I have always been cute. I am fit": Interview with Joan Price, author of *Better than I Ever Expected: Straight Talk About Sex After Sixty* (New York: Seal, 2005), Generation Ex, *The Globe and Mail* (Jan. 22, 2009).

Pg. 175: "It was in broad daylight": Quoted in Generation Ex, *The Globe and Mail* (Oct. 16, 2008).

Pg. 176: "Do not underestimate your confidence": Sarah Hampson, "You Go, Girl," *The Globe and Mail* (May 13, 2006).

Pg. 176: "Let's conjugate the verb *to come*": Quoted in Generation Ex, *The Globe and Mail* (Oct. 16, 2008).

Pg. 176: Best to see a man as icing to your cake: Some advice on how to date in mid-life from Judith Sills, *Getting Naked Again: Dating, Romance, Sex and Love When You've Been Divorced, Widowed, Dumped or Distracted* (New York: Springboard Press, 2009).

Pg. 177: "It's quite liberating": Quoted in Generation Ex, *The Globe and Mail* (Sept. 25, 2007).

Pg. 177: "An erection has no conscience": Quoted in Generation Ex, *The Globe and Mail* (Jan. 10, 2008).

Pg. 177: Maureen Dowd, *Are Men Necessary? When Sexes Collide* (New York: Berkley Trade, 2006).

Pg. 179: "The skirt stays": Generation Ex, *The Globe and Mail* (Jan. 15, 2009).

Pg. 179: "When I was younger these were just not the kind of conversations . . .": Quoted in Generation Ex, *The Globe and Mail* (Oct. 16, 2008).

Pg. 181: "Younger women are sperm foraging": Quoted in Generation Ex, *The Globe and Mail* (Nov. 29, 2007).

Pg. 183: "Hello? I have them, too": Quoted in Generation Ex, *The Globe and Mail* (Jan. 31, 2008).

Pg. 183: "We got to talking about this and that": Quoted in Generation Ex, *The Globe and Mail* (Nov. 29, 2007).

Chapter 14—Living Happily with My Bitch Wrinkle

Pg. 188: Maintenance is a "finger in the dike" . . . : Nora Ephron, *I Feel Bad About My Neck: And Other Thoughts on Being a Woman* (New York: Random House, 2006).

Pg. 190: "Just the feeling that I've earned the right not to": Interview with Ted Danson, the Hamspon Interview, *The Globe and Mail* (May 19, 2008).

Pg. 192: The gludgeons are the loose skin in the flabby armpit: *Vogue* Age-less issue (Aug. 2008).

Pg. 197: "If you're fifty and trying to look thirty . . .": Evie Gorenstein, mycustomtailor.com.

Pg. 197: "You have to cut open a redwood tree to know how old it is . . .": Nora Ephron, *I Feel Bad About My Neck*.

Pg. 197: Interview with Mireille Guiliano, author of *French Women*

Don't Get Fat: The Secret of Eating for Pleasure (New York: Vintage, 2007), the Hampson Interview, *The Globe and Mail* (May 28, 2005).

Pg. 198: We will remember that a fiftysomething man said that men who like MLWs . . .: Sarah Hampson, "You Go, Girl," *The Globe and Mail* (May 13, 2006).

Pg. 199: "If I pursued perfection, I'd have a facelift": Interview with Jane Fonda, *The Globe and Mail* (Apr. 23, 2005).

Pg. 199: "I would rather have a good chimera light . . .": Shirley MacLaine, the Hampson Interview, *The Globe and Mail* (Sept. 15, 2008).

Pg. 199: "like a vampire bat disturbed in mid-dinner": Diana Athill, *Somewhere Towards the End* (London: Granta, 2008).

Pg. 201: "Do you think you're a great beauty?": Interview with Nora Ephron, "The Older Woman," *The New York Times* (May 6, 2007).

Pg. 201: "It's because of my vanity and my pride . . .": Kristin Scott Thomas, quoted in *New York Times Magazine* (Aug. 2009).

Chapter 15—Vows of an Ex-Wife

Pg. 210: "Please let us not interfere with the other's work or play": Amelia Earhart, *The Fun of It: Random Records of My Own Flying and of Women in Aviation* (Chicago: Academy Chicago Publishers, 1932).

Pg. 210: Women and finances: Interview with Barbara Stanny, author of *Prince Charming Isn't Coming* (New York: Penguin, 2007), Currency column, "Nice Girls Don't Get Raises" by Sarah Hampson, *The Globe and Mail* (July 7, 2009).

Pg. 211: I allowed myself to slip out of that "nice girl" identity: Interview with Sara Laschever, co-author (with Linda Babcock) of *Ask for It: How Women Can Use the Power of Negotiation to Get What They Really Want* (New York: Bantam, 2009), Currency column,

"Nice Girls Don't Get Raises" by Sarah Hampson, *The Globe and Mail* (July 7, 2009).

Pg. 215: "I didn't know how much your heart is expanded as a mother": Interview with Rosanne Cash, the Hampson Interview, *The Globe and Mail* (Apr. 26, 2003).

Pg. 215: "Alimony is like being married": Jessica Cherniak, quoted in Generation Ex, *The Globe and Mail* (Sept. 25, 2007).

Pg. 217: "There are cases where women cry wolf . . .": Quoted in Generation Ex, *The Globe and Mail* (Nov. 13, 2008).

Pg. 218: "Work is what we're made for": Interview with Ruth Reichl, the Hampson Interview, *The Globe and Mail* (May 11, 2009).

Pg. 218: "When you're young, you give yourself obligations . . .": Interview with Isabella Rossellini (interviewed by Johanna Schneller), *The Globe and Mail* (Sept. 12, 2009).

Chapter 16—Neighbouring Solitudes

Pg. 222: "We shocked ourselves": Gloria Steinem, interview with CBS *Sunday Morning* (CBS News, Jan. 2006).

Pg. 222: "John is very rational": Interview with Rosanne Cash, the Hampson Interview, *The Globe and Mail* (Apr. 26, 2003).

Pg. 224: "We certainly didn't get married to have children": Marlene Hore, quoted in Generation Ex, *The Globe and Mail* (Jan. 22, 2009).

Pg. 225: "This dashing, silver-haired man walked into my line-dancing class . . .": Interview with Joan Price, Generation Ex, *The Globe and Mail* (Jan. 22, 2009).

Pg. 226: "Somewhere in the back of my head . . .": Interview with Joe Flaherty, *SCTV* comedian, the Hampson Interview, *The Globe and Mail* (July 24, 2004).

Pg. 228: "I asked Greg if he wanted me to wear . . .": Chris Evert, *Vogue* Age-less issue (Aug. 2008).

Pg. 229: "I think I was, a long time ago": Interview with Anne Carson, the Hampson Interview, *The Globe and Mail* (Sept. 14, 2000).

Chapter 17—Lessons in Love

Pg. 234: "I haven't ruled out the hope . . .": Daphne Merkin, "Memoirs of an Ex-Bride," *The Bitch in the House: 26 Women Tell the Truth About Sex, Solitude, Work, Motherhood and Marriage*, edited by Cathi Hanauer (New York: HarperCollins, 2002).

Pg. 235: "I married the man I married because . . .": Lynn Darling, "For Better and Worse," *Esquire* (May 1, 1996).

Pg. 238: Sex as communication of a man's vulnerability: Interview with Lou Paget, Generation Ex, *The Globe and Mail* (June 7, 2007).

Pg. 239: Shared housework as important factor in happy marriage: Pew Research, Survey about modern marriage (July 2007).

Pg. 240: "I'm learning to see marriage . . .": Phil Reinders, Generation Ex, *The Globe and Mail* (Oct. 11, 2007).

Chapter 18—In the Ring of My Own Light

Pg. 247: "it took me several years of such periods . . .": M.F.K. Fisher, quoted in *Alone in the Kitchen with an Eggplant: Confessions of Cooking for One and Dining Alone*, edited by Jenni Ferrari-Adler (New York: Riverhead, 2007).

Pg. 249: "I always say it was because I was angry . . .": Pema Chodron, *When Things Fall Apart: Heart Advice for Difficult Times* (Boston: Shambhala Publications, 1997).

Pg. 250: "It is a very selfish time": Interview with Shirley MacLaine, the Hampson Interview, *The Globe and Mail* (Sept. 15, 2008).

Pg. 250: "Whatever version of that longing there is . . .": Interview with Leonard Cohen; some material appeared in the *Globe and Mail* (May 26, 2007).

Pg. 251: Some believe that being in a relationship is a mark of mental health: Interview with Stephen B. Poulter, author of *Your Ex Factor: Overcome Heartbreak and Build a Better Life* (Amherst, NY: Prometheus Books, 2009), Generation Ex, *The Globe and Mail* (Aug. 21, 2009).

Pg. 253: it is mid-life men who often want the comfort of a permanent relationship: Interview with Neil Chethik, Generation Ex, *The Globe and Mail* (Jan. 10. 2008).

Pg. 254: "the terrible necessity of other people": Lynn Darling, "For Better and Worse," *Esquire* (May 1, 1996).

Chapter 19—Playing My Cards

Pg. 266: Forging new family rituals: Karen Stewart, Fairway Divorce Solutions, Calgary, quoted in Generation Ex, *The Globe and Mail* (Dec. 28, 2007).

Pg. 267: Katherine Jackson, *My Family, the Jacksons* (New York: St. Martin's, 1990).

Chapter 20—Life Is a Carnival

Pg. 273: "Does Divorce Make You Happy?" by Linda Waite, sociologist at the University of Chicago, Institute for American Values study (New York, 2008).

Pg. 274: separation . . . is not about self-expression . . . : Mark O'Connell, *The Marriage Benefit*.

Pg. 274: "It's a paradox between the intimacy and the distance . . .": Quoted in Generation Ex, *The Globe and Mail* (Mar. 6, 2008).

Pg. 275: Difficulty in grieving an ex: Kenneth Doka, professor of gerontology at New York's College of New Rochelle and editor of *Disenfranchised Grief: New Directions, Challenges and Strategies for Practice* (Champaign, IL: Research Press, 2002), quoted in Generation Ex, *The Globe and Mail* (Mar. 6, 2008).

Pg. 275: A connection to an ex never disappears: Ibid.

Pg. 277: Anne Morrow Lindbergh, *Gift from the Sea* (New York: Pantheon, 1991 [reissued edition]).

Pg. 277: "worldwide phenomenon" of divorce in later life: Deirdre Bair, *Calling It Quits: Late-Life Divorce and Starting Over* (New York: Random House, 2007).

Pg. 278: "I don't know that it's real regret": Deirdre Bair, Generation Ex, *The Globe and Mail* (Nov. 6, 2008).

ACKNOWLEDGMENTS

This is a work of non-fiction. However, many identifying details about individuals have been changed to protect people's identity and privacy. Some names are real names, which I have used with permission.

I'm lucky to have wonderful support and encouragement from friends, whom I would like to thank by name: Siri Agrell, Daphne Ballon, Willa Black, Janet Brown, Barbara Clerihue Carter, Cate Cochran, Charlene Codner, Jane Common, Beth Nowers Curtin, Gisela Curwen, Barbara Dawson, Wendy Dobson, Kathy Elder, Carolyn Ellis, Suzanne Etherington, Michael Gundy, Shauna Gundy, Anne Kingston, Nancy Lang, Susan Latremouille, Judy Lawrie, Rob Lawrie, Barbara Moore MacKinnon, Meg McCourt, Cinders McLeod, Debbie Oates, Charlie Part, Jennifer Warren Part, Sarah Scott, Molly Sheehan, Suzanne Spragge, Helga Stephenson, David Swaine, Susan Swan, Joy von Tiedemann, Amy Scowen Walsh and Gayle Woods. Knowing wise, funny people is such an asset.

Of course, none of this book would have been possible without the support of my editors at the *Globe and Mail*, who not only let me write what I want in my Generation Ex columns, interviews and other pieces, but also were generous to give me the time off to work on the project. They are Jill Borra, Kevin Siu, Cathrin Bradbury and Sylvia Stead. A special thanks goes to Sheree-lee Olson, who happily agreed to read several chapters while they were in development.

I also owe a debt of gratitude to the editors and publishers at Random House/Knopf Canada—Louise Dennys, Anne Collins, Diane Martin and Angelika Glover—who were always encouraging of my desire to write a book and ready to provide editorial insight whenever I asked, throughout the process. Without Angelika Glover, this would not be the book it is. She is brilliant. To the list of indispensable people, I add Rick Broadhead, my agent; editor Meg Taylor; copy editor Allyson Latta; production editorial assistant Amanda Lewis; and typesetter Erin Cooper.

Finally, I have so much to express to my family that it is difficult to put into words. Here, though, let me just say how blessed I am to have my parents' unwavering love for me and support for the creative process. They make me who I am in many ways and are never far from my mind. My siblings, Daphne, Geoffrey, Harry and Aimée, make brief appearances in the book but occupy a much larger space in my life. The list would not be complete without adding the memory of my two grandmothers, Margaret Evans and Geraldine Hampson, who had profound influences on me in different ways.

My beautiful boys, Nick, Tait and Luke, are so lovely. Without the man I call Eric in these pages, I could not have had them, so in that regard, I am thankful to him too. I am grateful for my boys' support in writing this book and their patience when it preoccupied me. They read the parts pertaining to them before it was published and encouraged me to write the story—without shame or hesitation. They have taught me so much, and given me more pleasure and love than I ever thought imaginable. Without them, my life would not have the purpose and fulfillment that sustain me.

SARAH HAMPSON is an award-winning journalist with the *Globe and Mail*. She has been writing the Hampson Interview column for over ten years. In 2007, she began her popular weekly Generation Ex column about marriage and divorce. Hampson has three sons and lives in Toronto.